IN DEWEY'S WAKE

IN DEWEY'S WAKE

Unfinished Work of Pragmatic Reconstruction

Edited by
William J. Gavin

STATE UNIVERSITY OF NEW YORK PRESS

For Cathy

Published by
State University of New York Press, Albany

Printed in the United States of America

For information, address State University of New York Press,
90 State Street, Suite 700, Albany, NY 12207

Production by Cathleen Collins
Marketing by Jennifer Giovani

Library of Congress Cataloging-in-Publication Data

In Dewey's wake : unfinished work of pragmatic reconstruction / edited by William J. Gavin.
p. cm.
Includes bibliographical references and index.
ISBN 0-7914-5629-3 (alk. paper) — ISBN 0-7914-5630-7 (pbk. : alk. paper)
1. Dewey, John, 1859–1952. I. Gavin, W. J. (William J.), 1943–

B945.D4 I5 2003
191—dc21

2002021754

10 9 8 7 6 5 4 3 2 1

Contents

Introduction

Passing Dewey By?

WILLIAM J. GAVIN

While some philosophers write for eternity, others are more humble, or perhaps more anticipatory, offering outlooks which stem from particular contexts. For the latter group of thinkers, any sense of becoming timeless stems from enduring *through* time rather than transcending it. One of the latter thinkers is John Dewey, whose work consistently alluded to and affirmed the importance of context. Contextualism is the opposite of certainty, that is, of the assumption than an apodictic point of view exists, or is even desirable. In opposition, Dewey has told us that "the most pervasive fallacy of philosophic thinking goes back to neglect of context."[1]

Taking this statement seriously requires several things on our part. By far the most important of these is realizing that contexts by their very nature are limited, and therefore in some sense and at some time they change and so must be "passed by." Applying this observation to the works of Dewey himself forces us to ask when, and in what sense, he should be passed by. To be sure, if done at all, this task should be approached respectfully, for Dewey's work remains at the pinnacle of the American tradition in philosophy. Still, Dewey himself would encourage us to take on this task; failure to do so would result in pragmatism degenerating into a form of antiquarianism, that is, a study of the past without realizing that the future will be different. In contrast, Dewey was constantly about the task of telling us how things have changed, for example, in a post-Darwinian universe. Going further, Dewey is best viewed as a social reformer, and his philosophy, as social criticism, is designed to be passed by, that is, to lead to some form of action. Philosophy for Dewey is mimetic; it reflects and perfects the concerns of a community, albeit it in a critical manner. It is "formed," and then it is "formative." "The distinctive office, problems, and subject matter of philosophy grow out of stresses and strains in the community life in which a given form of philosophy arises, and . . . accordingly, its specific problems vary with the changes in human life that are always going on and that at times constitute a crisis and a turning point in human history" (MW 12:256). Once again, such a stance places upon the reader the responsibility of not letting Dewey's work exist merely as "text," but rather of undertaking the task of uncovering how the text relates to contemporary *con*texts in the new millennium.

A comparison here may perhaps be enlightening. At the end of book one of Nietzsche's *Thus Spoke Zarathustra,* Zarathustra says: "Many die too late, and a few die too early. The doctrine still sounds strange: 'Die at the right time!'"[2] This is a somewhat tricky matter; no bell goes off to let one know just when the right time has arrived. In theory we know what characterizes the right time, i.e., when your death can function as a "spur and a promise to the survivors."[3] On the face of it, Zarathustra has given his gift (of uneasiness) to his disciples, and asked them to love the earth in its flawed entirety. Now it is time for him to go: "verily Zarathustra had a goal; he threw his ball: now you, my friends, are the heirs of my goal; to you I throw my golden ball."[4] But having said as much Zarathustra does not leave, asking his disciples to "forgive me for that."[5] His nondeparture forces the reader into reflection, thus insuring that s/he too is made uneasy. Zarathustra has urged his disciples to "pass him by." But as the text "progresses" it becomes more and more difficult to accomplish this task. For Zarathustra himself does not stand still long enough to be passed by, as he continues to take upon himself the seemingly impossible task of becoming the *Übermensch,* and affirming eternal recurrence, a task initially thought to be reserved for his successors. Hence the significance of the book's subtitle: "A Book for All and None."[6]

Dewey's texts, like Nietzsche's *Thus Spoke Zarathustra,* should be viewed as a spur or a prod. This is but another version of the pragmatic stance which stresses the interpenetration of thought and action. The thoughts and criticisms contained in Dewey's works are not meant merely to be studied, though that of course is necessary. The text is also meant to be directive in nature. But in order to do so the texts must tell a story, a narrative. Dewey is constantly telling the reader the tale of how we got from "there" to "here"—in *Reconstruction in Philosophy* and in "The Need for a Recovery in Philosophy," for example. By the time of Dewey's "Reconstruction As Seen Twenty-Five Years Later," written as a new Introduction to *Reconstruction in Philosophy* in the 1940s, the story has become more urgent, and Dewey calls for the reconstruction *of* philosophy rather than merely reconstruction *in* philosophy, saying that "the need for reconstruction is vastly more urgent than when the book was composed" (MW 12:256). In other words, the *context* has changed.

There is a sense in which we can feel urged to pass Dewey by, analogous to that urged by Zarathustra. With Nietzsche this sense becomes more formidable as it becomes apparent that Zarathustra's disciples will not be able to pass him by, and that he himself is being asked to become the over[wo]man. Analogously, it can seem easy and somewhat straightforward to suggest that Dewey be passed by; but doing so may prove more difficult than initially appeared to be the case. For Dewey himself anticipated and took on, to a remarkable degree, many of the issues now being debated in contemporary philosophy. Dewey, like Zarathustra, did not stand still, waiting passively to be "passed by" by a group of successors. Though in a sense he urged his followers to surpass him for good pedagogical reasons, Dewey also was remarkably anticipatory of some of the new "problems"[7] on the horizon of the new millennium.

In the following essays several Dewey scholars take up the issue of just how, and to what extent, his work is to be "passed by."

For one set of authors, Dewey's contextualism remains intact, requiring more to be amended than radically changed. Thus, in "Advancing American Philosophy: Pragmatism and Philosophical Scholarship," James Campbell considers the pragmatic meaning of philosophical scholarship at the present time, a time when many suggest that we are *preserving* rather than *advancing* American philosophy. Campbell begins with a formulation of this issue, and then compares efforts to advance American philosophy with what might be done to advance the American classical musical tradition. In a final section he "advances" matters significantly, by showing how a Deweyan approach might be effectively utilized in dealing with the contemporary issue of abortion. In "Dewey's Limited Shelf Life: A Consumer Warning," Michael Eldridge argues that Dewey's most significant contribution is his advocacy of "social intelligence." Using the latter, however, requires that we be sensitive to particular contexts. As a specific example of his point here, Eldridge argues that we not unqualifiedly accept an endorsement of unions in all situations—or assume that Dewey himself would do so in the context of the new millennium. In "New Directions and Uses in the Reconstruction of Dewey's Ethics," Gregory Pappas argues that, although we do not find an ethical theory per se in Dewey's writings, nonetheless there are new functions for an ethical theory which are not at odds with Dewey's criticism of traditional ethical theory. Rather, there is available from Dewey an alternative position which lies *between* divorcing ethical theory completely from moral practice, and on the other side, the pretensions of some normative ethical theories to dictate our moral conduct in a noncontextual manner. In "Contexts Vibrant and Contexts Souring in

Dewey's Philosophy," William Gavin notes that neglect of contexts and contextualism was deemed "the most pervasive fallacy in philosophic thinking" by Dewey. Contexts should be "fat" rather than "thin," offering a rich naturalism. Going further, contexts can go wrong or "sour" in several ways: by reducing the *con*text to the text alone; by turning interaction into control or domination; by replacing the environment of interaction with one of interacting with narcissistic "pseudo-events"; and by not realizing that the con*tent* of a con*text* has changed.

For a second group of authors, Dewey's work needs significant revision if he is to be relevant in the new millennium. Thus in "As Dewey Was Hegelian, So We Should Be Deweyan," Ray Boisvert faults Dewey's attempt to extend the method of the physical sciences to politics, education, and morals. While such a goal may have been comprehensible at the beginning of the twentieth century, it is not feasible in contexts confronted with "AIDS-type" issues. Dewey's attempt to universalize scientific method overgeneralizes from the specificity of different contexts and, going further, it immerses him in a "fresh start" view, that is, a new approach through science, which should be avoided. Dewey still has much to offer however, in the areas of "lived experience" and in his view of mediation which assumes "co-respondence" as primordial. In "(Re)construction Zone: Beware of Falling Statues," Shannon Sullivan argues that Dewey neglected the issues of race and racism in his philosophy. This, for Sullivan, is more than a mere gap or hole in his thought, for it perpetuates the conceptual and theoretical "whiteness" of his philosophy. Nonetheless, some resources do exist in Dewey's pragmatism which can be of assistance in going beyond it on the matter of race. The most powerful of these is "habit," understood as an organism's predisposition to transact with its physical, social, political and natural worlds in particular ways. In "Between Being and Emptiness: Toward an Eco-Ontology of Inhabitation," Tom Alexander argues that the thought of John Dewey is of exceptional value in relocating the quest for "knowledge" back where it belongs, that is, within the context of the general issue of "wisdom." Dewey dominates the twentieth century as the only thinker to articulate an eco-ontology compatible with democracy. Alexander offers a marriage of Dewey with the Buddhist doctrine of emptiness, especially as refined by Nagarjuna.

Still a third group of authors included here argues that we should not be overhasty in passing Dewey by, for he has much to offer that has still, even as we enter the new millennium, gone unnoticed or unappreciated. Thus, in "On Passing Dewey By: The New Millennium and the Climate of Pluralism," Sandra Rosenthal argues that Dewey's philosophy and his understanding of self offer a more useful balance of community and pluralism than do the more exclusive alternatives put forward by Alasdair

MacIntyre, John Rawls, and Richard Rorty. In contrast to Dewey, each of the latter philosophers offers a view of the self which seems unable to exercise its anointed community task. In "Pressing Dewey's Advantage," Joseph Margolis shows how the work of Richard Rorty and Hilary Putnam tend to cancel each other out. Each is a decisive critique of the other's particular form of relativism without, however, ever showing how relativism might be formulated in a coherent and defensible manner. In contrast, Margolis suggests that a coherent account of constructive relativism can be offered, one which is quite compatible with Dewey's realism stemming from *Experience and Nature*. In "Improving Life," John Lachs shows how Dewey's idea of " 'means-end' integrated actions" promises permanent improvements to the human condition. Rather than dispensing with undesired labor for a few people only as in, for example, Aristotle and Hegel, Dewey offers a strategy that is, in general, universally available. Rather than offering attitudinal change as in the Stoics, Dewey presents a way of objectively reconstructing our relations with our activities. But Lachs charges that Dewey's own account can offer only moderate progress, enabling us to achieve some, but by no means all, of the little improvements of which the human being is capable. In opposition, he suggests that we retain the "utopian" ideal that there are activities every element of which is rich in consequences and rewarding in experience. Finally, in "In the Wake of Darwin," Vincent Colapietro argues that Dewey is best viewed as a "critical traditionalist" who constantly emphasized the need for a pluralistic approach to the past. He turns to those occasions when Dewey mourned the loss of colleagues, such as James, Mead and Hocking, by reenacting the ritual of recollection, in order to emphasize that unbearable loss is oftentimes something that must be "worked" through. Dewey is indeed a "spur" for Colapietro, that is, he is a thinker who invites and demands further critical reflection, but one whose work must be married to Freud, Marx, and Nietzsche as we move into the future.

Hopefully, the "pragmatic upshot" of this pluralistic tapestry of approaches is a rich narrative—one indicating both where the context has changed, and also what needs to be preserved and nurtured in Dewey as we advance into the future.

NOTES

1. John Dewey, "Context and Thought" (LW 6:5). All references to Dewey's work in this volume are to the critical edition, *The Collected Works of John Dewey, 1882–1953* edited by Jo Ann Boydston (Carbondale: Southern Illinois University Press, 1969–91), and published as *The*

Early Works: 1881–1898 (EW); *The Middle Works, 1899–1924* (MW); and *The Later Works, 1925–1953* (LW). These designations are followed by volume and page number. Quotations in this section are cited from *The Collected Works of John Dewey, 1882–1953: The Electronic Edition,* edited by Larry A. Hickman (Charlottesville, Va.: IntelLex Corporation, 1996).

2. Friedrich Nietzsche, *Thus Spoke* Zarathustra, in The *Portable Nietzsche,* ed. and trans. Walter Kaufmann (New York: Penguin Books, 1976), 183.

3. Ibid.

4. Ibid., 186.

5. Ibid.

6. Ibid., 103.

7. Though Dewey was perhaps too ready to conceive every "situation" as at least potentially "problematic" in character. On the important difference between "having a problem" and "having trouble," see John McDermott, Introduction, *William and Henry James, Selected Letters,* ed. Ignas Skrupskelis and Elizabeth Berkeley (Charlottesville: University Press of Virginia, 1997), xxii.

PART ONE

Changing Contexts

ONE

Advancing American Philosophy

Pragmatism and Philosophical Scholarship

JAMES CAMPBELL

INTRODUCTION: PRESERVATION VERSUS ADVANCEMENT

The American philosophical tradition is a rich and varied one that offers to the historically oriented philosopher a limitless amount of potential research. There are numerous aspects of the tradition in need of study: questions to be addressed, themes to be reinterpreted, figures to be recovered, new developments to be incorporated. Much of this analysis is carried on in conjunction with the Society for the Advancement of American Philosophy (SAAP). It seems, however, that commentators on the history of American philosophy often feel themselves in a bind about the usefulness of further historical inquiry. I am not referring here to the mindless doubting of the value of historical efforts in any form, the belief that all important philosophical work is contemporary. Rather, my concern is the more specific question of the value of additional historical examination on pragmatism, the central strand in the American philosophical tradition. If, as non-pragmatists might suggest, the purpose of philosophical inquiry is to uncover truths about ultimate questions, then there is no problem with endless speculation; but, if the purpose of philosophical inquiry is to make the world a better place—a description that would seem to fit pragmatism—then we are led to wonder about the actual value of continuing historical scholarship about pragmatic (or any other) philosophy. At some point, it would seem, we have learned enough about the commentaries on *The Principles of Psychology* and the background to *A Common Faith;* now it is time to try to change the world. At some point, we need to move beyond "mere philosophizing." We philosophers need to stop talking to each other about the concepts of 'fuller experience' and 'moral growth' and to try to do something to expand the range of fuller experience and the likelihood of moral growth in our communities. As pragmatists, we need to resist the temptation to continue to reformulate our ideas until we think that they are in perfect shape. We must fight this temptation, so powerful to individuals of an intellectual bent, because we know that such endless refinement will keep us from any practical applications. We need to remind ourselves that our philosophical work has an overall purpose, and that our attempts to advance American philosophy must further this purpose.

In our search for the pragmatic value of philosophical scholarship, we can consider two initial stances, each of which has some value. On the one hand, there is merit to the position that in our work we cannot simply repeat what has been done so many times before. There would seem to be little need, for example, for an additional exposition of Peirce's essay on the fixation of belief, an essay that was never extremely hard to understand in the first place. There would similarly seem to be little value in yet another attempt to repair James's troubled essay on the will to believe, an essay that philosophers by the score have already repaired to their own, if not to each other's, satisfaction. Continuing to work on these and similar topics, topics that have either been settled adequately already or that give all indication of defying any possibility of settlement, makes of our philosophizing a kind of intellectual history in which our endless tinkering distracts us from any larger obligations. The pragmatic scholar recognizes that well-written intellectual history is a valuable product, but one that does not represent the full range of our potential activities as inheritors of the American tradition. On the other hand, there is merit to the position that extraordinary and valuable insights were achieved by past American philosophers and that these need to be passed on—explicated and made relevant—to the next generations of American thinkers. Evidence for the severity of the need to better understand the American philosophical tradition can be found in almost every philosophy journal and at almost every philosophy conference. Moreover, even when we leave this narrowly academic emphasis aside, there is still the need to engage our general undergraduate populations (and broader public audiences as well) on issues of great human importance like the source and justification of human valuing. Here the insights of the many figures in the American philosophical tradition would, if better known, provide valuable suggestions. To pass on these insights in the classroom requires instructors who are well grounded in the tradition. It requires, in other words, good intellectual history by scholars who are dedicated to putting their ideas to work to advance social goals.

The need to consider the pragmatic value of historical scholarship is particularly vital at present because the historical and pragmatic emphases have grown so different. The predominate mood, largely influenced by Richard Rorty, seems to be to abandon historical work and to concentrate on the latter task. Rorty himself has confessed that he does not really understand the tradition for which he has become the leading spokesperson;[1] and, further, his relaxed and playful style suggests that worrying over the historical niceties is wrongheaded. The pragmatic value of the American philosophical tradition, however, reveals itself fully only to those with a firm grounding in that tradition. I am not suggesting, of course, that Rorty's work is without value or that he does not have a place somewhere in the American philosophical tradition other than at the head. Even as uninformed as he is about the tradition, his work might draw individuals working outside it to reconsider the works of figures whom they had neglected or forgotten; and his work might result in the creation of new insights among those who are more solidly grounded. Still, the question remains whether recent developments demonstrate the advancement, or the kidnapping, of the American philosophical tradition.

What does it mean to advance the American philosophical tradition? How would this differ from attempts to preserve it? The *preservation* of a philosophical tradition would seem to be an easier task because the goal in preservation is simply to capture and embalm a set of ideas in its present state so that it remains available to others at a later date. Preserving philosophical traditions is certainly better than forgetting them; and, at times, we need to remind ourselves that SAAP was born at a particular time and in relation to a particular situation in which even the preservation of the American philosophical tradition was in doubt. At present, it would seem that this situation has changed for the better; now we can and must think about fulfilling the potential implied in "advancement." As might be expected, *advancement* is a much more complex and demanding task than preservation. Advancing the American philosophical tradition involves moving beyond negative aspects of the inherited tradition—minor ones like its ambivalence about esthetics and major ones like its lack of inclusiveness—while at the same time preserving the valuable aspects that are to remain vibrant in the reconstruction. It involves a close familiarity with the tradition that is being reconstructed so that it winds up being advanced rather than kidnapped. So far, however, I have barely scratched the surface. The goal of advancing American philosophy leaves us at present with many unsettled questions.

TWO PARALLEL CASES

We can consider the issues involved in advancing American philosophy in the light of a parallel case: the (fictional) Society for the Advancement of

American Music (SAAM). The question that I want to focus upon is what would distinguish such an organization from the (equally fictitious) Society for the Preservation of American Music (SPAM)? What would it mean to *advance* rather than *preserve* American music?

The work of SAAM would have to include a number of tasks. One of these would be to keep before the interested public the works of those American composers who have long been recognized to be central to the American classical tradition. I have in mind such individuals as: Charles Ives, Walter Piston, Howard Hanson, Virgil Thomson, George Gershwin, Roy Harris, Aaron Copland, Samuel Barber, William Schuman, and Leonard Bernstein. Another of the tasks of SAAM would be the work of building contemporary audiences for the compositions of other figures who have been largely forgotten over time. Here, part of the interest of SAAM would be in refamiliarizing the listening public with works that once had a fairly wide audience. Some examples here would be the compositions of George Whitefield Chadwick, Charles Martin Loeffler, Edward MacDowell, and Charles Tomlinson Griffes. At the same time, SAAM would also need to build the audience for composers who, for whatever reason, failed to garner the sort of critical regard during their lifetimes that these figures did. I have in mind here such neglected composers as William Dawson and Amy Marcy Cheney Beach, whose *Negro Folk Symphony* and *Gaelic Symphony* (among other works) deserve wider regard. SAAM should also work to expand the abilities of audiences to better appreciate those composers who have worked more on the fringes of the American classical tradition like: John Cage, Alan Hovaness, Philip Glass and John Adams. Ranging a bit further, SAAM should attempt to foster the "serious" appreciation of composers like Scott Joplin, Louis Thomas Hardin, and Edward Kennedy ("Duke") Ellington.

So far, it would seem that the tasks of SAAM and SPAM would be virtually interchangeable. Both organizations would work to make the American classical music tradition more popular with contemporary and future audiences. Rather than just preserving the historical content of the American classical tradition, however, SAAM would go further at this point and attempt to expand the body of works that makes up the tradition. These efforts to advance the tradition would most likely include competitions of various sorts that would result in performances, broadcasts, publication, and recordings of the new works that would make the victorious composers better known. The primary goal of these competitions would be to ensure that the tradition come to be understood as open-ended and evolving.

A fourth task of SAAM would be more indirect. This would be the deliberate attempt to pass on an appreciation for the tradition, as it had been enhanced in the efforts to satisfy the first three tasks, to the students who are to become the American musicians of the next generations. A major part of these efforts to increase appreciation would involve the establishment of workshops and master classes to foster personal interactions between these students and those interpreters of the American tradition—the composers and performers and commentators—who have helped to advance the tradition in the past. The goal here would be to pass on those elements of musical style that are in some sense extratextual. More than the words and notes on the page are the ideas, the references, and the intentions that shape the choices in composition and in performance. It is these intangible aspects of the tradition that, when passed on in a face-to-face manner, can help to create a skilled performance group and an informed audience that will advance the American classical tradition. And, it is these intangible aspects that, if neglected, will hamstring efforts to carry the tradition into the future.

With this analogy in mind, we can now consider SAAP in its task of the *advancement* of American philosophy; and, for the most part, the transference would seem to be quite straightforward. One task of SAAP would be to provide a forum for the evaluation and appreciation of the ideas of such central figures as Peirce, James, Dewey, Royce, Santayana, Mead, and Whitehead, who have long been seen as being at the center of the American philosophical tradition. Leaving aside questions of the relative emphases among them, SAAP seems to be doing quite well with regard to this task. A second task would be to develop greater interest in the neglected or forgotten works of the lesser known figures in the American philosophical tradition. The list of such individuals is not short. It would include, to offer just a baker's dozen of the more recent figures, such philosophers as: Hartley Burr Alexander, John Elof Boodin, Edgar Sheffield Brightman, Mary Whiton Calkins, James Edwin Creighton, Irwin Edman, William Ernest Hocking, Elijah Jordan, Alain Leroy Locke, Arthur Oncken Lovejoy, De Witt H. Parker, Edgar A. Singer, Jr., and James Hayden Tufts. While there may be legitimate reasons why these philosophers fell out of favor, an initial survey of recent SAAP activities would suggest that much more could be done to grant them all another hearing. With regard to the third task of SAAP, the attempt to develop and expand the body of ideas that comprises the American tradition through the fostering of new works, SAAP has done even less. Without any funds of its own to commission major new works or to subsidize their publication, SAAP can do little more than open its programs as a forum where individuals can present their novel ideas. Experience suggests, however, that the programs are molded to favor the historical over the novel, serving more to preserve than advance the tradition.

With regard to the fourth task, the indirect task of passing on a greater regard for the tradition to whose who are to be the philosophy teachers of the next generations, SAAP has been very successful. The cause of American philosophy is very strongly advanced by the ability of young scholars to interact with individuals who have long worked with the figures and ideas that have come to interest them. In my own case (and I am surely not alone here), I was able even as a young scholar to interact on an equal footing with any number of individuals whose articles and books were then powerfully active in my mind. (The equality of this relationship was due primarily to their graciousness.) Leaving aside those who are still prominent at SAAP meetings, I remember with great fondness and gratitude the interactions I had with such philosophers as: Elizabeth Flower, Darnell Rucker, and Ralph Sleeper. It is these interactions, during the sessions and in the hallways and at the meals, that make SAAP meetings high-energy seminars for American philosophy. By means of these interactions, young scholars reap many gains: direct answers to specific questions about written works; explanations for puzzlements that had not yet become problems; interpretations alternate to those that had been learned in graduate school; suggestions about where to look for further assistance; and so on. The particular impacts here may be slight since the words on the page remain the same; but these differences of emphasis and mood and shading can have a cumulative effect, leaving the resulting product greatly improved. As in the case of the fourth task of SAAM, what is transmitted in this face-to-face manner is a sense of the whole tradition that is broader and deeper and more diverse than is likely to be gained in the normal course of graduate studies. The primary result of fostering these intangible continuities is a new generation of scholars and teachers who can work within the developing American philosophical tradition and advance it.

ADVANCING THE AMERICAN PHILOSOPHICAL TRADITION

This inquiry into the advance of the American philosophical tradition, and more broadly into the pragmatic value of philosophic scholarship, is based upon the assumption that there is some value in the American tradition that has manifested itself to us in our attempts to solve our philosophical problems and that will be of assistance to others. We cannot offer any antecedent proof for this claim. We believe with James that "every philosopher . . . whose initiative counts for anything in the evolution of thought, has taken his stand on a sort of dumb conviction that the truth must lie in one direction rather than another, and a sort of preliminary assurance that his notion can be made to work. . . ."[2] Moreover, this belief is shared in a general way by all the members of any pluralistic philosophy department. In such a department, all the philosophers have the feeling that their own perspective is the one that yields answers to the serious problems of living; yet, at the same time, each recognizes that the others in the department have their own dumb convictions that the truth lies in other directions. As a department, these philosophers hope that, by presenting their students with a number of approaches to philosophical inquiry, the students will both find one that helps them to deal with their inchoate philosophical problems and develop respect for other approaches to philosophizing.

This consideration of the nature of philosophical traditions and the means to their advancement indicates that a necessary component of advancement must be some element of novelty. The process of advancement requires the development of new ideas, or the application of old ideas to new situations, or their interaction with new rivals. As examples of each of these, we can consider an attempt to expand upon the ideas of Mead to explicate better than he was able to the social origins of the self, or an effort to apply the insights gained from the study of Dewey's ethical thought to a contemporary problem like abortion, or an encounter between Royce's understanding of community as a social process and the more geographically based understanding of community present in the work of Wendell Berry. Without some element of novelty, the American philosophical tradition, or any tradition, would not be advanced but simply preserved. Still, it remains important to remember that what is being advanced is a philosophical tradition, an historical entity with its own profile and contours and inertia. As such, a philosophical tradition must be mastered before it can be advanced. Otherwise, elements of it are simply being abducted and put to another purpose.

In the examination of the question of pragmatism and scholarship, Dewey's work has a special sort of primacy because of his own direct consideration of this issue. In "The Need for a Recovery of Philosophy" of 1917, for example, he pointed to the widening distance between the problems of philosophers as an academic group increasingly focused on its own internal professional issues and the problems of ordinary people; and he suggested that this trend toward greater separation needed to be reversed. As he wrote, philosophy will recover itself "when it ceases to be a device for dealing with the problems of philosophers and becomes a method, cultivated by philosophers, for dealing with the problems of men." While at present avoiding the problems that arise "in the vicissitudes of life" by busying ourselves with problems that are "supposed to depend upon Reality as such, or its distinction from a world of Appearance, or its relation to a Knower as such" might not be as popular as it was in 1917 (MW 10:46–47),[3] the possibility for philosophers to avoid the problems of ordinary people by dealing with philosophers' problems remains. Among this latter class would seem to be the problem of scholarly hyper-preparation that we considered early on.

Dewey, at times, may have failed to appreciate the importance of the tradition of which he was a part to his own way of thinking. Moreover, it is surely unnecessary to point out that philosophers are persons very much like nonphilosophers, with many interests and problems that are in no way narrowly academic, and that one of the fundamental tenets of all philosophers in the American tradition is that no individual lives more than a shadow life without an ongoing component of philosophical inquiry. Still, there remains something of great importance to his position. As Dewey develops this theme in *Reconstruction in Philosophy* in 1920, he emphasized the need for philosophers to select very carefully the problems on which they are to work. Evaluation among philosophical problems is just as important as evaluation within them. As he writes, "the task of future philosophy is to clarify men's ideas as to the social and moral strifes of their own day." Rather than continuing to puzzle over issues inherited from their philosophical tradition, philosophers should devote themselves to "enlightening the moral forces which move mankind and . . . contributing to the aspirations of men to attain to a more ordered and intelligent happiness" (MW 12:94). In this way, Dewey hoped that philosophical work would not be devoted to preserving its present status in our inherited culture but rather to earning a place in the ongoing life of society, thus advancing both social life and itself.

An initial attempt to translate Dewey's position might be through a separation of the philosophers' academic task into two large groups. On the one hand, there is the need for them to teach undergraduates. These students for the most part will take only one course, almost always at a general or introductory level; and teachers need to select a level of historical precision that will build student interest. Here, our attempts to advance the American philosophical tradition would seem most successful if we emphasize the *spirit* of pragmatic inquiry. Consequently, instead of doing explicitly historical work, we should try to "cash in" our concepts and ideas in terms of our students' experiences. Further, we should make it a central point of our inquiry to examine and challenge our students' ideas and values to see both what these ideas mean in the contemporary world and whether they have retained any value. What value does marriage, for example, retain in our emerging world? Is it possible to see the course of nature as containing a plan? What is the contribution of song, and other forms of art, to human life? These are issues that matter deeply to our students and issues with which a grounding in the American philosophical tradition can help us. Similarly, it is necessary to challenge the growing belief that information and data are enough to settle our social questions. This popular, if mistaken, belief rests on the unfounded assumption that science has uncovered—or soon will uncover—all the answers that we need to live our lives and organize our social practices. It is admittedly hard to see, except perhaps occasionally, how our efforts at this level would do much to advance American philosophy. In most of our work with undergraduates, our primary interest must be to advance society.

Still, in addition to undergraduate teaching, academic philosophers have an obligation to carry their discipline forward in a more direct fashion. For those who are interested in American philosophy, this obligation requires ongoing research in the primary and secondary literature of the tradition to understand what has been done in the past and what needs to be done in the future. By writing their own interpretations of what has happened and contributing their own thoughts to the process—by, as Santayana suggests, "joining the procession wherever one happens to come upon it, and following it as long as one's legs hold out"[4]—these philosophers do their part to help the tradition advance. Whether their efforts are directed to increasing our understanding of the central figures of the tradition, or extending our familiarity with those who are currently neglected, or presenting their own novel ideas, these philosophers can advance the tradition. Moreover, if they are very fortunate in their academic situation, they can contribute directly to the preparation of the next generations of philosophers interested in American thought by personally introducing advanced undergraduates and graduate students to the inherited ways of thinking that constitute the tradition. In dealing with these students, they may even be justified on occasion to undertake expositions of "The Fixation of Belief" and to ask students to attempt to repair "The Will to Believe."

We also need to consider directly the relationship of this academic work to the larger interests of society. Here, much of what needs to be said can be pulled together from what we have already seen. Philosophers, as citizens, have obligations of service to their broader communities. Philosophical scholarship, although important in itself, must be evaluated among the other goods of society. More important than what interests me is what I ought to be interested in, and here the criteria must be social. Our conceptual work needs to incorporate wider social experience, and our tendency to play with ideas must be countered with our recognition of the needs of our social situation. Of course, our attempts to pass on the insights contained in the American philosophical tradition—understanding the nature of community and its problems, understanding the nature of the self and the good life, and so on—will go a long way toward validating the pragmatic value of historical scholarship.

A DEWEYAN APPROACH TO ABORTION

So far, this examination of pragmatism and philosophical scholarship has been devoted to a general consideration of largely informal methods for advancing the American philosophical tradition. It is also possible to consider a more formal method. What I have in mind is to attempt to address a contemporary issue through the voice of one of the central figures in the American tradition. How, for example, might Dewey deal with a problem like abortion? Any attempt to answer such a question is, of course, largely speculative. We cannot *know* how Dewey might address any contemporary problem. We can, however, attempt to extrapolate upon what we believe to be the basic core of his work; and explicating this core is the point of the exercise. Whether in the form of an individual or group writing assignment, or of a critique of a document with which they are presented, this sort of teaching device might help advanced students to climb inside the tradition and try it out as a means for dealing with their problems. A discussion of the issue of abortion, in the style of Dewey, might run as follows.

At the present time, America is in the grips of a major crisis centering around the issue of abortion. Politicians and the media, religious and civic groups wrestle with facts and values, definitions and procedures, surveys and predictions. In spite of all of this public activity, the two centers of contradictory opinion remain as divided as ever. This polarity of opinion would seem to leave the inquiring individual unable to make use of the values of one position without condemning the other position out of hand. On one side stand those who are "pro-life"—the defenders of human life in any form or degree possible. They identify personhood with the *conceptus* and consider any prevention of maturation and birth to be "murder." Since the "rights" of the "child" are seen as primary, the circumstances of the situation need hardly be considered. From the child's point of view, after all, poverty or disability is a small price to pay for life. Circumstances only cloud a very simple situation in which a "person" is either allowed to live or prevented from living. Within such a mind-set, to have an abortion is purely and simply to commit murder. On the other side stand those who maintain that to have an abortion is a woman's prerogative whenever she chooses to do so. Current medical technology has made early abortion a simple and safe procedure, far safer in fact than carrying a fetus to term. Whereas for those who are pro-life, no justification for abortion is good enough—no reason could condemn an innocent child to death—for those who are "pro-choice," no justification is needed. The body of a woman is her "property," and what she does with it is exclusively her own business. The fetus is perhaps a person of some sort, but it has no right to make the serious demands of pregnancy on any woman.

Each of these positions demonstrates an understanding of abortion so simple in nature that the failure of one side to grasp the other's position defies intellectual analysis. This perhaps explains each side's emotional condemnation of its opponent as "immoral" or "totalitarian." But as far from each other as they may be, and as radically different in their conclusions, the two positions share a common assumption. This joint starting point is the belief that the abortion problem has *an* answer. This answer may be either that abortion is wrong—and therefore never to be permitted—or that abortion, while not a positive good, is not wrong—and therefore permissible when a woman desires to obtain one. The essence of both cases, however, is that there is a fixed answer: abortion itself is either right or wrong.

The weakness of this right/wrong approach is that it makes the abortion problem all too simple: the only problematic aspect is how to deal with the recalcitrance of the opponent. In both instances, the answer to the question arises *outside of the situation*. Certain possible outcomes to the question are rejected out of hand as wrong without any knowledge of the situation itself. This approach falsifies the actual situation because it speaks of goods and evils prior to our analysis: and, prior to analysis, there are only goods which compete as means for our ends-in-view. Life is good. Children are good. Motherhood is good. Freedom and a career are goods. None of these in itself is an evil. "The worse or evil is a rejected good. . . . Until it is rejected, it is a competing good" (MW 14:193). People then do not deliberate over goods and evils, but over what they experience as competing goods. "Choice is not the emergence of preference out of indifference. It is the emergence of a unified preference out of competing preferences" (MW 14:134). Moral choice is not the adoption of some inherent good and the rejection of many inherent evils.

Traditional morality opposes abortion, equating it with murder. This position seems extreme to many; but, rather than simply denying that abortion is murder (as the pro-choice position does), we should try to see how abortion came to be equated with murder. Then perhaps we will be able to deal rationally with the absolutism of the pro-life position. We must realize that there were reasons why abortion came to be seen as an evil that society had a legitimate interest in preventing, and may still have an interest in preventing in some cases. In an attempt to evaluate the history of the abortion question, we must first consider the role of medical factors. If abortion is now safer than full-term pregnancy, it has only become so in the last few decades. At the time that traditional morality evolved its prohibition against abortion, obtaining an abortion was risking death. Moreover, the desire of traditional morality to prevent abortions grew out of sociomedical conditions under which all too frequently the child died anyway. When our control over life and death was often no more direct than to shake beads and burn incense, our efforts to respect life were restricted to maximizing *lives* rather than maximizing the quality of any one's *life*. We have now reached such a level of technical sophistication, however, that we can prolong virtually all lives, and produce infinite numbers of new ones, by mechanical means. Mere control of life can no longer be seen as our goal; we have all but reached it.

Unfortunately, the sociomedical aspects of the abortion issue are not the only ones. There is also a tradition of antifeminism that runs through our society, a tradition that sees pregnancy and childbirth as a woman's duty in life. She owes children to her husband as her contribution to the family, and to the country as her contribution to the state. For a woman to obtain an abortion is to shirk this sacred obligation. Whatever pain she might suffer, whatever else she might have to forgo to be a mother, should be seen as minor since she is fulfilling her natural role. And, should a woman ever become pregnant without a husband, then the pain and social dislocation she suffers is both a just punishment for her sin and a justification for the further suffering which the society then heaps upon her. The reaction to these strictures on women is now being felt in the romanticism of that segment of the woman's rights movement that maintains that each woman is a unique individual free from all familial and social commitments; but such a position would never have been suggested were it not for our prior antifeminine orientation.

When children were born and died for reasons which were not known, and women were either pregnant or nursing most of their short adult lives, rules were formed to deal with abortion. While these rules have been called into question by medical developments and social changes, because of the strength of the impulse to respect life, they live on in custom. "Rules formed accidentally or under the pressure of conditions long past, are protected from criticism and thus perpetuated" (MW 14:167). The impulse to respect life should not be blindly discharged in efforts to prolong all lives as long as possible, or to accumulate as many human beings as possible; nor should the impulse be denied entirely. Rather, the impulse to respect life should be worked through to decide how best we can respect life in any particular situation. Any such inquiry immediately calls into question the old methods of valuing life. Is any rule justified? Not solely by its being a rule. Authority is no argument; it is history. We need to overcome the position that "while an open mind may be desirable in respect to physical truths, a completely settled and closed mind is needed in moral matters" (LW 7:329). But the necessity to justify any rule should not call into question the necessity for rules of some sort. Social life requires that we take others into account when we act and vice versa: although "*a* law is always questionable," law itself is necessary because people "are born and live in social relationships . . ." (LW 7:227).

This position denies the possibility of a final, complete, perfect, and certain moral code that we could apply to all people and all actions at all times. The grounds for this denial have two sources. The first is in the discoveries of Darwin, yielding proof of the pervasiveness of change and of the natural origins of humanity; the second, in a general fallibilistic position that rejects claims to certainty. The purpose of morality is to make human life more secure and valuable, not to satisfy some presumed prehuman code; and, if we are honest about recognizing our relationship to a changing environment, we must admit that we can never be sure that we have achieved an answer so secure that we need no longer continue to question. Rather than resting behind moral codes, moralists should look to people's lives.

On the one hand, it is important to recognize that different people have different values. Different people value life in different ways. This is a fact of human experience. But such a fact cannot be seen to solve the abortion problem, it only poses it. Given that people feel differently about abortion, our question must be to see if and when some ways are better than others. The question then becomes one of deciding how people *should* value life—a question as vital for us as for our premedical ancestors. It is also important that we recognize the power of habit in conduct. People are creatures of habit, and operate to a great extent on the fund of past actions, both personal and social. People learn their moral codes from a community, which "becomes a forum and tribunal within . . ." (MW 14:216). Unfortunately, there are times when customary morality "simply lives off the funded results of some once-moving examination of life" (EW 3:96), thereby losing its vitality and usefulness to us. Thus we can see how "the rigid character of past custom has unfavorably influenced beliefs, emotions and purposes having to do with morals" (MW 14:46). We do not want to do away with habits and customs, only to get more appropriate ones. Precedents should not be *followed* but *studied*. The fact that some people once felt a certain mode of valuing life was good is a useful datum for all circumspect moralists; but a datum as such imposes no duty on us beyond encouraging us to take it under advisement when we attempt to evaluate current situations. After all, "a man's duty is never to obey certain rules; his duty is always to respond to the nature of the actual demands which he finds made upon him . . ." (EW 3:106). Life is to be valued; so is motherhood. The freedom and responsibility of each life outside the home is also desirable. But as goods they are a means to a better life, "not goods to be possessed as they would be if they expressed fixed ends to be attained. They are directions of change in the quality of experience. Growth itself is the only moral 'end'" (MW 12:181).

Morality tends to be a highly emotional matter; but an honest commitment to an experimental approach to abortion would do much to lift this question out of the realm of emotional condemnation into an area of intelligent analysis. "Mistakes" at times will no doubt be made, or so things will seem to us when others act as we would not. We must come to respect the decisions of these women as honest attempts to do what they see as best. We must remember that "moral science is *not* a collection of abstract laws. . . . It is [her] perception of the acts that need doing . . ." (EW 3:99). We can expect no more than honest effort. Life offers no better choice. Moreover, before we can make an intelligent decision on the role that abortion should play in current society, we will need data. Data on intelligence and education. Data on the relations of the interactions of mothers and children. Data on population growth and the environment. Data on the world's resources and future population growth. Without such data, any choice which we make will be myopic, if not blind. We can no longer tolerate the divorce of "practical" and "ethical" matters. "Probably the great need of the present time is that the traditional barriers between scientific and moral knowledge be broken down, so that there will be organized and consecutive endeavor to use all available scientific knowledge for humane and social ends" (LW 7:283).

Since all we can change is the future, such an experimental approach to morality emphasizes the *future* over the *past*. Such an approach to morality also de-emphasizes the negative aspects of punishment and guilt, since it sees ethics as less interested in prohibitions than in the discovery and realization of values. This approach to morality also emphasizes that we have not yet achieved morality: "No individual or group will be judged by whether they come up to or fall short of some fixed result, but by the direction in which they are moving" (MW 12:180). All of this is but a realization that we are slowly, piece by piece, building our future—for better or worse—with each individual choice. "Our world does not so obviously hang upon any one of [our minor decisions]; but put together they make the world what it is in meaning for each one of us. Crucial decisions can hardly be more than a disclosure of the cumulative force of trivial choices" (MW 14:150). Of course, there will be those who will maintain that abortion is too important a matter for any experimental approach, that the wrongs or rights of the situation transcend the possible value of study. To these people we can only answer that abortion is such an important matter that we *must* adopt an experimental approach. The method of intelligence, "the same ordinary intelligence that measures dry-goods, drives nails, sells wheat, and invents the telephone" (EW 3:94–95), is all that we have beyond our blind emotions, and our unthinking habits.

So might run an attempt to deal with the problem of abortion in a Deweyan voice. Surely, Dewey would have done a better job himself; and even the students who consider this étude—or who prepare one of their own—will no doubt suggest improvements to this version. Still, if it is a reasonably successful attempt to present Deweyan thinking on a serious social issue, if it captures the core of his thought, then it will advance our inquiry by suggesting to students the power of, and the potential problems with, his approach to ethics. This interaction, and similar ones with other issues and other figures in the American tradition, will help our students to grow in their understanding of the tradition. Moreover, because of the novelty that this or any similar endeavor would bring to our philosophy, we would not be piling up more scholastic monuments but would be putting our historical scholarship to work in hopes of advancing the tradition and benefiting the communities of which we are a part.

NOTES

1. Cf. Rorty's comments to SAAP in the early 1980s: "I am out of my depth in addressing this audience. . . . [P]ractically everyone in this room has read more James and Dewey than I have, and read them more recently. . . . My excuse for invoking their names despite being relatively unlearned in their works is as follows. For some years, whenever I thought I had found something general and useful to say, it sounded like an echo of something I had once read. When I tried to run it down, I was constantly led back to Dewey. . . . Perhaps it would have been better not to have taken Dewey's name, or the term 'pragmatism,' in vain, or at least not until I had done enough homework to count myself a student of the history of American philosophy" ("Comments on Sleeper and Eden," *Transactions of the Charles S. Peirce Society* 11, no. 1 [winter 1985]: 39).

2. William James, *The Will to Believe* (Cambridge: Harvard University Press, [1897] 1979), 77–78.

3. In this piece, I will be quoting passages from Dewey's writings from the critical edition of his works edited by Jo Ann Boydston, abbreviated as follows: (EW) *The Early Works, 1882–1898* (Carbondale: Southern Illinois University Press, 1969–1972), five volumes; (MW) *The Middle Works, 1899–1924* (Carbondale: Southern Illinois University Press, 1976–1983), fifteen volumes; (LW) *The Later Works, 1925–1953* (Carbondale: Southern Illinois University Press, 1981–1990), seventeen volumes.

4. George Santayana, *Scepticism and Animal Faith* (New York: Dover Publications, [1923] 1955), 1.

TWO

Dewey's Limited Shelf Life

A Consumer Warning

MICHAEL ELDRIDGE

There are several reasons why John Dewey's social and political proposals may need a consumer warning. Some think that they were wrongheaded to begin with and should never have been made available. Some think they are well intentioned but not very workable. So they should be recalled and redesigned. But the best reason, in my view, is that they were intended for specific situations. Those situations have now passed; so they are no longer usable as originally formulated. There is, however, a second-order proposal, the advocacy of social intelligence, that is of continuing value. But even this has its critics; and its advocates, such as myself, caution that it is to be used with care. Thus some consumer warnings definitely seem to be in order.

BAD IDEAS

Many would warn consumers because they think Dewey's secular, scientific and democratic approach is wrong. They find his proposals antitraditional, antireligious, anti-intellectual or defective in other ways—scientistic, unduly optimistic, or incoherent. From the left he has been attacked as naïve, relying too much on education, and too complacent toward American society. These criticisms have been well advertised and need not be rehearsed here.[1]

IMPRACTICAL

Of greater interest is the concern that, while Dewey may have been well motivated, informative, and insightful and thus should be taken seriously, his proposals have shown themselves to be impractical or less than complete in terms of effectiveness. This consumer warning is worth attention and I will consider it by examining what John Herman Randall, Jr., and H. S. Thayer have had to say. Both philosophers were sympathetic to Dewey's project but found it wanting in an important respect.

RANDALL AND THE NEED FOR A POLITICAL TECHNOLOGY

In "Dewey's Interpretations of the History of Philosophy," Randall, who was Dewey's student and then colleague at Columbia University, cited a series of passages from *Liberalism and Social Action,* in which Dewey called for the use of a social intelligence to change the institutions that had been inherited from a premodern age.[2] Randall suggested that if Dewey's analysis was right and his program adequate, then "the most insistent problem today is precisely this one of political education" in the broad sense of intelligent, directed institutional change. He chided Dewey for having failed to inquire into the requisite political skills: "Instead of many fine generalities about the 'method of coöperative intelligence,' Dewey might well direct attention to this crucial problem of extending our political skill. For political skill can itself be taken as a technological problem to which inquiry can hope to bring an answer. . . . Thus by rights Dewey's philosophy should culminate in the earnest consideration of the social techniques for reorganizing beliefs and behavior—techniques very different from those dealing with natural materials. It should issue in a social engineering, in an applied science of political education—and not merely in the hope that someday we may develop one."[3] The logic of Dewey's "intelligized practice" and his insistence on the use of the sort of thinking one finds in science to transform prescientific institutions required an attention to the methods of social change.

Dewey readily accepted the criticism. In a footnote in his rejoinder in the Schilpp volume he wrote: "I wish to take this opportunity to express my full agreement with what Dr. Randall says in his paper about the importance of developing the skills that, if they were produced, would constitute political technology. The fact—which he points out—that I have myself done little or nothing in this direction does not detract from my recognition that in the concrete the invention of such a technology is the heart of the problem of intelligent action in political matters" (p. 592,

n. 57 LW 14:75)[4]. Dewey could have replied to his younger Columbia University colleague that it was enough for him as a cultural critic to have pointed out the need for integration of thought and action and that it was the work of someone other than a philosopher to develop a political technology. Dewey had often declined in the past to get into the specifics, the political machinery, of institutional change. He had often contented himself with the conceptual reconstruction that was prior to actual political change, leaving to others or a later time the invention of the needed political means. This time, although not accepting the challenge for himself (he was eighty years old), he readily agreed that "in the concrete the invention of such a technology is the heart of the problem of intelligent action in political matters."

Intelligent, political action requires a political technology, a specification of the means to the ends desired. In late 1939, if not before, Dewey knew that democratic ends required democratic means, and he could describe both—to a point. But he admitted in his response to Randall that he could not specify "in the concrete" the political means to effect the democratic ends. Therefore, there was a hiatus in his thinking. But it was not a necessary one. Far from it, for his project of intelligizing practice permitted none. Moreover, he had many useful things to say about how one would intelligize practice. The problem was not how one would go about developing a political technology. The problem was that this itself was a subject for inquiry. It was not that it could not be done or that doing it would have been inconsistent with or beyond his philosophy. Rather, it had not been done by him or others, at least not to the point that it could be formulated as a technology.

But we must not make too much of this admission. All along Dewey had been insisting on the need to understand democracy as something more than the existing political machinery. He often pointed to the need for such an enlarged understanding in order to counter the tendency of some, if not most, to reduce it to the actions of voters, politicians, and government officials. His admission is the corollary of that long-standing practice. What was new was his way of putting the matter and a shift of emphasis. Always before he would say, in effect, "I am going to concentrate on the non-political aspects of democracy as a way of life," without denying the need for improved political techniques. But in the response to Randall, he said that the problem of an effective politics was also important.

To be sure he had himself paid attention to politics, significantly so in the 1930s. In public statements and articles and in service on various committees he had engaged in political action. But he had not reflected on this political practice in the same way that he had on education. The situation was this: His cultural instrumentalism required that practice, including political practice, be intelligized. He had himself engaged in political practice. But he had not made explicit the political technology employed in the same way that he and others had developed an educational technology. Accordingly, his cultural instrumentalism was incomplete. It lacked the political edge it needed to be the truly intelligized practice that he proposed. What he admitted to Randall was what he had long realized and had been moving toward—"the invention of such a technology"—but had never himself developed "in the concrete."

THAYER AND THE NEED FOR A POLITICAL PROGRAM

Thayer's criticism is an extension of Randall's, requiring that Dewey offer a program of political action. In his critical history of pragmatism, he faults Dewey in particular for not developing an effective social and political program. Noting Dewey's persistent plea for social intelligence, Thayer declares that this is the right answer, but that it is "much too general to inspire great confidence in particular undertakings. . . . What was wanted but never forthcoming from pragmatists practicing intelligence was a social program, something more concrete and pragmatically meaningful than 'growth' or 'intelligence.' For without some program of specific objectives, social engineering is hardly possible."[5]

One response to this criticism is the one that Dewey made to Randall. There does need to be a working out of the means and ends of political action—a political technology. Another is that of James Campbell, who, noting Thayer's criticism, as well as those of Charles Frankel and Morton White, argues that we can discover in Dewey's voluminous writing "a rather thorough program for social reconstruction."[6] But then Campbell rightly observes that to focus on the program is to mistake what Dewey was all about. We can piece together what Dewey said in various places and we can formulate a fairly complete program. But in so doing we miss the point of Dewey's proposal and run the risk of treating his social and political proposals as products to be consumed. Dewey's recommendations were responses to specific situations.[7] As the situations change, as they no doubt have since the early part of the twentieth century, then his proposals are no longer relevant as substantive proposals. Rather, as Campbell suggests, we should be looking at what Dewey proposed as examples of the method he recommended. We should be interested not so much in the content but in the working out of his proposals as responses to various socially and politically problematic situations. Then we would have models of how to engage in social reconstruction.

The danger of Thayer's criticism is that we could be asking for something that smacks of an ideology, a readily understandable and applicable program of action, that requires little of its adherents beyond commitment and ingenuity in implementation. But, and this is the consumer warning, what Dewey would have us do is develop in our own time and place an intelligent response to our social and political difficulties. We do need means and ends—a political technology—but we can not take off the shelf a political technology that has been developed by prior generations. We can benefit from a store of such technologies, but we can never be relatively unthinking consumers.

A TEST CASE—DEWEY, UNION ORGANIZING AND A NONUNION BUT DEWEYAN APPROACH

To illustrate the contextual nature of Dewey's advocacy of social intelligence I want to consider the possibility of an alternative to union organizing that is Deweyan in approach but contrary to what Dewey usually proposed in such situations. I begin with a reminder of Dewey's extensive involvement in the union movement. I then consider a case in which a Deweyan could well decide that an alternative approach is needed. I conclude this section with some lessons we can draw from this for a Deweyan understanding of social intelligence.

Dewey and Unions

Dewey had a long association with the New York teachers' union, from its organization in 1912 as the Teachers League of New York through its affiliation with the American Federation of Labor and the internal battles of the 1930s.[8] A casual thumbing through of the collected works turns up many expressions of support for the union movement. In 1916 Dewey wrote that "every teacher should feel proud to be affiliated with the labor unions" (MW 10:172). His 1929 address, "Why I Am a Member of the Teachers Union" (LW 5:269–75), was, according to the textual commentary of Patricia Baysinger, reprinted by the American Federation of Teachers and included in their recruitment brochures (LW 5:441; Baysinger's observation was made in 1984). But the most uncompromising statement that I have noticed was a radio address in 1935.

New York City radio station WEVD, as a part of its "University of the Air" series to be broadcast over the NBC radio network, invited Dewey to speak on three occasions. The second of these addresses, "The

Teacher and the Public," was published in *Vital Speeches of the Day* (28 January 1935) and began with several questions, "Who is a worker? Are teachers workers? Do workers have common ties to unite them? Should these ties be expressed in action?" (LW 11:158). Dewey answered that teachers are workers—they produce "the goods of character, intelligence and skill"—and they should make common cause with other workers (LW 11:161). But then he noted that the lack of these goods raised the question: "Is not this fact proof, it may be asked, of a widespread failure of teachers to accomplish their task?" It is his answer to this question that is worthy of some consideration.

He acknowledged that teachers had failed in their task, but he said the cause for this failure was not with the teachers but with "the excessive control . . . exercised by the small and powerful class that is economically privileged." Independent-minded teachers were subject to dismissal and were branded as "subversives." Then, turning to the last question, the one about the actions that teachers needed to take, Dewey continued his forthright class analysis: "The answer is short and inclusive. Ally themselves with their friends against their common foe, the privileged class, and in the alliance develop the character, skill and intelligence that are necessary to make a democratic social order a fact." He then closed with these words: "In union is strength, and without the strength of union and united effort, the state of servility, of undemocratic administration, adherence to tradition, and unresponsiveness to the needs of the community . . . will persist. And in the degree in which they continue, teachers will of necessity fail in the special kind of productive work that is entrusted to them" (LW 11:161). Dewey's pro-union stance could not be clearer.

A Deweyan, but Nonunion Solution to the Problematic Situation of Adjunct University Instructors

Yet, a few years ago, I made a proposal that I thought was Deweyan in approach, but did not propose a teachers' union.

This proposal came about when I was employed as a "full-time part-time" teacher. I was teaching four or five sections a semester but at part-time wages. My total salary for four sections was just under $10,000 a semester—and there were no benefits. So, when the American Philosophical Association formed a committee on the priorities and problems of the APA, I spoke, in December 1998, to the chair about the adjunct teacher situation. Then I followed up with an e-mail in which I outlined my proposal. Here is what I wrote:

1. We have drifted into a situation in which increasingly large numbers of academics are employed as adjuncts. I realize that many individuals and institutions have been quite intentional, but collectively there has not been much deliberation. On the whole, it is an accidental development.
2. Our current self-understanding of adjuncts as temporary is inaccurate. Some institutions apparently have come to rely on "adjuncts" as a significant minority (if not majority) of their faculty. As I mentioned to you, I have been employed as a "full-time part-time" teacher (except for one semester when I taught only one course) since the fall of 1995. I have an office, phone, and computer access and regularly teach four or five sections. Technically, I am employed on a semester-to-semester basis, but effectively, I am a continuing employee—albeit one without much status, rights, or benefits. (I am well aware that I have it pretty good relative to those who are teaching in more than one institution and lack an office.)
3. We need a new model. In North Carolina enrollments are up. There are an increasing number of eighteen-year olds and a larger percentage are choosing to go to college. But universities are reluctant to add tenure-track lines in the humanities and social sciences. So the "adjunct" lines get expanded to meet the need, creating a situation in which people like me are lumped with those who may teach only for a semester or two or who may be employed full-time elsewhere and teach a course "on the side."
4. This new model should be constructed by those involved—adjuncts, regular faculty, administrators, and professional organizations. Assuming good will rather than malevolence—administrators do not set out to harm people like me; they are just trying to cope with the various pressures—we don't need to confront one another. Rather we need to figure out who are the interested parties and get them to work together on possible solutions.
5. The organizing impetus should come from the professional associations—the American Philosophical Association and its counterparts in the other disciplines. Most adjuncts are vulnerable to the whims of those who hire them and are reluctant to confront the powers that be. Also they lack time and resources. These vulnerable individuals need to be represented by their professional organizations.

6. The mechanism should be a task force/project that is composed of the professional associations not only for the disciplines (philosophy, history, English, psychology, etc.) but also of the administrators.
7. This project could pick a region/metropolitan area that has willing administrators and one or more schools of education doing (or willing to do) research on adjunct teaching. Additionally, the project could be conducted in an area that includes a state capitol, thus creating an opportunity to involve state legislators.
8. A collaborative research/action effort could then be carried out with representatives of the professional associations, the school of education researchers, and local participants, including administrators, regular faculty, and adjuncts.
9. Funding could come not only from the associations but also from foundations.
10. If a better system could be devised, then universities in other regions could adopt it. Hence, there is no need to mount a national effort in the sense of implementing a nationwide, once-for-all solution. It would be, however, a national effort in the sense that national institutions would be involved.

This proposal is Deweyan in that it is deliberative, collaborative, experimental, and meliorative in approach. Readers of Dewey will recognize the contrast between the accidental development of the current situation and the call for a *deliberative* approach. Rather than just accepting the current situation, Deweyans will note that this situation was constructed, or more precisely, was the result of a host of individual efforts. But we do not have to acquiesce in the given situation. We can reconstruct it. But this time we will do so in a *collaborative* fashion. This does not mean we must get everybody into one big room and take a vote. Rather we would proceed in an *experimental* fashion, constructing and publicizing fairer and more productive alternatives to the present accidental arrangement. Over time we could modify the present situation on the basis of these various experiments. Thus the proposal is *meliorative*.

I proposed this to a committee of a professional association. If I were to be asked by someone else what I think should be done, I might well construct a variation that did not give such a prominent role to the professional associations. This is another respect in which this is a Deweyan proposal. Dewey often addressed particular situations, shaping what he had to say to the occasion. But there were continuing themes. Clearly his participation in unions was one and his insistence on the need for social intelligence was another. So how can my nonunion approach to a problem that Dewey would have apparently solved by organizing be a Deweyan one?

Dewey, Unions and the Need for Social Intelligence

Earlier I cited many passages that indicated Dewey's commitment to union organizing. Now I want to qualify that picture. Dewey was a good union man, but he was not an unthinking supporter. If one pays attention to what he actually said, s/he can find room for alternative approaches, particularly in changed circumstances. Context, as should be clear by now, can make a big difference for Dewey. Earlier I was selective in my citations, passing over any qualifications that may have made Dewey other than an uncompromising union supporter. Now I want to go back and notice some of those qualifications.

In 1927, in "Why I Am a Member of the Teachers Union," Dewey addressed the members of the New York teachers' union, noting that the question had arisen in past discussions of admitting "educational officials" to membership. He observed that a similar question had arisen in the American Association of University Professors, which he had helped to organize. The AAUP had decided not to admit college presidents into the Association. But he expected that "the time will come when the professors' association will be sufficiently large and sufficiently powerful so that they will feel safe to admit them" (LW 3:270). The clear impression is that Dewey was among the "active minority" that favored their inclusion. Apparently his unionism was more inclusive than that of others.

In the revised edition of the *Ethics,* which he coauthored with James H. Tufts, there is a chapter devoted to "Collective Bargaining and the Labor Union." That there is such a chapter is an indication of Dewey's interest in the issue. Moreover, the tone of the chapter is one that takes seriously the rights of working people, including their right to organize. But Dewey and Tufts do not think that working people should be given the upper hand. Rather, they recognize three competing interests: owner-employers, working people, and consumers. They accept that each group has claims. The problem they find with the present situation, that is, with the modern industrial period viewed from their vantage point in the 1930s, was that "the immense gains made by modern industrial processes, including those due to science, to invention, and to education, have gone to the owner-employer group" (LW 7:388).

In other words, in recent centuries an imbalance had occurred, one that favored the owner-employers. This suggests that Dewey's commitment to workers and to their unions was not absolute. In a different time and place he might side with a different group. What he thought desirable was a balancing of these groups' interests.

No doubt we are still in a period of imbalance in favor of the economic elite that control our corporations and unduly influence our political institutions. But the point is that one does not divide workers and others into two classes—the good guys and the bad guys. At least not initially. Rather one attempts to be inclusive, insuring that each party has an equal say in the resolution of common problems.

The important question is not, *Is this proposal one that relies on union organizing?* Rather, *Is it an intelligent response to the situation?* Dewey, in the first part of the twentieth century, given the economic and political inequities of the time, tilted in favor of unions. But the overriding consideration was one of democratic participation involving all the affected parties. So one cannot simply look to what Dewey usually said and did and assume that since our situation is sufficiently similar, the same approach is needed. Maybe yes; maybe no.

This is why Thayer's criticism is mistaken. He, in effect, can be understood to be arguing that unless Dewey gives us a ready-made solution, we will not know what to do. Dewey's advocacy of social intelligence is much too vague to be action-guiding. But this criticism assumes that ordinary citizens, working with experts, cannot formulate programmatic responses to problematic situations. They need experts, such as Dewey, to work out programs for them. Admittedly, programs must be devised, but it is not the responsibility of the intellectual to do this *for* people and *for all time*.

This is the issue in terms of what is enduring in Dewey's pragmatism. One can study what he said and did *and why*. But what one most needs to understand is Dewey's approach to social problems. And a key feature of this approach is its situatedness. One constructs solutions to specific problems. Hence the one Deweyan "product" (other than his naturalism, but that is another story for another time) with a long shelf life is social intelligence, and this is a product that requires knowledgeable users. Moreover its use will produce solutions that will vary with the circumstances.

This, of course, is judged to be a weakness by many. They think that such plasticity is too amorphous to be a useful approach. One needs programs, formulas, recipes for success. But Dewey thinks that we can learn to make good judgments about our practices. He thinks we can learn to exercise wisdom. So perhaps a better title for this essay would be "Dewey's Limited Value," for his approach is one that cannot be mass marketed. It requires skill, insight, study, collaboration, and wisdom. Whether good judgment can be widely practiced is yet to be determined.

On the basis of my experience I would say, "Not now and not for the foreseeable future." But we make a mistake if we judge the success of an effort on the basis of what has happened to date or in our lifetime. Dewey concluded an autobiographical essay with these words:

> I do not expect to see in my day a genuine, as distinct from a forced and artificial, integration of thought. But a mind that is not too egotistically impatient can have faith that this unification will issue in its season. Meantime a chief task of those who call themselves philosophers is to help get rid of the useless lumber that blocks our highways of thought, and strive to make straight and open the paths that lead to the future. Forty years spent in wandering in a wilderness like that of the present is not a sad fate—unless one attempts to make himself believe that the wilderness is after all itself the promised land. (LW 5:159f)

Neither Dewey nor we live in the promised land, and we cannot expect that what Dewey worked out in his own time and place would have enduring value, unless it is of a general nature and thus speaks to both transitory situations. His diagnosis of the need for intelligent action and his recommendation as to what constitutes such action are valuable over time—but not necessarily the specific proposals that he made at the time. Hence the need for us to be wary of what we take from Dewey and how we use it.

DEWEY'S METHOD AS A BAD IDEA

Earlier I was rather dismissive of those who think Dewey's instrumentalism is a bad idea. There I had in mind those who reject Dewey's approach because they think it is fundamentally mistaken. There are, however, two more limited rejections, ones that react negatively at precisely the level of method. Some find themselves more or less in agreement with some of Dewey's social and political proposals (or they may not), but they react specifically to his method of inquiry.

Richard Rorty thinks that for all of Dewey's talk of method there is really no method there. In "Pragmatism Without Method," an essay he wrote for a Festschrift honoring Sidney Hook, one of Dewey's prominent students, Rorty argues that the method Dewey and Hook advocated was neither as well defined nor as effective as they thought. It amounted to little more than muddling through various social problems.[9] Rorty has little problem with what Dewey and Hook did; his problem is with their description of their activity. Hence, he wants a pragmatism without method. This is made clear in Rorty's response to James Gouinlock's contribution to *Rorty and Pragmatism.* Rorty thinks a method would be "a set of concrete, teachable techniques." But what Dewey proposes falls short of this, occupying "an unfindable middle ground between a set of virtuous habits" and a discrete method with "formal properties."[10] In *Transforming Experience* I defend Dewey's use of method and his self-understanding, arguing that Dewey "had a complex understanding of intelligence that included attitudes, beliefs, and activities." It is not easily reducible to a set of readily transferable techniques. But if one must produce something discrete I proposed this: "Deweyan intelligence uses conditions and consequences that it has identified to institute means and ends" (17). This, of course, is too vague to satisfy Rorty. But, in *Transforming Experience* I gave it some specificity by doing what I took Campbell to be recommending—namely, looking at several instances of Deweyan political involvement to see what he actually did. What one finds is that Dewey was constantly attempting to discover actual conditions and consequences and turn them into means and ends. This procedure is what he thought scientists did and it was extendable to social and political problems.[11]

It is precisely at this point that C. A. Bowers charges that Dewey's advocacy of social intelligence is "ideological." But where Rorty takes Dewey's method just to be one of muddling through (and so no real method at all), Bowers understands Dewey to be an ardent progressive, recommending the use of the scientific method in all areas of life. His Dewey is antitraditional, dismissing out-of-hand alternative ways of knowing. Bowers is interested in education for a just and environmentally sustainable society and is convinced that Dewey's "epistemology" is one of "high-status" knowledge that supports our modern industrial way of life which is neither fair nor ecologically sensitive.[12]

If Dewey were the linear, anticulture, scientistic thinker that Bowers believes him to be, then Dewey would hold little interest for me, for I share Bowers's concern for the environment, justice, and a pluralistic culture. But Dewey deserves a more nuanced reading, one that I cannot now supply, except on the one point which is at issue here—Dewey's understanding of social intelligence. Dewey did think that science provides us the best example of intelligence to date, but he did not mean by that we were to bring the laboratory method of experimentation into other areas of life. Rather, what he found significant about science was its ability to generate from within experience the methods and norms necessary for knowledge. With the advent of science experience had become self-regulative.[13] The task for us is not to become scientists but to learn from science how to be more intelligent in our on-going activities.

At age ninety, in a piece with familiar Deweyan themes, "Philosophy's Future in Our Scientific Age: Never Was Its Role More Critical," Dewey called once again for the "extension" of the scientific method into other areas of life, for "the development of *methods* of inquiry into *human* conditions." Then, after repeating and italicizing once again the word "methods," he added this footnote: "The word 'methods' is italicized as a precaution against a possible misunderstanding which would be contrary to what is intended. What is needed is not the carrying over of procedures that have approved themselves in physical science, but *new* methods as adapted to *human* issues and problems, as methods already in scientific use have shown themselves to be in physical subject-matter" (LW 16:379). From bitter experience he had learned that his "scientific method" talk could be misunderstood. This 1949 footnote is one last effort to forestall this misunderstanding.

DEWEY'S LIMITED VALUE

Bowers's mistake is in thinking that Dewey's philosophy is an ideology, the sort of program that Thayer thought the pragmatists should have developed. As such, it can be expected to be well defined and implementable. But Dewey, as Thayer rightly understands, did not develop such a program. At best, he made many programmatic suggestions which can, as Campbell argues, be gathered together into a comprehensive program. But to do so is to miss the point. We should not take his suggestions as suggestions *for us*. Rather we should look to his approach to the problems of his time and learn from the method he employed. There is enduring value in what Dewey did. As he said, in an often quoted sentence, "Philosophy recovers itself when it ceases to be a device for dealing with the problems of philosophers and becomes a method, cultivated by philosophers, for dealing with the problems of men" (MW 10:46). It is the task of philosophy to cultivate methods for dealing with human problems; it is the task of everyone to work on our common problems. The mistake some make is to confuse the two, to think that Dewey was telling us how to live. That he did, but indirectly and his advice was carefully qualified. He spoke to particular situations, using his philosophically cultivated methods. That advice does not stand for all time and for everyone. It is limited as to time and place.

So the consumer warning that I am issuing is this: Don't buy what Dewey recommended—except as he is telling and showing us how to solve our common problems intelligently.

NOTES

1. See J. E. Tiles, ed., *John Dewey: Critical Assessments* (London: Routledge, 1992), for a collection, in four volumes, of a variety of criticisms

of Dewey's work. Also see John Patrick Diggins, *The Promise of Pragmatism: Modernism and the Crisis of Knowledge and Authority* (Chicago: University of Chicago Press, 1994). I respond to some of Diggins's criticisms in my study *Transforming Experience: John Dewey's Cultural Instrumentalism* (Nashville, Tenn.: Vanderbilt University Press, 1998), 184–94.

2. This paragraph and the following four paragraphs, slightly modified, are taken from Eldridge, *Transforming Experience,* 82–84.

3. In Paul Arthur Schilpp, *The Philosophy of John Dewey* (Evanston, Ill.: Northwestern University Press, 1939), 90f.

4. References to Dewey's works are to the critical edition edited by Jo Ann Boydston and published by Southern Illinois University Press at Carbondale. There are thirty-seven volumes in three series—*The Early Works, The Middle Works,* and *The Later works*. Thus, the citation LW 14:75 is to volume fourteen, page 75 of *The Later Works*.

5. H. S. Thayer, *Meaning and Action: A Study of American Pragmatism,* abr. ed. (Indianapolis, Ind.: Bobbs-Merrill Company, 1973), 242.

6. "Dewey's Method of Social Reconstruction," in James Campbell, *The Community Reconstructs: The Meaning of Pragmatic Social Thought* (Urbana: University of Illinois Press, 1992), 39–42.

7. See William J. Gavin's essay in this volume and Eldridge, *Transforming Experience,* 62–67.

8. See George Dykhuizen, *The Life and Mind of John Dewey* (Carbondale: Southern Illinois University Press, 1973), 145–46, and Eldridge, Transforming Experience, 91–97.

9. In Paul Kurtz, ed., *Sidney Hook: Philosopher of Democracy and Humanism* (Buffalo, N.Y.: Prometheus Books, 1983), 259–73; reprinted in Richard Rorty, *Objectivity, Relativism and Truth: Philosophical Papers* (Cambridge: Cambridge University Press, 1991), 63–77.

10. Herman Saatkamp, ed., *Rorty and Pragmatism* (Nashville, Tenn.: Vanderbilt University Press), 92–93.

11. The reader may gain some clarity by referring above to the nonunion but Deweyan proposal that I put forward to deal with the problem of adjunct teachers. I attempt to come to terms with the logic of this approach in my contribution to the *New Essays on Dewey's Logic* (Nashville, Tenn.: Vanderbilt University Press, forthcoming), edited by Tom Burke, Micah Hester, and Robert Talisse.

12. My knowledge of Bowers comes from interaction with him at the first Central European Pragmatist Forum, held in Slovakia in late May-early June 2000, and from an examination of his many books, which develop these themes. The paper he prepared for our session was titled "The Double Binds in Using Dewey's Epistemology to Address Eco-Justice Issues." In *Critical Essays on Education, Modernity, and the Recovery of*

the Ecological Imperative (New York: Teachers College Press, 1993), he refers to Dewey, along with Marx and Freire as an "ideologue" (84). The idea of "high-status knowledge" appears not only in the conference paper but in his books; see *Critical Essays,* 176. The John Dewey Society thought enough of Bowers's work to ask him to deliver the nineteenth John Dewey Lecture, which was published as *The Promise of Theory: Education and the Politics of Cultural Change* (New York: Longman, 1984).

13. See Eldridge, *Transforming Experience,* 30f, 179–81, and 186–89.

THREE

New Directions and Uses in the Reconstruction of Dewey's Ethics

GREGORY PAPPAS

Dewey once wrote that "the truest reverence we can render any of the heroes of thought is to use his thinking to forward our own struggle."[1] As we celebrate the beginning of a new millennium it is time to reexamine where we are in our forward "use" of Dewey's ethical theory. The difficulty with this is that we do not find an ethical theory in his writings, at least not in its traditional normative form.[2] In fact, most of what he had to say about normative ethics is negative and critical of such an endeavor. But what may be puzzling is that he was also at times positive and encouraging about finding new ways in which ethical theory can assist moral practice. The alternatives in this apparent tension in Dewey suggest two different ways in which present Deweyans can be critical of Dewey and thereby "pass him by." We can either drop his positive hope or we can work on trying to find the ways in which ethical theory is not a misuse or waste of intelligence. For those of us willing to resurrect (reconstruct) moral theory and put it to some "use," Dewey's texts on ethics are of very little help. He believed that even though moral theory cannot take the place of personal decision, nonetheless there are many ways in which it can "render personal choice more intelligent."[3] He hoped that in ethics, "theory having learned what it cannot do, is made responsible for the better performance of what needs to be done"(MW 4:45). But there is no explicit, systematic, or detailed explanation of what form a reconstructed ethical theory might take in order for it to be useful.[4] What, if anything, can we expect from a Deweyan-based ethical theory in terms of a positive and normative ethical theory?

To "pass Dewey by" in ethics does not require that we radically break away from his basic insights about morality and philosophy, but it does mean that we must test them by using them to complete tasks that he left largely undone and in light of our present experience. There are some features of an adequate and useful normative moral theory that are implicit in Dewey's criticism of traditional ethics. We need to make those explicit and suggest what positive tasks and functions ethical theory might play in our life today; otherwise, our silence will continue to be interpreted as total scepticism regarding any theory.

The challenge is really twofold. On the one hand, one must offer new functions for ethical theory that are consistent or not at odds with Dewey's criticisms of traditional ethical theory; otherwise, "passing Dewey by" is more like a total abandonment or a misuse of his name and ideas "to forward one's own struggle." On the other hand, there is the difficulty of presenting something substantial enough to be taken seriously as an alternative. Can there be a normative ethical theory that is "thin" enough not to fall into another rule-guided absolutist ethical system but "thick" enough to be taken seriously as an ethics that, in some indirect way, can at least illuminate moral practice?

The "thickness" of traditional normative ethical theories is problematic because it amounts to pretending to determine right action prior to and across situations. For Dewey this is an overestimation of what a moral theory can do in handling real-life moral decisions. This overestimation is due in part to an oversimplified view of moral experience. The experienced uniqueness of each morally problematic situation, as well as the fact that in most of them what one has is a plurality of irreducible moral forces with no common denominator, precludes the very possibility of this type of ethical theory. But the pretensions of traditional moral theory are also the result of a failure to have an adequate empirical conception of what a theory is. Dewey's criticism of this issue is illuminating regarding the positive functions of ethical theory.

MORAL THEORY AND MORAL PRACTICE

In an early essay Dewey explains the functional relation between theory and practice by using the example of an engineer building a tunnel. No matter how many times the engineer has done the "same" tunnel, what s/he is building is not a tunnel in general. It is a tunnel having its own special end and called for by its own set of circumstances—a set of circumstances not capable of being precisely duplicated anywhere else in the world. The work has to be done under conditions imposed by the given environment (EW 3:156).

However, because similar tunnels have been built under functionally similar circumstances, one may develop theories or techniques that, because of their generality, can function as tools of analysis for particular cases. Hence, the general character of theories is not a limitation but the key to their possible functional importance for practice. To be sure, not all of the theoretical resources available to the engineer bear the same kind of instrumental value. The most immediate "ready at hand" tools are principles or rules of thumb that provide a suggestion as to what to do when one is building this particular kind of tunnel. But an engineer might also have a very general theory about the nature of the materials that make up the tunnel. Even if this theory has no direct bearing on or makes no reference to the practice of building tunnels, it is not entirely divorced from or irrelevant to that practice. In general, Dewey claims that theory cannot be divorced from the context of practice. For theory arises from, is informed by, and affects practice. In other words, theory is not something that belongs to a different realm than the situational facts to be dealt with in a particular situation.[5] Moral theory is not "something apart from the practice of which it is a theory" (EW 3:96). The intelligence required in both moral deliberation and in the construction of a moral theory is the "same ordinary intelligence that measures dry-goods, drives nails, sells wheat, and invents the telephone" (EW 3:95).[6] It is true that theoretical moral inquiry has its own theoretical problems, very different in nature from the concrete moral conflicts which are the origin of personal moral deliberation. But theoretical inquiry is not the quest for a "foundation for moral activity in something beyond that activity itself" (EW 3:94). To think otherwise is to commit a philosophical fallacy. For Dewey, moral philosophy is invariably and inevitably enmeshed in a particular context, that is, it is a function of and within moral life. The refined conclusions (i.e., "secondary products") of moral theory are, like the theoretical resources of the engineer, instrumentalities by which we might be able to indirectly assist or illuminate the decisions and problems encountered in primary moral experience. When theory is conceived as something within practice it takes on the responsibility of being a part of the available means for the intelligent amelioration of practice. "Theory located within progressive practice instead of reigning statically supreme over it, means practice itself made responsible to intelligence; to intelligence which relentlessly scrutinizes the consequences of every practice" (MW 4:48).

The conception of moral theory as somehow existing "outside" or "above" the context of moral practice is the source of recent scepticism against theory. Bernard Williams, for example, criticizes the history of moral philosophy for its futile attempt to find an "Archimedean point."[7] This "outside-god's eye view" spot is the place from which 1) one can "objectively" evaluate competing answers about how to live; or 2) discover a universal criteria of right or wrong action; or 3) where one can argue that anyone (even the moral sceptic or anarchist) has reasons to live an ethical life. Indeed, traditional ethical theory usually assumes that to have a normative ethics is to have a philosophical answer to these issues. For Williams, we must come to terms with the fact that "our point of view, is inevitably from here, and not from a 'mid-air position.'"[8] This should deflate significantly our expectations in regard to what moral theory can do for moral practice. Williams asserts the Deweyan thesis that ethical theories "still have to start from somewhere, and the only starting point left is ethical experience itself,"[9] but he fails to appreciate the more positive and constructive implications of the conception of theory "within" moral practice.[10] Dewey's criticism, on the other hand, has positive implications regarding the scope and legitimate functions of ethical theory. There is an alternative which lies between divorcing ethical theory completely from moral practice and the pretensions of some normative ethical theories to dictate our moral conduct.

THE EMPIRICAL-INSTRUMENTAL CONCEPTION OF MORAL THEORY

The view that moral theory is both in and for moral life has important implications regarding how to evaluate ethical theories and their most productive functions. The most straightforward of these is that one cannot determine what adequate ethical theory is without considering what kind of moral theory is better for our moral lives. In other words, the worth of a theory is determined not only in terms of its intellectual consistency and coherence or its explanatory power, but also in terms of its instrumental-ameliorative powers in the context of practice. This allows us to propose hypotheses about when, and in what form, moral theory helps and when it hinders moral practice. Of course, any suggestion in this regard ultimately would have to be an empirical claim. That is, it should be tested in the moral lives of agents, remain open for future inquiry, and be evaluated in light of the particular theories available at any give time. Dewey's own evaluation of some of the ethical theories of his time led him to some general hypotheses about this issue.

Dewey believed that our moral lives are better served if ethical theory becomes empirical.[11] This means primarily that ethics must take morally problematic situations in their qualitative uniqueness as the starting point and end point of inquiry and not adopt any kind of axiomatic "first principles." Theory must have a dynamic, open, and learning relation with respect to the practice out of which it arises and in which it is embedded. However, one might accept the general claim that empirical theories are better than nonempirical ones and still remain sceptical about the point of ethical theory. For it is not clear what role there is left for ethics, once one gives up the traditional goals. Does this mean that philosophers should redirect their concern with theory to a more direct and exclusive concern with specific practical problems, as in what is called today "applied ethics"? This issue needs to be considered so as to avoid saddling a Deweyan approach to ethics with a narrow kind of instrumentalism about moral theory.

Ethical theory is not necessarily made more practical simply by having as its direct end "being practical." In philosophy, just as in science, a constant fixation and concern with practical problems and ends could undermine practical effectiveness. One might even argue that productive inquiry requires a division of labor where there are individuals who are directly involved in doing theory, as we say, for "theory's own sake." This is not to deny that there are excesses and dangers that result when intellectuals are so in love with their theories that they completely forget the place of theory within the context of moral practice. But the failure to be empirical is perhaps the result of being seduced by one's interest as a theoretician.

If the function of moral theory is to assist in some way or to illuminate our moral practice, then the operations and selectivity of a theoretician should be guided by purposes that enhance this function.[12] But the temptation of the ethical theorist is always to guide his or her selectivity by theoretical-academic purposes that are irrelevant, secondary, or even counterproductive to the improvement of moral practice. For instance, selecting only those features of moral life that can be quantified, universalized, or made commensurable in terms of a theory is not in the best interest of morality. For it results in theories that, in spite of their theoretical elegance, are for those who have narrow and oversimplified moral experiences. Moral theories are bad tools if they suggest that the complexity, uncertainty, and incommensurability that we experience in our moral lives are illusory. One is more likely to direct the changes in experience intelligently if one is faithful to its present traits. As Dewey says, "projection of a better life must be based upon reflection of the life already lived" (MW 4:32).

The counterpart to the idea that the moral theorist must not aim at just more theory is the assumption that moral theory becomes of use for moral practice only if it becomes applied ethics, that is, if it addresses particular problems instead of the usual general ones. The underlying assumption seems to be that the nonpractical character of a philosophy is proportional to how comprehensive, general, and speculative it is. However, there is no reason to think that, for example, a moral theory about the problem of abortion will better assist particular decisions about abortion than a theory that addresses the generic traits of all moral problems. Dewey would be even more suspicious of the former because it usually tries to replace context-sensitive reflection. In a view of theories as tools, there is room for specialized tools as well as for tools that have a wide range of application and reference, and either type of tool can conceivably be an obstacle or an aid to moral practice. Hence, philosophy cannot be disregarded as a speculative waste of time simply because it is concerned with formulating hypotheses that have the widest possible range of reference. On the contrary, Dewey found this to be one of the reasons why philosophy is important. He said,

> It is designated "philosophy" when its area of application is so comprehensive that it is not possible for it to pass directly into formulations of such form and content as to be serviceable in immediate conduct of specific inquiry. This fact does not signify its futility; on the contrary. . . . Historical facts prove that discussions that have not been carried, because of their very comprehensive and penetrating scope, to the point of detail characteristic of science, have done a work without which science would not be what it now is.[13]

Of course, this is not to deny the futility of philosophical inquiries that are so abstract as to be completely detached from everyday moral experience. But usually the problem with these inquiries from a practical point of view has nothing to do with their being abstract or general per se, but rather in the fact that they usually reify their theoretical abstractions over the things of ordinary experience. Here Dewey's view can be contrasted to that of Bernard Williams. Williams contrasts the "thickness" of ethical terms and deliberation of concrete moral agents with the "thinness" of ethical theories. Williams seems to think that ethical theory can be discredited because it "looks characteristically for considerations that are very general and have as little distinctive content as possible."[14] But for Dewey the problem with the abstract and general categories of traditional ethical theories is not that they are "thin" or general, but that these reflective products are used to discredit, ignore, and replace the richness of concrete moral experience. The implication is that so long as ethical theory recognizes that our actual ethical lives are richer, more variegated, "thicker" than our theoretical articulations, it can indulge in "thinness" and speculation without undermining its legitimate instrumental function.

We do not want to suggest the equally implausible view that the degree of abstractness and generality or specificity of an ethical theory is totally irrelevant to its instrumental potentialities. But it would be futile to try to lay out any universal and fixed rule about this issue. Dewey does propose a general "rule of thumb" or vague hypothesis in this matter. He claims that the kind of ethical theory that is adequate and capable of functioning as a tool for our moral life has to avoid becoming either so general as to be abstract or so specific as to attempt to replace the particularity of our lived experience. In other words, ethical theories and rules can become bad tools when they are either too abstract or too specific. In one of his early ethical writings Dewey said,

> The difficulty, then, is to find the place intermediate between a theory general to the point of abstractness, a theory which provides help to action, and a theory which attempts to further action, but does so at the expense of its spontaneity and breath. I do not know of any theory, however, which is quite consistent to either point of view. (EW 3:155)

This is a claim that can be understood in terms of both the descriptive and the normative functions of ethical theories. A metaphysics of morals (as a description of what there is in moral experience) is undesirable in ethics when it consists of excessively abstract generalities that "remain remote from contact with actual experience" (EW 3:159). But a metaphysics that can illuminate practice is "such a general statement of the nature of the facts to be dealt with as enables us to anticipate the actual happening, and thereby deal with it intelligently and freely" (EW 3:159). Dewey's reference to metaphysics as a "ground map of criticism" provides a useful analogy to make this point. A map can be general to the point of becoming a useless abstraction. On the other hand, a map that pretends to capture the uniqueness of the streets we are about to travel or to tell us where to go becomes a bad tool. Furthermore, the fact that a map cannot have this kind of precision is hardly a good excuse for not using or making maps. Dewey would use this same argument to support the construction and use of moral theory.

Ethical theories can become so abstract and general as to be of no use to moral practice. In spite of this, for Dewey ethical theories can only be of use to moral practice if they are concerned with the general character of moral situations. "Ethical theory must be a general statement of the reality involved in every moral situation. It must be action stated in its more generic terms" (EW 3:158).

Dewey took the general character of theory not as a limitation, but as a precondition which rendered individual experiences luminous but was also fructified by them.[15] The capacity for theory to inform practice and be informed by it mark two different but dependent phases of a fruitful ongoing relationship. Dewey's conception of an empirical ethical theory assumes a complementary and dynamic relation between theory and practice: "the former enlarges, releases and gives significance to the latter; while practice supplies theory with its materials and with the test and check which keep it sincere and vital" (LW 2:58).

What has been made explicit thus far is only the most general features of an adequate moral theory that are implicit in Dewey's criticism of traditional ethics. The alternative to an ethical theory that stands aloof and has nothing to do with moral practice, a theory that pretends to lay down in advance fixed rules applicable to every case, is one that is empirical, concerned with the generic in moral experience, and that offers only indirect assistance to moral practice. These seem to be rather formal or methodological conditions of a theory. The type of theory that meets these conditions cannot solve moral problems. Neither can it adopt the kind of standpoint where it can convince a moral sceptic that it is rational to be moral; nor can it provide a rational proof that Hitler's conduct was wrong. But is there anything it can do? What sort of "indirect assistance" can be proposed? If one wishes to confront the sceptic about the potentialities of ethical theory once the traditional pretensions are abandoned, it is necessary to suggest some specific positive functions that a Deweyean ethics can perform. There are at least two. An ethical theory can function as a tool of criticism, and it can propose hypotheses about what the conditions are for living a better moral life.

ETHICAL THEORY AS CRITICISM

For Dewey philosophy is criticism. Philosophy as criticism relies on subjecting the more refined reflective products of philosophical inquiry to the test of primary experience. But it can also subject what at any time is taken as primary experience to criticism. This is done either by arguing that it is not really primary, or by unveiling factors that condition our experience in an unwanted way. In other words, experience as method relies on what is experienced but what is experienced not only changes but can be modified and improved by the same method. What cannot be subjected to criticism is *all* of our primary experience, this is the "Cartesian dream." Reflective criticism always takes place in the noncognitive context of a situation that cannot be transcended. Nevertheless, effective criticism and modification of what we do experience needs to begin with what we do experience, and its point is to enhance what we do experience. All of this can be used to understand the potentialities of ethical theory within moral life.

Although too much reflective criticism might sometimes be harmful to moral practice, Dewey understood that without it the quality ("spirit and life") of our moral life suffers.[16] Moral ideas degenerate into petrifications or mechanical rules when they are not subject to reflective criticism in light of present experience. It might be argued that, even if one accepts that a moral life affected by reflection is desirable, and that theoretical reflection is continuous with ordinary reflection, it does not follow that theoretical reflection can have a useful function in our moral life. True, but what makes theoretical reflection indispensable is that it can take a wider and broader perspective, one that is not provided by ordinary reflection. This is why Dewey calls philosophy "criticism of criticism." To be sure, "wider-broader" does not mean or imply "outside."

Dewey declared as illusory the notion of ethical theory as performing criticism from an "outside" privileged standpoint, but he never doubted the possibility of criticism "from within." This is the possibility that seems to be ruled out or ignored by recent skeptics of theory, such as Richard Rorty and Bernard Williams. This has left them in an awkward position. For many have questioned whether the narrow role they have left for philosophical reflection is sufficient to engage (or make possible) the kind of social criticism and reflective moral life to which they seem to be committed. In effect, their repudiation of ethical theorizing is interpreted as moral conservatism, insofar as it seems to imply that we should leave moral practice as it is. To be sure, Dewey did not hold the view that ethical theory is necessary for a reflective moral life. However, he hoped that it would be, once reconstructed, a potentially useful resource for such a life. This was a resource he used in his criticism of traditional moral philosophy and of the society and times in which he lived. The theoretical use of intelligence cannot make contextual decisions, but it might be able to undermine misleading assumptions and beliefs that could be operative in making such decisions.

In the capacity of moral theory as a tool of criticism we can distinguish two different tasks: the descriptive and the normative. The descriptive function is to provide a generic but faithful description of the generic traits of moral experience. The point of this is not to provide a picture of how "things really are" but to provide a basis for reconstructing traditional notions of character, moral deliberation, and moral problems that usually presuppose dualisms. These dualisms are not mere intellectual problems. They reflect or reinforce ways of conceiving moral life that are obstacles for the present amelioration of our moral experience.[17] Furthermore, the descriptive-metaphysical task is an important precondition and basis for making any criticism of positive proposals about how to live. Dewey said, "The more sure one is that the world which encompasses human life is of such and such a character (no matter what his definition), the more one is committed to try to direct the conduct of life, that of others as well as himself, upon the basis of the character assigned to the world" (LW 1:309).

But criticism from the point of view of how things are (i.e., descriptive) can be complemented by criticism from the point of view of how things should be (i.e., normative). "No just or pertinent criticism in its negative phase can possibly be made, however, except upon the basis of a heightened appreciation of the positive goods which human experience has achieved and offers" (LW 1:308). Hence, a moral theory can also take the form of articulating and making explicit a moral ideal that could be used for criticism of present beliefs and institutions. This task also serves the purpose of making such an ideal both available and subject to criticism. This is the only way we can preserve the "life and spirit"[18] of a worthwhile ideal. This being said, there is bound to be some scepticism about the adoption of such a traditional notion as that of "ideals" by a pragmatist. How can this be compatible with the commitment to a situational contextualism?

Pragmatism recognizes the reality and necessary role of ideals in human life. They are "as natural to man as his aches and his clothes" (LW 1:312). They are real because potentialities and possibilities are part of experience. They are not made out of "subjective stuff"; nor do they come from a Platonic heaven; they are active instrumentalities in experience. About ideals, James said, "they ought to aim at the transformation of reality—no less."[19] For the pragmatist, ideals are ends but they are not "ends in themselves," that is, ends that are not also means. They are not fixed or final ends; they are subject to refinement (change) and their achievement is not a finality. They are not states of ultimate repose, nor do they have antecedent existence. Dewey put this eloquently when he said, "men do not shoot because a target exists, but they set up targets in order that throwing and shooting may be more effective and significant."[20]

Ideals can be distinguished from other ends by their inclusive nature. In an ideal, constructive imagination puts together into a coherent whole values that have been previously experienced. Thus, ideals are instrumental in the melioristic effort of making more secure what has been experienced accidentally. Every ideal, Dewey says, "projects in a securer and wider and fuller form some good which has been previously experienced in a precarious, accidental, fleeting way" (MW 14:20)—for the purposes of criticism. So, for example, by projecting the positive traits of actual forms of community life into an ideal, we can use the ideal to criticize undesirable features of our community and suggest improvement.[21] Ideals serve as a "basis for criticism of institutions as they exist and of plans of betterment" (LW 7:349).

It is dangerous for ethical theory to take the formulation of ideals as its major task. Dewey warned us that "the trouble with ideals of remote perfection is that they tend to make us negligent of the significance of the special situations in which we have to act" (LW 7:273). However, a pragmatic understanding of the proper function of ideals makes the commitment to an ideal compatible with the commitment to the amelioration of present situations. For neither one of these commitments is a mere end for the other. Projected ideals and goals give a general direction; they provide an additional continuity from situation to situation, that is, our present efforts are served by an ideal. But ideals are also served and informed by their application. We can set up ideals in order to improve our actual conditions, but they do not demarcate the absolute limits of improvement. For they are themselves subject to constant improvement. Ideals give coherence and stability to our lives, but a "mobile" one, that is, the ideal itself unfolds and expands.

Ideals can be obstacles but they can also be effective instrumentalities. Ideals can be vacuous, mere utopias, and arbitrary if they are formed without taking account of actual, present conditions. Dewey says, "Any ideal that is a genuine help in carrying on activity must rest upon a prior knowledge of concrete actual occurrences. A metallurgist's ideal of the best possible steel must rest upon knowledge of actual ores and natural processes. Otherwise, his ideal is not a directive idea but a fantasy."[22] Ideals can also become idle and impotent fantasies if we consider them independently of the means of their realization. It is through an explicit articulation and evaluation of ideals in terms of concrete existential requirements and the means of their realization that we can begin making ideals relevant and effective.

What is the origin of ideals? We depend on what others have done before us. Most of our ideals, like democracy, are inherited as possibilities from tradition. Our creative task is both to modify actual conditions with them and to reconstruct them so as to fit the actual situation. In other words, both the actual and the ideal are open to modification and improvement by an experimental and continuous process.[23]

In today's intellectual environment, the philosophical articulation of an ideal seems like a gratuitous theoretical and speculative indulgence. But for Dewey, ideals are integral parts of any worthwhile philosophy. The contemporary resistance to associating philosophy with moral ideals has as its source the neglect of the contextual nature of all philosophical reflection, and is also based on the assumption that philosophy is a "form of knowledge" (LW 6:43). But Dewey pleads that "we should return to the original and etymological sense of the word, and recognize that philosophy is a form of desire, of effort at action—a love, namely, of wisdom . . ." (LW 6:43). This view of philosophy as wisdom is consistent with the view of theory within practice. It conceives of philosophical inquiry as arising out of or assuming a moral concern or commitment.[24]

If philosophy is wisdom, then a philosopher is the intellectual with a moral conviction or a sense of a better kind of life to be led. He or she resorts to "the best knowledge and the best intellectual methods available in their day" (LW 6:44) for its articulation, support, and to persuade himself or herself and others of its reasonableness. Here we can "pass Dewey by" in the sense that we can add "thickness" to his vague and generally ("thin") but profound moral vision in terms of an ideal character and community. This does not mean that we have to provide the specifics or fine details; recall that Dewey thought this could be counterproductive.[25] Dewey has been criticized by Randall and Westbrook for not specifying "'in the concrete' the political means to effect the democratic ends."[26] But from the point of view of Dewey's ethics, this is a virtue. Dewey was a committed contextualist, and the lack of specific instructions is what allows us to develop the specifics as they pertain to our present experience without abandoning Dewey's vision. Critics wanted to know from Dewey "what to think"; instead Dewey would tell them "how to think," because the latter was more useful. Ethical theory can betray its practical function if it abandons its generic character and pretends to provide specific instructions. But to a large extent Deweyans today suffer from the other extreme. It might be argued that, overall, we have not moved very far beyond repeating the same general and abstract statements that Dewey repeated throughout his life about Democracy as a way of life. The challenge in doing the sort of theory that is not a waste of intelligence is to strike a balance that may well be very difficult to find and sustain. One must say enough to be useful, but not so much that it spoils context-sensitive reflection. One promising way to do this is to inquire into the conditions of moral experience.

ETHICAL THEORY AS INQUIRY INTO CONDITIONS

Dewey hoped that ethical theory would shift its concern from trying to make decisions for individuals and reducing moral experience to abstractions, to the study of the conditions of these experiences and their betterment. The persistent attempt by ethicists to lay down rules or universal criteria is a misuse of intelligence and needs to be replaced by the effort to "devote themselves to studying the conditions and effects of the changing situations in which men actually live" (MW 3:57).

For Dewey, it is an experiential datum that there is moral experience; a philosophical empiricism can only point to and describe these experiences as they are had. "Definition by pointing or denotation is indeed the ultimate recourse in all empirical matters" (LW 2:79). But beyond the operations of designation and description we can inquire into the conditions of their occurrence and amelioration. We can formulate hypotheses about what would enhance or what would be obstacles to having certain experiences without having a theory of the precise necessary and sufficient conditions that define those experiences.

Inquiry into conditions in ethics assumes a conception of ethical theory within practice. For it assumes that this kind of theory will be meaningful only to those who have had moral experiences. For those of us who are in moral life, convincing a radical sceptic can only be an activity secondary to inquiry into the conditions for improving experiences we already have.

The inquiry about conditions can be explained in terms of an important functional distinction between "what" and "how" we experience. We can establish a functional distinction in a situation between the way of experiencing and what is experienced, that is, between method and subject matter, without abandoning the notion of a situation as the locus of moral experience.[27] The recognition that what is experienced is not independent from what we bring into a situation (e.g., our habits) was a great modern discovery. However, instead of using it to regulate the course of experience, philosophers have used it to defend the reductions of experience to experiencing, that is, to subjectivism. For Dewey the purpose of this functional distinction is to provide some control over the direction or quality of our moral experience. The concern with conditions in morality is attention to "method," in the sense of the habits, character, ways of life, kinds of relationships, or any other notion that is relevant to the issue of "how" to interact with and participate in situations.[28] The pragmatist can recover or reconstruct these ethical notions and give them their due importance without assuming the usual dualisms and disregard for concrete situational experience that usually accompany ethical discourse about them.

Given the uniqueness of our characters, each one of us has unique ways of interacting with situations, but we can also distinguish generic ways. For example, approaching a situation with "openness" is a generic trait even though each one of us is "open" in a different way. Moreover, under "how," we can distinguish different levels of generality, for example, habits as particular ways of interacting, and character as a complex unity that defines how an organism interacts. We can even move to another level and speak of a "way of life" as a shared general way of interacting. These are abstract but very useful distinctions when we inquire about conditions.

There are good reasons why ethics in this new function should focus on character.[29] Although Dewey never completed the project, he thought that an "inventory of the different characteristic dispositions; and an account of how each is connected . . ." is needed.[30] Moral philosophy has had the tendency to either overestimate or underestimate the importance of character. The underestimation is a result of denying our participatory role in moral experience. On the other hand, the overestimation is usually a result of overestimating how much the direction of moral experience is within our control, or of making character an end in itself (and of morality). In both instances, the mistake is both one of not having an empirical starting point, and of having a mistaken notion of character. In Dewey's ethics, character and habits are central but not because they have ontological or epistemological primacy. They should be the foremost concern of moral reflection and theory simply because, of all the factors that come to determine the direction and moral quality of experience, habits are the most controllable factor we have. But, as Dewey warned us, we must be careful not to seek the sort of theoretical control that undermines the ability to arrive at judgments attentive to the uniqueness of each situation. The task to add "thickness" to a Deweyan ethical theory in terms of virtues (as habits) is more promising than coming up with "operational instructions"[31] because they are more general and therefore less liable to interfere with the qualitative sensitivity and reflection needed to confront each situation. In fact, Dewey thought that this sensitivity is procured by cultivating habits. The most important instrumentalities for morality, the "cardinal" virtues, are the traits of character that can make it possible to determine what morality requires here and now (i.e., in a situation).

The inclusion of the study of conditions as a normative function of ethical theory might be met with the objection that this is a reduction of ethics to psychology (or science). Furthermore, since the study of conditions is the study of what *is* the case, the new "normative" function of ethical theory outlined above, while legitimate, is not really "normative." In order to answer to this objection one needs to recall Dewey's conception of philosophy.

Dewey understood the task of philosophy to be one of utilizing the best available knowledge of its own time and place for human good. The mere study of human habits as the condition for moral experience might be just psychology or any other science, but when this study is carried out with an eye on or purpose of ameliorating our moral life (in light of moral ideals), it is ethical philosophy. Ethics might rely on science in its study of conditions.[32] But this does not reduce ethics to science, or eliminate the normative element implicit in Dewey's view of ethics as "wisdom."

PRAGMATISM AND HOW WE SHOULD LIVE

The above understanding of the "how" of experience allows a pragmatist to recover the normative ethical issue of "how to live" in a way that is consistent with its philosophical approach. This issue is best understood as "how to interact," and not as "what is the good life?" Whereas the latter usually assumes an "Archimedean point of view," the former merely assumes that we are one of the conditions of moral experience, and that these can be evaluated. Although the pragmatist gives up the assumption that there is an all-inclusive fixed and final end to our lives or an abstract and antecedent notion of the "good life," she or he can maintain that the question of "how" to live is meaningful and important when it is asked in the context of experience and when it is understood as an inquiry into conditions. For the purpose of having some control in the direction and quality of our lives we can discriminate between "how to live" (or ways of life) and our circumstances, even if, concretely speaking, there is no ideal "way of life" independent of concrete living. This means that a philosophical investigation of this question starts from where we are. The question is not how "we," as human beings or as beings with a human nature considered independently of present actual experience (i.e, of time, culture, and history), should lead our lives. In the context of experience the question requiring an answer is a matter of choice and not just idle speculation. For it needs to be answered in terms of what our present "living" options are,[33] where we are, and what we can do. The issue is a "momentous" and "forced" one because we are not subjects that can stand outside the course of events; participation in some form or another is unavoidable. The only choice available to us is between modes of participation. As Dewey says, "one cannot escape the problem of how to engage in life, since in any case he must engage in it some way or another—or else quit and get out" (MW 14:58). This does not mean that we are "trapped"—unless we presuppose a nonrelational, noncontextual notion of ourselves. However, it does mean that the question of "how" cannot be answered once and for all; there is no final resting place because our options and conditions can change. Therefore the pragmatic approach has to be tentative. There is no final answer to the question of how we should live. But this is not a good enough reason to neglect the question.

It might be objected that once one gives up the "Archimedean" standpoint, one also has to give up the normative task of being concerned with the issue of how we should live, since there is no justified way to engage in nonarbitrary criticism about this issue. Recently, Richard Rorty, a self-proclaimed pragmatist, has asserted that a pragmatist needs to admit that "there is no ahistorical standpoint from which to endorse the habits of modern democracies he wishes to praise,"[34] that there is no "demonstration of the 'objective' superiority of our way of life over all other alternatives."[35] For Rorty, the only alternative to an ahistorical "objective" justification is not despair, but "solidarity." We need to learn to be "ethnocentric," to "privilege our own group, even though there can be no noncircular justification for doing so."[36] Since it is idle to have a desire to stand outside our particular community "and look down at it from a more universal standpoint,"[37] we should cultivate the desire to stand by our traditional liberal habits and hopes simply because they are ours. Neither James nor Dewey would deny the futility of "objective" justification, but the alternative is not a "blind" solidarity that merely justifies the "status quo." In short, Rorty places us in a false dilemma. We do not have to stand outside experience or assume a "god's eye point of view" in order to assess the options available at a particular time. Neither is there a field of experience which provides all the considerations relevant to the evaluation of a "mode of participation." We can use past experience and our knowledge of actual conditions in order to evaluate our options. We need to start from where "we are," but we can also learn from where "we have been." The options we have today are not strictly the same as the ones our ancestors had, but they are not always so different that learning from past experience is impossible. We can, for example, rely on the fact that there have been many undesirable consequences resulting from rigid dogmatic adherence to beliefs.

But we can also conduct a philosophical investigation in which, in light of where we are, and the predominant traits of present experience, we can construct a hypothesis about which general habits are better than others. Even if experience is fairly hospitable and tolerant to all types of character and "ways of life," it might not lend itself equally to all ideals. For example, if experience is such that things usually do not turn out like we want or expect them, can we not use this to develop a hypothesis about what dispositions would fare better? In talking about such "traits of experience" we are appealing to metaphysics as a hypothesis about the generic traits of present existence, not as a traditional form of foundationalism. In this respect we can adopt Dewey's description of experience as being "precarious" and "stable." But we seem afraid that such a terminology might not capture what seems very simple and straightforward. There are indeed less sophisticated ways to describe our everyday life. Minimally, we assume that life is change, that it has consummations and fulfillments, and that even with our best efforts, disappointments, new problems and difficulties, failures, risk, and the unexpected seem unavoidable. Is it an excessive claim then, to say, that in such a world a character that goes forth to meet new demands, that welcomes untried situations, that is capable of constant readjustment, is in better shape than a fixed static character?

It is mostly in terms of general and tentative proposals about "how" to interact in situations that one can add "thickness" to a Deweyan ethics so as to significantly assist moral practice. Proposing how to best approach moral problems and engage in moral situations should be distinguished from the traditional ethical tasks of providing the answer to moral problems, or proposing a mechanical decision procedure by which we can resolve all problems. These are not universally-fixed prescriptions but rather are instruments at the disposal of persons already caught up in the moral life. There is no reason why this "weaker" or more humble task cannot be as normative (or as prescriptive) as the table of commandments of some ethical theories. There is a difference between a theory that states what to do, and one that recommends in a very general and tentative way how to live in the sense of what might be better. Whereas the content of the first kind consists of rules, formulas, or imperatives, the latter claims only general proposals that ultimately have to be tested in the lives of individuals. Ethical inquiry can propose hypotheses about dispositions and intrumentalities that can assist individual reflection and are likely to improve (enhance) moral life. These proposals are nothing more than hypotheses of the form, "if you try to cultivate *x* you will be likely to be better prepared to meet the demands of morality than if you do not."

If a Deweyan ethics can be normative in the "humble" sense outlined above, then how can we evaluate the adequacy of such a view? We cannot test its adequacy via the usual use of counterexamples (for example, by considering whether it is able to rule out the actions of someone like Hitler as moral). Instead, it has to be the sort of philosophical inquiry that, if successful, provides good philosophical reasons why something is worth trying, and is presented with enough specificity to know when it is being tried. For Dewey the most controlled environment for testing his hypotheses was the classroom. This is why, for him, moral theory and moral education were interdependent. Deweyans today may not have a positive and full proposal to be tested. This does not show that Dewey was wrong, but only that Deweyans have perhaps failed to "to use his thinking to forward our own struggle." To "pass Dewey by" in ethics we must be bold and imaginative, but also open in the sense of not losing sight of the fact that whatever we come up with is a hypothesis to be tested and modified by its means and application.

NOTES

1. John Dewey (EW 3:170).

2. But this task is complicated by the fact that Dewey did not consolidate his ideas about ethics into any single work. He scattered his ideas throughout his many books and essays. In some cases he even presented them in a paragraph or two placed almost parenthetically in the midst of a

passage devoted to another philosophical topic. The few books in which Dewey focused explicitly on ethics were textbooks and syllabi, written primarily for classroom work. They were therefore not intended to be systematic, theoretical formulations of his views.

3. See Dewey (LW 7:166).

4. In his *Ethics* Dewey does claim that ethical theory can "(i) generalize the types of moral conflicts which arise, thus enabling a perplexed and doubtful individual to clarify his own particular problem by placing it in a larger context; . . . (ii) state the leading ways in which such problems have been intellectually dealt with by those who have thought upon such matters; . . . (iii) render personal reflection more systematic and enlightened, suggesting alternatives that might otherwise be overlooked, and stimulating greater consistency in judgment" (LW 7:166). But if this is all that Dewey had to say about this issue, then these are hardly convincing reasons to resurrect the need for theory. For it seems that these indirect sorts of assistance can be better fulfilled by educators without the need of moral theory.

5. This follows from Dewey's general view of experience. For Dewey, thinking, knowing, and its products are things that occur within the noncognitive practical context of everyday experience.

6. There is continuity (difference of degree and not in kind) between theory as a "reflective and systematic account of things" and the general ideas about what could be done in a situation. See (EW 3:100–103).

7. Bernard Williams, *Ethics and the Limits of Philosophy* (Cambridge: Harvard University Press, 1985), 29.

8. Susan Wolf, "The Deflation of Moral Philosophy," *Ethics* 97 (July 1987): 827.

9. Williams, *Ethics and the Limits of Philosophy,* 93.

10. Williams' "deflation" of theories has been received with both enthusiasm and disappointment by the philosophical community. The source of disappointment is that Williams and other contemporary sceptics do not have much to say about the direction (if any) that moral theory should take. See Susan Wolf, "Deflation of Moral Philosophy"; Samuel Scheffler, "Morality Through Thick and Thin: A Critical Notice of Ethics and the Limits of Philosophy," *Philosophical Review,* 96, no. 3 (July 1987): 411–34.

11. For a more thorough explanation of what this means see my "Dewey's Moral Theory: Experience as Method," *Transactions of the Charles Sanders Peirce Society* 33 (summer 1997): 411–34.

12. In general it can be said that what purposes are adequate in the control and selectivity of a particular kind of inquiry are determined by what interests are thought more likely to resolve or ameliorate the kinds of

problems that set out that inquiry. A scientist, for example, is trained to select out of a total situation only those "qualities that are capable of being treated as signs of definite interactions" in order to "facilitate and control inference" (LW 12:268). Qualities are unique but the scientist is not interested in their uniqueness but in their functional sameness and quantifiability so as to allow prediction and control of events. It is this and other theoretical interests that guide their selectivity in observation and experimentation. An honest empiricist would make explicit the purposes and places where selectivity took place so that others can repeat the experiments. If the problem is how to biologically or chemically control and predict the spread of a particular disease in our society, then the scientist is better served by the kind of selectivity and purposes that is more likely to help solve this problem. For example, if scientists' observations are guided by what is common and quantifiable to all cases of the virus, they might be better served than if they were interested in and observed only what is unique to each case.

13. (MW 12:263–64).

14. Williams, *Ethics and the Limits of Philosophy,* 116–17.

15. Standard moral theories do not assist practice, not because they are not useful in telling us precisely what to do, but because such a theory, "as a statement of the character of all moral action . . . does not lend itself to uncovering . . . the reality of specific cases as they arise . . . on the other hand, these special cases . . . [by not offering] the detailed exhibition of the same reality that is stated generally in the theory, do not react upon the theory and fructify it for further use" (EW 3:158).

16. It is important to notice how different this is from traditional moral theory. For Dewey, reflective criticism is important because it is a constituent element of a meaningful growing moral life, and *not* because it is a means to moral knowledge or to avoid being duped. Again, it is the quality of our moral life that ultimately concerned Dewey.

17. Dewey, for example, was very perceptive about how dualism has affected moral education.

18. See (EW 3:101–2).

19. William James, *The Letters of William James,* edited by his son Henry James (Boston: Atlantic Monthly Press, 1920), 1:270.

20. See (MW 14:156).

21. See (MW 9:89).

22. (LW 9: 194).

23. Dewey tells us that: "Interaction between aim and existent conditions improves and tests the ideal; and conditions are at the same time modified. Ideals change as they are applied in existent conditions. The process endures and advances with the life of humanity. What one person

and one group accomplish becomes the standing ground and starting point of those who succeed them" (LW 9:34).

24. Dewey explains that: "By wisdom we mean not systematic and proved knowledge of fact and truth, but a conviction about moral values. Wisdom is a moral term. . . . As a moral term it refers to a choice about something to be done, a preference for living this sort of life rather than that. . . . The philosophies embodied not colorless intellectual readings of reality, but men's most passionate desires and hopes, their basic beliefs about the sort of life to be lived" (LW 6:44).

25. In this regard I find any attempt to come up with any procedural rules dangerous, including even Michael Eldridge's recent well-intended effort to provide a "political technology" (a manual for democracy). See Michael Eldridge, *Transforming Experience: John Dewey's Cultural Instrumentalism* (Nashville, Tenn.: Vanderbilt University Press, 1998), 70.

26. Ibid., 83.

27. See (MW 9:172–74).

28. It therefore has nothing to do with "method" as a fixed procedure for answering or deciding moral questions.

29. One should again emphasize that Dewey's ethical inquiry about character relies on abstracting the "how" from the full-integrated moral experience for instrumental purposes. Hence, it is not to be confused with moral experience *as* it is experienced. Dewey explains this in the following way:

> psychology of course does not aim at reinstating the immediate experience of the individual; nor does it aim at describing that experience in its immediate values, whether aesthetic, social, or ethical. It reduces the immediate experience to a series of dispositions, attitudes, or states which are taken as either conditions or signatures of life-experience. It is not the full experience-of-seeing-a-tree it is concerned with, but the experience reduced by abstraction to an attitude. (MW 3:29)

30. "Since character is a fact entering into any moral judgment passed, ability of control depends upon our power to state character in terms of generic relations of conditions" (MW 3:927).

31. See Eldridge, *Transforming Experience,* 117. I have nothing against getting on with "the task of developing a democratic political technology" (117), as long as the "operational instructions" remain general enough not to interfere with the qualitative sensitivity and reflection of each individual and unique situation that Dewey stressed so much in his ethics.

32. Dewey said "the conclusions of science about matter-of-fact efficiencies of nature are its indispensable instruments" (LW 1:305).

33. On "living," "momentous" and "forced" options, see William James, *The Will to Believe and Other Popular Essays* (Cambridge: Harvard University Press, 1979), 14.

34. Richard Rorty, "Contingency and Solidarity," in *Post-Analytic Philosophy,* ed. Cornel West (New York: Columbia University Press, 1985), 12.

35. Ibid., 16.

36. Ibid., 12.

37. Ibid., 13.

FOUR

Contexts Vibrant and Contexts Souring in Dewey's Philosophy

WILLIAM J. GAVIN

For John Dewey, philosophy is not a self-subsistent study; it rather reflects and perfects via critical analysis the concerns and values of a specific community.

> The distinctive office, problems and subject matter of philosophygrow out of stresses and strains in the community live in which a given form of philosophy arises, and . . . accordingly, its specific problems vary with the changes in human life that are always going on and that at times constitute a crisis and a turning point in human history.[1]

From this perspective, it follows that there is no such an entity as a noncontextual philosophy. Indeed, the attempt to find such an outlook is in actually an attempt to find certainty. Such an outlook would transcend all contexts and, as such, would be relevant to none. On the other hand, when "context is taken into account, it is seen that every generalization occurs under limiting conditions set by the contextual situation."[2] Certainty must be rejected as a quest, for it fosters several false dualisms. The most important of these is the subject/object dichotomy, the ripping of an organism out of its specific environmental context so as to see him or her as an impartial spectator viewing experience or being in a detached, supposedly objective fashion. Dewey does not mince words here; he tells us that ". . . the most pervasive fallacy of philosophic thinking goes back to neglect of context."[3]

Like a good tuning fork, this criticism has several prongs of development. First, what is the specific context of philosophy now? Second, how does this compare and/or contrast with other contextual situations? And finally, how have matters changed since the time that Dewey wrote? And how will they change in the future?

For Dewey, Darwin's *Origin of Species* is a watershed in philosophy. It marks a fundamental turning point in human culture. Change in human intellectual history takes place in two ways: usually, it merely means an advance in the knowledge we have about old conceptions. But at other times intellectual change is qualitative or cataclysmic in nature; it indicates that while old ideas, old problems were not solved, they were no longer considered important; they were turned away from. Such qualitative change occurred, in Dewey's opinion, with the birth of Darwin's thesis. Prior to Darwin, the conception of "species" had reigned supreme in philosophy, and with it went the notions of fixed form and of final cause. Change was viewed as indicative of defect and unreality. All of this was undetermined by Darwin's outlook. The perfect was no longer identified with the fixed and the absolute. As a result, a post-Darwinian world is a truly experimental world, one wherein change and process are real. Transitions are at least as important as substances.

> The influence of Darwin upon philosophy resides in his having conquered the phenomena of life for the principle of transition, and thereby freed the new logic for application to mind and morals and life. When he said of species what Galileo had said of the earth, *e pur se muove,* he emancipated, once for all, genetic and experimental ideas as an organon of asking questions and looking for explanations.[4]

While advocating this as a model, however, Dewey realized that old frameworks would not simply go away, and indeed the new outlook would be resisted for "psychological" reasons as well as logical ones:

> Men cannot easily throw off their old habits of thinking, and never can throw off all of them at once. In developing, teaching and receiving new ideas we are compelled to use some of the old ones as tools of understanding and communication. Only piecemeal, step-by-step, could the full import of the new science be grasped.[5]

In other words, while the disjunctive transitions must be articulated, thereby indicating a new context, this cannot be done in a *completely* cataclysmic manner, but rather must be approached dialectically, by indicating what the old context(s) were and how the new is continuous, how different. One reason this approach is necessary is because philosophers cannot make a context a complete object of reflection. They are involved *with* what they are looking *at*. But the philosophizer can recognize the existence of a background, a context, and in so doing at least refrain from making dogmatic, acontextual generalizations. On the other hand, overly naive subjectivity can be avoided by comparing the present specific context to others. To make this point more clearly, let us take as our second example Dewey's analysis of "experience."

For Dewey, there are three historic conceptions of "experience" in the West: the Greek; the modern (Locke); and the contemporary (still developing). For the Greek, experience was the "accumulated information of the past, not merely the individual's own past but the social past, transmitted through language and even more through apprenticeship in the various crafts."[6] Experience was basically a type of knowledge acquired via practice, or habit. As such, experience began to be contrasted with a higher type of knowledge; namely, casual analysis. "Experience and empirical knowledge were set in very definite contrast with science, since science meant . . . understanding or rational comprehension."[7] In short, experience consists of information accumulated via repetition; as such it is not the final court of appeal. Experience is not self-sustaining; reason and science are self-sustaining.

In the notion of experience found in John Locke, this outlook is reversed. Not reason, but experience is taken as self-sustaining. "What had passed for rational truths seemed . . . infected with stale repetition and blind acceptance of authority. In contrast 'experience' suggested something fresh and personal."[8] There is a tendency to view the individual, the atomic, as the "really real," and the general, or the universal, as abstraction. For Locke, experience is observational: it proceeds through the senses. We see (passively) one "idea" at a time. "What characterizes sensation and observation, and hence experience, is, in Locke's thought, their coerciveness."[9] Here experience is the final court of appeal; it functions in a critical fashion. Experience serves as that to which thought is ultimately reducible. Our rationalizations, or constructed ideas, are subject to the check of experience. Such an outlook, as it developed in Locke's successors, became highly particularistic and nominalistic. Ironically enough, this "empirical" outlook is actually antiscientific. Sensationalism cannot explain experimentation in science. "For all experiment involves regulated activity, directed by ideas."[10] Scientific theories are not merely descriptions of sensations or copies of observations. Therefore, either science does not depend upon experience or experience must be articulated in a fashion different from the Lockean notion.

The last notion of experience for Dewey is that of our present context. It is still more or less inchoate, because it is still in the making. However, it can as least be partially characterized as biological rather than introspectionist. Viewed in a biological context, experience is interaction, "an affair of the intercourse of a living being with its physical and social environment."[11] Experience is now seen as experimental, as "an effort to change the given; it is characterized by projection, by reaching forward into the unknown; connection with a future is its salient trait."[12] As experimental, experience recognizes both the disjunctive and conjunctive transitions; viewed as an "undergoing of an environment and a striving for its control in new directions, [experience] is pregnant with connections."[13] It is inferential.

This outlook is a sustained attempt by Dewey to present a view of experience that is beneath the subject/object dichotomy, and the thought/action dichotomy. These are retrospective categorizations that cannot do justice to the primordial event. That event is one of interaction, of simultaneous doings and sufferings. Experience here is considerably broadened; it includes the Greek notion of accumulated information and the Lockean notion of experience as the final court of appeal. But experience is not exclusively regulated to being a matter of knowledge. A deeper portrait is envisioned wherein the concrete organism interacts with environment.

> Life itself consists of phases in which the organism falls out of step with the march of surrounding things and then recovers unison with it—either through effort or by some happy chance. . . . Life grows when a temporary falling out is a transition to a more extensive balance of the energies of the organism with those of the conditions under which it lives.[14]

Dewey's new notion of experience caused many critics to term his outlook excessively anthropomorphic. In *Experience and Nature,* he responds by telling the reader:

> Experience is of as well as in nature. It is not experience which is experienced, but nature—stones, plants, animals, diseases, health, temperature, electricity, and so on. Things interacting in certain ways are experience; they are what is experienced. Linked in certain other ways with another natural object—the human organism—they are how things are experienced as well. Experience thus reaches down into nature; it has depth. It also has breadth and to an indefinitely elastic extent. It stretches. That stretch constitutes inference.[15]

What Dewey is saying here is that there is more to nature than experience, that there is no evidence that experience goes on all the time in nature. But, in addition, when experience does occur as one of the events in nature, it occurs, or can occur, in such a way as to reach down into the depth of nature and investigate some aspects of nature "in such a manner as to render other of its precincts accessible."[16]

FAT VERSUS THIN CONTEXTS

In order to make this point more clearly, Dewey describes nature as an "affair of affairs" and begins to talk of three different types of interactions which take place in nature:

> The first [level], the scene of narrower and more external interactions . . . is physical; its distinctive properties are those of the mathematical-mechanical system discovered by physics. . . . The second level is that of [plant and animal] life. . . . They have qualities in common which define the psycho-physical. [This level exhibits need-demand-satisfaction activity.] The third plateau is that of association, communication, participation. . . . It is marked . . . by common properties, which define mind as intellect; possession of and response to meanings.[17]

It is important to stress that these are all transactional activities constituted by the activity, and not vice versa. Secondly, the difference among the various levels of transaction is one of degree, not of kind. Here Dewey advocates a fat, rich, naturalism, one wherein human communicative transactions, and need/demand/satisfaction transactions must not be reduced to mass/energy transactions. Dewey "does not think that there is one type of transaction—the physico-chemical—which is the only real type of transaction and to which others are to be completely reduced."[18]

More positively stated, we must recognize and uphold both the disjunctive and the conjunctive transactions found within nature, without turning from nature to an exclusively acontextual transcendental philosophy. The different levels in nature run from the less complex to the more complex. The latter experience, generally associated with human experience, is characterized as being able to deal with things which are not immediately present. It can do so through the ability to use language, or symbols, to re-present, that is, make present in some sense, items from the past in such a fashion as to prepare for the future. Human cognitive experience consists of one type of transaction with nature located within a larger context of physicochemical and psychophysical transactions. But such human (cognitive) experience, while not self-sufficient, is also of nature, in the sense that "it is a type of transaction in which the variety of other natural transactions participate."[19] Human experience can grow by its edges, so as inferentially, that is, through linguistic symbols, to contain more and more of nature while still remaining within nature.

The above review can stand as an illustration of Dewey's general method of procedure, and of his emphasis upon the importance of context. What remains to be done is an analysis of how things might change, or "go wrong," within the context of our experience.

CONTEXT VERSUS TEXT

In Dewey's time it was important to guard against reduction of symbolic interaction and need/demand/satisfaction interaction to mere physicochemical interaction. Today the opposite is also true—and perhaps more dangerous in contemporary contexts. One must guard equally against reducing the physicochemical and "felt need" types of transaction to symbolic, that is, linguistic, transactions. One must resist the temptation to reduce the context to the written text—and assert that "there is nothing outside of the text" *(Il n'y a pas de hors texte)*.[20] The human organism, taken in its fullest sense, is more than a linguistic or cognitive entity. He or she has not only cognitive relations with the environment, but also aesthetic, ethical, and religious interactions. Dewey himself was aware of this potential danger. In *Experience and Nature* he says:

> What is really "in" experience extends much further than that which at any time is known. From the standpoint of knowledge, objects must be distinct; their traits must be explicit; the vague and unrevealed is a limitation. Hence whenever the habit of identifying reality with the object of knowledge as such prevails, the obscure and vague are explained away. It is important for philosophic theory to be aware that the distinct and evident are prized and why they are. But it is equally important to note that the dark and twilight abound.[21]

For Dewey then, any transactional experience which becomes exclusively cognitive or linguistic or textual, leaves out dimensions of the situation. Anything which we interact with in experience, or better stated, anything which is constituted through transactions in experience, can become the "object" of intellectual analysis. When this happens, the item takes on an additional increment of meaning. The item is "seen" in terms of its relational properties—at least some of those properties. But when it is all said and done, neither experience per se, nor nature per se is to be viewed as completely identical with the cognitive, linguistic, or symbolic. As Dewey puts it in *Experience and Nature:*

> It is not denied that any experienced subject-matter whatever may become an object of reflection and cognitive inspection. But the emphasis is upon "become"; the cognitive never is all-inclusive: that is, when the material of a prior non-cognitive experience is the object of knowledge, it and the act of knowing are themselves included within a new and wider non-cognitive experience—and this situation can never be transcended.[22]

Taking this last quote seriously requires some honesty on our part. Our conceptual schemas will never come to completely dominate nature. While liberating, they are also insulating. Language does not go all the way down, Rorty to the contrary.[23] Philosophy is more than "keeping up the conversation."[24] The conversation points beyond itself, to praxis. Those philosophy texts are best which disclose this by acting as a "spur" or an "inspiration," pointing beyond themselves toward the situation which they wish to change or interact with. Rorty is right, however, in his rejection of Pierce's dictum that some opinion is ultimately fated to be agreed upon by all who practice the scientific method.[25] Dewey too is sometimes guilty of accepting Peirce's dictum too readily. Doing so would come at the price of rejecting contextualism as described above, of collapsing a realism into an idealism, of "internalizing" a situation or transaction. What is, for Dewey, should always remain broader and bigger than what is known. At their strongest, Dewey's texts do serve as an invitation or a call to action. At the end of the chapter on "Renascent Liberalism" in *Liberalism and Social Action,* for example, Dewey notes that the

> question [of an energized radical form of liberalism coming into existence and utilizing intelligence rather than force as its method] cannot be answered by argument. Experimental method means experiment, and the question can be answered only by trying, by organized effort. The reasons for making the trial are not abstract or recondite. They are found in the confusion, uncertainty, and conflict that mark the modern world.[26]

Failure to acknowledge and affirm the richness and the stubbornness of nature can result in the context "going sour" on us in one of several ways, in addition to the aforementioned reduction of the context to the text. There are at least three additional ways in which contextualism can be soured.

INTERACTION VERSUS DOMINATION/CONTROL

First, we can assert that we no longer interact with our context(s), but can now control and manipulate it completely. Recall the experimental flavor of the words of Sir John Winthrop, on the ship called the Arabella, outside Boston Harbor in 1630, when he says:

> We shall be as a City upon a Hill, the eyes of all people are upon us, so that if we shall deal falsely with our God in this work we have undertaken and so cause him to withdraw his present help from us, we shall be made a story and a by-word through the world.[27]

This theme of acting upon and in turn being acted upon by one's environment is repeated in Thoreau's statement that

> All things invite this Earth inhabitants
> To rear their lives to an unheard of height
> And meet the expectation of the land.[28]

Contrast these texts with the more recent one by Robert McNamara in a book called *The Essence of Security,* which reads as follows:

> Some critics today worry that our democratic, free societies are becoming over managed. I would argue that the opposite is true. . . . The real threat to democracy comes, not from overmanagement, but from undermanagement. To undermanage reality is not to keep free.[29]

Such an outlook, which signals and applauds the move from interacting with a context to trying to control and manipulate that context from outside, had already been foreseen and criticized by Joseph Wood Krutch in his book called *Grand Canyon*. Krutch writes:

> No age before ours would have made such an assumption. Man has always before thought of himself as puny by comparison with natural forces, and he was humble before them. But we have been so impressed by the achieve'ment of technology that we are likely to think we can do more than nature herself. We dug the Panama Canal, didn't we? Why not the Grand Canyon?[30]

Dewey himself was occasionally guilty of "control" language of this type. Thus in *Reconstruction in Philosophy,* for example, he says that "only indefinite substitution and convertibility regardless of quality render nature manageable. The mechanization of nature is the condition of a practical and progressive idealism in action."[31] Earlier in this text he had said: "the patient and experimental study of nature, bearing fruit in inventions which control nature and subdue her forces to social uses, is the method by which progress is made. Knowledge is power and knowledge is achieved by sending the mind to school to nature to learn her processes of change."[32] Elsewhere he tells the reader: "we cannot too much insist on the fact that until man got control of natural forces civilization was a local accident."[33] But alongside these texts there exist others where Dewey is more careful not to adopt the language of complete control. In *The Quest for Certainty,* for example, he says:

> Ability, through a definite or measured correlation of changes, to connect one with another as sign or evidence is the precondition of control. It does not of itself provide direct control; reading the index hand of a barometer as a sign of probable rain does not enable us to stop the coming of the rain. But it does enable us to change our relations to it: to plant a garden, to carry an umbrella on going out, to direct the course of a vessel at sea, etc. It enables preparatory acts to be undertaken which make values less insecure.[34]

In sum, while Dewey offers for the most part an interactionist model wherein nature retains her relative intrepidness, there are moments when the social reformer in him almost succumbs to a management model or image. Like Marx, Dewey as social reformer wanted to bring about significant social change. Like Marx, he sometimes grew frustrated with mere theory which did not lead to praxis. His key to effective social change was the scientific method, which could, he said, direct change so as to bring about progress. But his desire to transform the scientific method from the natural sciences to the social sciences sometimes betrays a lack of awareness of the very contextualism he so often espoused.

Dewey does recognize that things have changed, and not necessarily for the better, in the twentieth century. In "Reconstruction As Seen Twenty-Five Years Later," written in 1948, he says:

> The First World War was a decided shock to the earlier period of optimism, in which there prevailed widespread belief in continued progress toward mutual understanding among peoples and classes, and hence a sure movement to harmony and peace. Today the shock is almost incredibly greater. Insecurity and strife are so general that the prevailing attitude is one of anxious and pessimistic uncertainty. Uncertainty as to what the future has in store casts its heavy and black shadow over all the aspects of the present.[35]

Here, grounds for optimism here seem virtually nonexistent. Dewey's solution however, is to ask that we redouble our efforts; he calls for reconstruction *of* philosophy rather than reconstruction *in* philosophy.[36] In short, there are times when Dewey does seem to look into the abyss and not like what he sees. To his credit, he does look. But sometimes he seems to want to "will" control over a context rather than interacting with it.

Another example of this occurs in *Liberalism and Social Action*. There Dewey recognizes that we have the technological ability to obliterate poverty, but not the "will" to do so. "Thanks to science and technology we now live in an age of potential plenty."[37] While it is true that scarcity does cause insecurity, "the conditions that generate insecurity for the many no longer spring from nature. They are found in institutions and arrangements that are within deliberate human control. Surely this change marks one of the greatest revolutions that has taken place in all human history. Because of it, insecurity is not now the motive to work and sacrifice but to despair."[38] While he realizes that the context has changed radically Dewey here can only say, once again, try harder to employ organized intelligent action rather than violence, force, or class struggle. The idea is that it is easier to control social institutions than it is to control nature, since we are responsible for creating the former. But institutions too have been known to demonstrate their own intractability, that is, their own unwillingness to be dominated or controlled.

CONTEXTUALISM VERSUS "PSEUDO-EVENTS"

The second way in which Dewey's interactionist model can be ruined is by replacing the picture of interactions of an organism and its multiple environment with one of interaction with a series of "pseudo-events." The danger of such a posture is vividly brought out by Philip Slater in his work *The Pursuit of Loneliness: American Culture at the Breaking Point*. Slater holds that Americans have fundamental desires for community, for engagement, and for interdependence—desires which we continually repress.[39] As a result of this, for Slater, we as Americans are systematically pursuing loneliness. Regarding the second of these, engagement, defined as "the wish to come directly to grips with one's social and physical environment," Slater says the following:

> Human beings evolved as organisms geared to mastery of the natural environment. Within the past few years we have learned to perform this function so well that the natural environment possess very little threat to civilized peoples. Our dangers are self-made ones—subtle, insidious, and meaningless. We die from our own machines, our own poisons, our own weapons, our own despair. . . . We still long for and enjoy struggling

> against the elements, even though such activity can only occasionally be considered meaningful or functional. We cross the ocean in artificially primitive boats, climb mountains we could fly over, kill animals we do not eat. Natural disasters, such as floods, hurricanes, blizzards, and so on generate a cheerfulness which would seem inappropriate if we did not all share it. . . . Like the cat that prefers to play with a ball around the obstacle of a chair leg, so man seems to derive some perverse joy from having a snowstorm force him to use the most primitive mode of transportation. It's particularly amusing to observe people following the course of an approaching hurricane, and affecting a proper and prudent desire that it veer off somewhere, in the face of an ill-conceived craving that it do nothing of the kind.[40]

Such seemingly funny quirks of human character reveal more than we realize, namely that for the most part, discounting these aberrations, we "interact largely with extensions of our own egos. . . . Our world is only a mirror, and our efforts mere shadowboxing—yet shadowboxing in which we frequently manage to hurt ourselves. . . . We encounter primarily our own fantasies: we have a concept and image of a mountain, a lake, or a forest almost before we ever see one."[41]

Nowhere is this impoverishment of context through vicarious replacement more obvious than through the use of TV and computers. In *The Necessity of Experience,* Edward Reed has argued that we are slowly losing our minds because we as humans need to experience things and others at the primary level, but that, more and more, we are engaged in a secondary, that is, processed, modified, and packaged experience.[42] This imbalance is a pervasive one. Education for example has moved from a focus upon hands-on experience to an emphasis on users' manuals. Even physical intimacy now comes packaged in the form of phone sex. Most children spend more than half of their waking hours plugged into the processed information box of television.[43] TV, video, and computer displays offer us a montage, that is, a reconstruction of experience so scripted that the causal structure of actual experience is replaced by a narrative structure and voice.[44] Experience, in Dewey's terms, is no longer seen as both precarious and stable, or as experimental, but as bland and anticipated. The environment we are leaving our children is therefore both degraded and dangerous. "Our post-modern world is thus achieving the reverse of what Dewey called for. Instead of using our information technology to create workplaces within which human experience can grow and thrive, we are using the technology to manufacture jobs that are often little more than glorified pigeonholes, with all opportunity for growth and reflection eliminated."[45] A standard refrain in many work situations is: "the computer won't let us do that." Intelligence in general has, as a result, been redefined so as to mean "reliability, rapidity, and repeatability," while at the same time pretending to value wisdom and creativity.[46] Such mechanized experience is both limited and limiting.[47] To the extent that public relations, television, drama, and life become indistinguishable, "virtual reality" begins to dominate, and Slater's words return to haunt us with the spectre of boredom. He says: "The story of Pygmalion is thus the story of modern man, in love with his own product."[48]

As noted by Reed in the above quote, this was a danger which Dewey himself was sometimes keenly aware of. In *Individualism Old and New,* he argues against an overly essentialist account of the concept of individuality—one which does not take account of changes in context. "Our material culture," he says, "is verging upon the collective and corporate. Our moral culture, along with our ideology, is, on the other hand, still saturated with ideals and values of an individualism derived from the pre-scientific, pre-technological age."[49] We are, in short, schizophrenic, unable to interact due to an overly romanticized view of nature. "Where is the wilderness which now beckons creative energy and affords untold opportunity to initiative and vigor? . . . The wilderness exists in the movie and the novel."[50] Dewey continues by saying: "I see little social unrest which is the straining of energy for outlet in action. I find rather the protest against a weakening of vigor and a sapping of energy that emanate from absence of constructive opportunity."[51]

For Dewey then, there is no possibility for action here, because the context has become internalized: we are interacting with our own projections. Dewey terms the loss of the individual a "tragedy,"[52] but one we can do something about. We must, of course, renounce an essentialist account of individualism as "something static, having a uniform content."[53] Going further, "a new individualism can be achieved only through the controlled use of all the resources of the science and technology that have mastered the physical forces of nature."[54] While we now control nature through technology, "control of power through the machine is not control of the machine itself. Control of the energies of nature by science is not controlled use of science."[55] In short, the lost individual can be recovered through the scientific method. Such a recovery will require recognition on our part that the scientific method is not intrinsically tied to private economic gain. While Dewey does not want science to become a new theology here,[56] nonetheless he continues to have enormous faith in the scientific method, and that method, once again, is articulated in language requesting more and more "control." In an interesting choice of an example, Dewey says: "Since we must in any case approach nature in some fashion and by some path—if only that of death—I confess my total inability to understand those who object to an intelligently controlled approach—for that is what science is."[57] Whether death can be controlled or managed as a problem will be taken up below. For the moment let us note that Dewey's faith in science results in his presenting the reader with an either-or. "The opposite of intelligent method is no method at all or blind and stupid method."[58] One is tempted to reply here, à la James, that the butter and the pancakes and the syrup of the universe do not come so neatly parceled out, and that, indeed, we would view them with scientific suspicion if they did.[59] Ray Boisvert has made this point well. He tells us that "Dewey speaks regularly as if there were only two choices. His formulation of these leaves no room for the tragic."[60] In short, one may, and perhaps should, wonder about the binary as it is presented.

CONTENT VERSUS CONTEXT

The third, and final way in which we can be untrue to the spirit of Dewey's philosophy is by not realizing that the context has changed again. Our attention to the content of a past context can result in mere antiquarianism. There are at least three ways in which the content of the context has changed, in the sense that factors either once nonexistent, or thought insignificant, have now become very significant.

First, the biological context, which Dewey was so aware of and influenced by, has now changed significantly. It is becoming more and more difficult, if not impossible, to determine with precision when life begins and when it ends. Robert Veatch has pointed out that it is "logically impossible to offer a strictly biological argument for the status of the fetus."[61] It is, of course, possible to argue normatively that some factor ought to be given privileged significance, and a plethora of events have been suggested. These include: fertilization; fixation of the genetic code; implantation; last chance for change of the genetic code (two to four weeks); central nervous system activity (detectable by electroencephalogram at about eight weeks); spontaneous movement (ten weeks); brain structure complete (twelve weeks); cardiac system activity (electrocardiogram at twelve weeks); quickening (thirteen to sixteen weeks); viability (as early as twenty weeks); integrated functioning of the nervous system; birth; breathing; consciousness; social interaction; acceptance by other people; development of language; and a development of a complete nervous system.[62] Analogously, there are at least four competing definitions of death in existence today, with no complete agreement as to which should be given priority, if any, and for what reasons. These are: departure of the soul from the body; respiratory and circulatory failure; so-called "whole brain death"; and, finally, failure of the neocortex, or upper part of the brain.[63] There are, in addition, those who point out that death is only the final moment in the process of dying, which we have all been doing for years, and who assert that it is the process, ambiguous and changing as it is, which we need to focus upon.[64] All of this contextual complexity about life and death, living and dying, the possible metamorphosis of one into the other, does not even mention the myriad ramifications of the situation made possible through competing interpretations of the developments in genetics and in recombinant DNA.[65]

Though Dewey himself wrote no separate treatise on the subject of death and dying, there are instances in his corpus where he reveals a surprisingly nuanced approach to the subject. In an early essay entitled "The Superstition of Necessity," written in 1893, Dewey is at pains to show that the term "necessity" is teleological in nature, that is, that "necessity" really means "needed." "Necessity is a device by which we both conceal from ourselves the unreal character of what we have called real, and also get rid of the practical evil consequences of hypostatizing a fragment into an independent whole."[66] As a way of illustrating his point Dewey takes up a seemingly acontextual and indubitable "fact," namely, the death of an enemy for a savage or a practical man:

> The "general result," the death of the hated enemy, is at first the fact; all else is mere accidental circumstance. Indeed, the other circumstances at first are hardly that; they do not attract attention, having no importance. Not only the savage, but also the common-sense man of today, I conceive, would say that any attempt to extend the definition of the "fact" beyond the mere occurrance of death is metaphysical refinement; that the fact is the killing, the death, and that that "fact" remains quite the same, however it is brought about.[67]

In other words, death is death, period, end of report. Dewey, however, strongly objects to this reification of the situation. "What has been done . . . is to abstract part of the real fact, part of this death, and set up the trait or universal thus abstracted as itself fact, and not only as fact, but as the fact, par excellence, with reference to which all the factors which constitute the reality, the concrete fact, of this death, are circumstantial and 'accidental'."[68] Important for our purposes is Dewey's strong refusal to essentialize or Platonize the concept of death. "These deaths in general do not occur,"[69] he says. And again, "all actual deaths have a certain amount of detail in them."[70] Dewey then attempts to "recover" a fat or thick context within which the death in question has occurred. "The savage has to hit his enemy with a club or spear, or perform a magic incantation, before he can attain that all-important end of getting rid of him. Moreover, a man with a coat of armor on will not die just the same way as the man who is defenseless. These circumstances have to be taken into account. . . . In other words, the real fact would be under constant process of identification, of 'production'."[71] The original or primordial death is a highly complex affair; one doesn't just kill in general. "Having, after all, to kill a man of certain characteristics and surroundings in life, having to choose time and place, etc., it becomes necessary, if I am to succeed, that I kill him in a certain way, say, with poison, or a dynamite bomb. Thus we get our concrete individual fact again."[72] For Dewey, the decision required to turn some aspect of a rich, concrete fact into a supposed necessity is a masked one. What pretends to be a necessity is really teleological in nature, though refusing to own up to any responsibility for a decision taken. The "full fact" includes both the "what" and the "how"—both the instance and the process via which the culmination occurred. The fact of "death in general" is taken as a necessity by those in need of a form of certainty in their lives. Dewey seems to be arguing, almost prenascently, that how one dies is at least partly constitutive of what death is, or, in more contemporary parlance, that the process of dying is more important, more real, than the abstract concept of death. While death may seem to be the item necessary to deal with, for Dewey, "contingent and necessary are . . . the correlative aspects of one and the same fact; conditions are accidental so far as we have abstracted a fragment and set it up as the whole; they are necessary the moment it is required to pass from this abstraction back to the concrete fact."[73] In short, while the issue of death and dying has moved to center stage in the new millennium, Dewey had already taken significant steps in that direction. This richer, more contextual model is a far cry from the "control" model of death referred to by Dewey in the previous section.

Second, at least two forces have now come into being which make the content of the context, in some sense, global. These are the development of electronic communications circuitry and the presence of nuclear power. The microelectronics featured in computers has, and will, significantly alter the economics of the previous industrial era, and the political ideologies such as capitalism, socialism, and communism insofar as these are based on the assumptions of that industrial era. Nuclear weapons, the existence of which threaten the very meaning of national boundaries, have now grown to alarming proportions. Most important, the fact that nonnuclear powers can start a nuclear war renders the question of who possesses such armaments in some sense an obsolete one.

Dewey did realize that the context had changed from nonnuclear to nuclear. In 1948, that is, at the end of World War II, in his new Introduction to *Reconstruction in Philosophy,* he says: "the destructive use made of the fission of the nucleus of an atom has become the stock-in-trade of the assault upon science."[74] His comment on this, however, indicates an underestimation of how radical a sea change was involved. "What is so ignored as to be denied," he says, "is that this destructive consequence occurred not only in a war but because of the existence of war, and that war as an institution antedates by unknown millennia the appearance on the human scene of anything remotely resembling scientific inquiry. That in this case destructive consequences are directly due to pre-existent institutional conditions is too obvious to call for argument. It does not prove that such is the case everywhere and at all times; but it certainly cautions us against the irresponsible and indiscriminate dogmatism now current."[75] Here, as elsewhere, Dewey hopes that a change in institutional practices will alleviate the situation. But if, as we now see, the issues are not exclusively socioeconomic but also ethnic and/or religious in nature, then the situation or context takes on a much more obstreperous hue.

A second issue of globalization concerns Dewey's desire "to prevent wage-slavery from destroying the hope of equality."[76] But, as Richard Rorty has noted:

> A problem Dewey . . . never envisaged has taken place, and measures which might cope with this new problem have hardly been sketched. The problem is that the wage levels, and the social benefits, enjoyed by workers in Europe, Japan, and North America no longer bear any relation to the newly fluid global labor market. Globalization is producing a world economy in which any attempt by any one country to prevent the immiseration of its workers may result only in depriving them of employment. This world economy will soon be owned by a cosmopolitan upper class which has no more sense of community with any workers anywhere than the great American capitalists of the year 1900 had with the immigrants who manned their enterprises.[77]

In other words, saying that the context has become global does not necessarily mean that we have become more unified, or are in the process of becoming so. Saying that the context is now global means that the issues we face and the decisions we make now have at least potentially global ramifications. As one publication put it:

> There is nothing new or unusual about cultural change. This observation, however, can easily blind us to the fact that we do indeed stand at an unprecedented turning point. The depth, per-

> vasiveness, and speed of the changes we are experiencing far exceed any previous time in history. Comparable transitions—the agricultural revolution, begun some 8000 years ago; the move to cities and urban civilization, begun some 5500 years ago; and the industrial revolution, begun some 200 years ago—all took place over centuries. Today we are in the midst of even greater cultural shifts which are taking, at most, a few decades.[78]

While one might think that recognition of these global factors would promote awareness of the finitude of our situation and of the disparate need to interact wisely with the limited resources of the globe, in actuality the temptation to react in the opposite manner also grows with this awareness. The pervasiveness and rapidity of change promote the temptation to overmanage, to turn from interaction to manipulation of the situation and hence, supposedly, to achieve certainty and security. This temptation must be resisted, particularly in its most manifest form, that is, the attempt to achieve a monistic outlook, or the attempt to assume that we are all essentially alike, as "cosmic citizens." As John McDermott has put it:

> The world and its creatures are not a 'block-universe', inert substances awaiting definition and management. Rather the world comes to us as a delicately woven fabric, related in a myriad of ways, and, although susceptible to human change it carries with it its own set of affairs.[79]

More positively stated, care must be taken to preserve a pluralistic contextualism, that is, a fat, or thick, or diversified view of reality where, although all of the different views of the universe have meaning and some connections among them do exist, nonetheless there is no one basic conceptual connection underlying all the various interpretations. No one way to attain control is either possible or desirable.

Third, the context is now gendered. Dewey once said that "philosophy recovers itself when it ceases to be a device for dealing with the problems of philosophers and becomes a method, cultivated by philosophers, for dealing with the problems of men."[80] This statement, should not be taken literally, that is, it is not the case that only men have problems, nor more importantly, that only men's problems which are the proper concern of philosophy. Differently stated, the content of philosophy is not the eternal acontextual features of human nature, for such characteristics, for Dewey, do not exist. As he says:

> The alleged unchangeableness of human nature cannot be admitted. For while certain needs in human nature are constant, the

> consequences they produce (because of the existing state of culture—of science, morals, religion, art, industry, legal rules) react back into the original components of human nature to shape them into new forms. The total pattern is thereby modified.[81]

While Dewey affirmed the model of the human being as an organism growing through interaction within an environment, he clearly realized that social and political relationships, which arise in the process of such interactions, cannot be reduced back to their original constituents, or ignored as marginal, or worse, preserved from criticism. This is especially true if, in the course of such interactions, a model of domination arises under the mask of seeming universal neutrality. To his credit, Dewey did foresee a change in content regarding gender. In a statement made in 1919 in "Philosophy and Democracy," Dewey noted that "women have as yet made little contribution to philosophy." But, he added, "when women who are not mere students of other persons' philosophy set out to write it, we cannot conceive that it will be the same in viewpoint or tenor as that composed from the standpoint of the different masculine experience of things."[82] As Charlene Haddock Seigfried has noted in detail, the first part of this statement can now be challenged. "Women have led interesting lives and have lots of stories to tell. Pragmatism has more resources than have yet been tapped. We just need to ask the right questions."[83] In Deweyan terminology, we must be careful about "inventing the problematic." If a problem "well put" is half-solved, a problem "badly put" offers true solutions to false questions; and a problem not "put" at all results in a form of domination or suppression.[84] Dewey argued against the dangers of domination in many ways, but perhaps did not clearly realize how deeply rooted it is in discussion of gender. The context has now changed, at least in terms of the legitimacy or nonlegitimacy of pronouns applicable or nonapplicable to it.

The above list is by no means an inclusive one, but it is illustrative. If we loathe our context, or do not pay attention to how it changes, ultimately we will destroy it.

At the end of his 1907 essay on "The Need for a Recovery of Philosophy," Dewey says:

> I believe that philosophy in America will be lost between chewing a historic cud long since reduced to woody fiber, or an apologetics for lost causes (lost to natural science), or a scholastic, schematic formalism, unless it can somehow bring to consciousness America's own needs and its own implicit principle of successful action.[85]

More than any other philosopher in the classic American tradition, Dewey realized how precarious and subtle the relation of philosophy to its environment actually is. Philosophical systems do arise from cultural contexts, and yet, when they do not envision themselves as exclusively transcendental, philosophical outlooks have the power to critically analyze and project ramifications of a given cultural stance and to do so in a concretely meaningful way. The texts of Dewey point beyond themselves and demand a constant reevaluation and interpretation of a continuous yet changing context. They ask us to see what Emerson would have termed the miraculous in the commonplace,[86] that is, of our ordinary experience. The written words of Dewey are a set of texts which are inviting and annoying, simultaneously, for, in the last analysis, they ask us to *do* something more than merely read them, or reread them. It is an invitation to which we dearly need to respond.[87]

NOTES

1. John Dewey, MW 12: 256. All references to Dewey's work are to the critical edition, *The Collected Works of John Dewey, 1882–1953,* edited by Jo Ann Boydston (Carbondale: Southern Illinois University Press, 1969–1991), and published as *The Early Works: 1881–1898* (EW); *The Middle Works, 1899–1924* (MW); and *The Later Works, 1925–1953* (LW). These designations are followed by volume and page number. Quotations in this chapter are cited from *The Collected Works of John Dewey, 1882–1953: The Electronic Edition,* edited by Larry A. Hickman (Charlottesville, Va.: IntelLex Corporation, 1996).

2. John Dewey, "Context and Thought" (LW 6:8).

3. Ibid., (LW 6:5).

4. John Dewey, "The Influence of Darwinism on Philosophy" (MW 4:7–8).

5. Dewey, *Reconstruction in Philosophy* (MW 12:122).

6. Dewey, "An Empirical Survey of Empiricisms" (LW 11:70). For an excellent analysis of Dewey's article, see John E. Smith, "Three Types and Two Dogmas of Empiricism," in *Themes in American Philosophy* (New York: Harper Torchbooks, 1970), 42–60.

7. Ibid. (LW 11:70).

8. Ibid. (LW 11:76).

9. Ibid. (LW 11:77).

10. Ibid. (LW 11:82).

11. John Dewey, "The Need for a Recovery of Philosophy" (MW 10:6).

12. Ibid. (MW 10:6).

13. Ibid. (MW 10:6).

14. John Dewey, *Art as Experience* (LW 10:19–20).

15. John Dewey, *Experience and Nature* (LW 1:12–13).

16. Ibid. (LW 1:12).

17. Ibid. (LW 1:208).

18. Richard J. Bernstein, *John Dewey* (New York: Washington Square Press, 1967), 85.

19. Ibid., 87.

20. Jacques Derrida, *Of Grammatology,* trans. Gayatri C. Spivak (Baltimore: Johns Hopkins University Press, 1976), 158.

21. John Dewey, *Experience and Nature* (LW 1:27–28).

22. Ibid., (LW 1:431–37).

23. See Richard Rorty, "Introduction: Pragmatism and Philosophy," in *Consequences of Pragmatism* (Minneapolis: University of Minnesota Press, 1982), xxx.

24. See Rorty, "Pragmatism, Relativism, and Irrationalism," in *Consequences,* 68.

25. See Rorty, "Pragmatism, Relativism, and Irrationalism, in *Consequences,* 173. See Charles Sanders Peirce, "How to Make Our Ideas Clear," in *Philosophical Writings of Peirce,* ed. Justus Buchler (New York: Dover Publications, 1955), 38.

26. John Dewey, *Liberalism and Social Action* (LW 11:64).

27. Cf. Daniel J. Boorstin, *The Americans: The Colonial Experience* (New York: Vintage Books, 1958), 3. (Spelling changed from original text quoted.)

28. Henry Thoreau, "Our Country," *Collected Poems,* ed. Carl Bode (Baltimore: Johns Hopkins University Press, 1964), 135.

29. As quoted in Theodore Roszak, *The Making of a Counter Culture* (New York: Anchor Books, Doubleday and Company, 1969), 11–12. Original reference Robert S. McNamara, *The Essence of Security* (New York: Harper & Row, 1968), 109–10.

30. As quoted in Roszak, 226. Original reference, Joseph Wood Krutch, *Grand Canyon* (New York: William Sloane Associates, 1958), 25.

31. John Dewey, *Reconstruction in Philosophy* (MW 12:120–21). For the notion of "controlling" nature as it is found in Dewey, see Raymond Boisvert, "The Nemesis of Necessity: Tragedy's Challenge to Deweyan Pragmatism," in *Dewey Reconfigured: Essays on Deweyan Pragmatism,* ed. Casey Haskins and David I. Seiple (Albany: State University of New York Press, 1999), 157 ff.

32. Dewey, *Reconstruction in Philosophy* (MW 12:107).

33. Dewey, "Progress" (MW 10:236).

34. John Dewey, *The Quest for Certainty* (LW 4:106).

35. Dewey, "Reconstruction As Seen Twenty-Five Years Later" (MW 12:256).

36. Ibid. (MW 12:256).

37. John Dewey, *Liberalism and Social Action* (LW 11:42).

38. Ibid. (LW 11:43).

39. Cf. Philip I. Slater, *The Pursuit of Loneliness, American Culture at the Breaking Point* (Boston: Beacon Press, 1970), 5ff.

40. Ibid., 17–18.

41. Ibid., 18–19.

42. See Edward S. Reed, *The Necessity of Experience* (New Haven: Yale University Press, 1996), 2–3, 158.

43. Ibid., 2–3.

44. See ibid., 111.

45. Ibid., 64.

46. Ibid., 80.

47. Ibid., 91.

48. Slater, *Pursuit of Loneliness,* 19.

49. John Dewey, *Individualism Old and New* (LW 5:77).

50. Ibid. (LW 5:80).

51. Ibid. (LW 5:80).

52. Ibid. (LW 5:81).

53. Ibid. (LW 5:80).

54. Ibid. (LW 5:86).

55. Ibid. (LW 5:86).

56. See ibid. (LW 5:88).

57. Ibid. (LW 5:88).

58. Ibid. (LW 5:88).

59. See William James, "The Will to Believe," in *The Will to Believe and Other Essays in Popular Philosophy* (New York: Longmans, Green and Co., 1896), 22.

60. Raymond Boisvert, "The Nemesis of Necessity," in *Dewey Reconfigured,* 162.

61. Robert M. Veatch, *Case Studies in Medical Ethics* (Cambridge: Harvard University Press, 1977), 169–70.

62. This listing is from Veatch, *Case Studies,* 170.

63. Cf. Veatch, *Case Studies,* 321ff. for a discussion of these four definitions. Some states have adopted a "conscience clause" allowing a person to choose between whole brain death and respiratory/circulatory failure, but not between whole brain death and neocortical failure. See, for example, "Brain Death, Religious Freedom, and Public Policy: New Jersey's Landmark Legislative Initiative," in *Ethical Issues in Death and Dying,*

2nd ed., ed. Tom Beauchamp and Robert Veatch (Upper Saddle River, N.J.: Prentice Hall, 1996), 52–60.

64. Cf., for example, Robert S. Morison, "Death: Process or Event?" in *Death Inside Out,* ed. Peter Steinfels and Robert M. Veatch (New York: Harper & Row, 1974), 63–70. See also William Joseph Gavin, "Death vs. Dying," chap. 7 in *Cuttin' the Body Loose: Historical, Biological, and Personal Approaches to Death and Dying* (Philadelphia: Temple University Press, 1995), 123–46

65. For a discussion of this issue, see chap. 10 in *Biomedical Ethics,* ed. Thomas A. Mappes and Jane S. Zembaty (New York: McGraw-Hill Book Company, 1981), 452 ff.

66. John Dewey, "The Superstition of Necessity" (EW 4:29).

67. Ibid. (EW 4:27). The language employed here, referring to "savages," is of course extremely problematic, and would nowadays need to be corrected.

68. Ibid. (EW 4:27).

69. Ibid. (EW 4:27).

70. Ibid. (EW 4:27).

71. Ibid. (EW 4:27–28).

72. Ibid. (EW 4:28).

73. Ibid. (EW 4:29).

74. Dewey, "Reconstruction As Seen Twenty-Five Years Later" (MW 12:267).

75. Ibid. (MW 12:267).

76. Richard Rorty, *Achieving Our Country* (Cambridge: Harvard University Press, 1998), 84.

77. Ibid., 85.

78. *At the Crossroads* (Spokane, Wash.: Communications Era Task Force, 1983), 5.

79. John J. McDermott, "Classical American Philosophy: A Reflective Bequest to the Twenty-first Century," *Journal of Philosophy* 81, no. 11 (November 1984): 669.

80. John Dewey, "The Need for a Recovery of Philosophy" (MW 10:46).

81. John Dewey, *Freedom and Culture* (LW 13:143).

82. John Dewey, "Philosophy and Democracy" (MW 11:45).

83. Charlene Haddock Seigfried, *Pragmatism and Feminism* (Chicago: University of Chicago Press, 1996), 29

84. For the topic of badly put problems, or problems not put at all, see the present author's "How Things Go Wrong in Our Experience: John Dewey vs. Franz Kafka vs. William Carlos Williams, " *Transactions of the Charles S. Peirce Society* 35, no. 1 (winter 1999): 39–68.

85. John Dewey, "The Need for a Recovery of Philosophy" (MW 10:47).

86. Cf. Ralph Waldo Emerson, "Nature," in *Selected Writings of Ralph Waldo Emerson,* edited with a foreword by William H. Gilman (New York: New American Library, 1965), 222.

87. A part of this chapter was presented as "John Dewey: Philosophy as *Con*text and the Con*text* of Philosophy," 3rd Walter E. Russell Endowed Chair Lecture, University of Southern Maine, March 26, 1985.

PART TWO

Radical Reconstruction

FIVE

As Dewey Was Hegelian, So We Should Be Deweyan

RAYMOND D. BOISVERT

TEMPUS INTERRUPTUS

Imagine a trans-temporal set of pen pals with an interest in philosophy. A simple empirical question is the subject of their latest correspondence: when did Plato live? The first correspondent is Roman: "Plato," he writes, "lived from 326 to 406 A.U.C." That is to say, he was born 326 years after the founding of Rome. The second writes from medieval Paris. "Plato lived from 427 to 347 B.C." For some reason, the writer does not seem to mind that these dates go backward, paradoxically supplying younger and younger numbers as Plato gets older and older. Our third correspondent lives in the same building as did the second one. When she looks out his window, however, what she sees is no longer the cathedral of Notre Dame, it is now the Temple of Reason. She joins the fray by declaring: "Plato lived from 2219 to 2139 B.F.R." (before the French Republic). Once again, the pen pal is not surprised to use numbers running backwards. The only confusion comes from the annoying need to calculate by adding or subtracting 1792.[1] Poor Plato! Even in death he is not left to rest in a secure temporal niche. Not only does he move around on the graph of the past, but the last two correspondents place him ignominiously in a realm where the best title to which he can aspire is "precursor."

The strange habit of resetting the counter for time seems to be a legacy of the Stoics. For them, history moved in cycles, culminating with a cataclysmic conflagration followed by a restart, all of it within the context of eternal return. The Romans transformed the cataclysmic conflagration into a special event, their city's founding. They also turned the circle into a line. *A.U.C. (ab urbe condita),* from the founding of the city, became one touchstone from which to count time. But the Roman line did not hold. So long as thinking about history was dominated by the idea of a cataclysmic event effecting a cosmic change, established time lines were constantly subject to revision. New groups, proclaiming a world-shattering event, were bound to emerge, and restart the temporal clock. This erase and recalculate approach, I will call the "fresh start" view of time. Fascination with terms and expressions like "radical," "overcoming," "shake the foundations," "tabula rasa," "new man," "presuppositionless beginnings," "utopia," and "post" as a prominent prefix, give an indication of the grip this notion of time had on thinkers. Rorty's description of the "mirror of nature," namely, that it held "traditional philosophy captive" and leading intellectuals found it "presupposed by every page" they read, can, I would claim, be applied as well to the "fresh start" view of time.[2]

Dewey was no exception. He did not go so far as to launch a movement for recalculating the calendar. Had he done so, however, we have a pretty good idea that his fresh start would date from 1564, the year of Galileo's birth.[3] Empirical science marked, for Dewey, a major world-historical event. Listen to him, in a book where the fresh start view is especially well entrenched, *Reconstruction in Philosophy*. He is waxing euphoric about empirical knowledge: "It has itself become an organ of inspiring imagination through introducing ideas of boundless possibility, indefinite progress, free movement, equal opportunity irrespective of fixed limits. It has reshaped social institutions, and in so far developed a new morale. It has achieved ideal values. It is convertible into creative and constructive philosophy" (MW 12:122). Reading this, one would think that prosperity, social harmony, justice, and equality were just around the corner. One little stumbling block lay in the way, our failure to apply systematically the scientific method to all areas of humane concern. "Put in the language of Bacon, this means that while we have been reasonably successful in obtaining command of nature by means of science, our science is not yet such that this command is systematically and preeminently applied to the relief of the human estate." Extending the field of application "defines the specific problem of philosophical reconstruction at the present time" (MW 12:103).

All of this would be well and good if (1) extending the field of application were noncontroversially possible, and (2) by "relief of the human estate" Dewey meant using technology and medicine to help feed the hungry, give work to the unemployed, cure the sick, and minimize the pain of those who cannot be cured. However, it is not this improvement in physical conditions alone that concerns Dewey. Nor is it what concerns him primarily. A new standard of success has been set by the achievements of science. Philosophical reconstruction must now work to extend the standard and the successes to wider areas of human interest, especially in those sticky areas involving the need for defining and living a good life.[4] After admitting that the revolution "wrought in physical science" had brought both progress and difficulties, he identifies the causes of the problems as a gap between the refined level of science and the rather primitive level of work in the social and political sphere. "These considerations indicate to us how undeveloped are our politics, how crude and primitive our education, how passive and inert our morals" (MW 12:152). The cosmic chronometer has once again been reset. Unfortunately, only science has so far caught on. It has advanced while social and political philosophy continue to live according to the anterior, more "primitive" epoch.

Just what can Dewey be thinking here? He is hoping for an era in which the progress made in the physical and biological sciences will be matched by a similar progress in all areas of human concern. Such an attitude was understandable in the first half of the twentieth century. Wonderful results had accrued from discoveries in the sciences. Heavenly occurrences like comets and eclipses could be both predicted and retrodicted. Electricity had been harnessed. Antibiotics and inoculations were making life easier. As we look back, we can sympathize with the hope expressed by Dewey. Who wouldn't want the successes of experimental methods to be duplicated in education, in politics, and in morals? But here we face the issue of how closely correlated are subject-matters and the means available for addressing them. The parallel works only if the problems that arise in the social and political spheres are amenable to the sort of treatments which have resulted in the marvelous gains in science and medicine. Several contemporary signs give us pause here. For one, even in the sciences, some of the initial optimism about having relegated certain problems to an outmoded past have had to be reassessed. In 1969, the U.S. surgeon general could claim un-ironically that "the war against infectious diseases has been won."[5] Such a pronouncement now sounds strange to our ears, accustomed as they are to the ravages of AIDS, and worries about other emerging viruses like dengue hemorrhagic fever and the hantavirus. When we leave the sciences, the contrast with a stepladder understanding of history (neatly sorting out the "undeveloped" from the developed) is even harder to sustain. Scholarship in history and anthropology now makes us less inclined to accept, in a blanket way, a progressive understanding of human cultures. We now realize that this was not only a scholarly mistake, but that it had serious political implications. The connection between "chronopolitics" and "geopolitics" has been well articulated by one anthropologist. He is discussing the conditions within which traditional anthropological theory arose:

> The expansive, aggressive, and oppressive societies which we collectively and inaccurately call the West needed Space to occupy. More profoundly and problematically, they required Time to accommodate the schemes of a one-way history: progress, development, modernity (and their negative mirror images: stagnation, underdevelopment, tradition). In short, *geopolitics* has its ideological foundations in *chronopolitics*."[6]

Dewey could with honest hope express his project for parallel achievements in the physical sciences and in sociopolitical situations with few reservations about its controversial nature. He was, after all, a child of the nineteenth century, writing in the first half of the twentieth. We, having learned from experience, are inclined to tell a more complicated story. As the euphoria associated with great advances in technology and medicine begins to fade, and as we learn from history and anthropology how our understanding of both non-Western and pre-Modern societies cannot be subsumed under the nineteenth-century narrative of progress from primitive to civilized, we must distance ourselves from this Deweyan project.

Dewey's search for a parallel between progress in the sciences and progress in politics, education, and morals assumes that one model for investigation and one set of expectations about results can apply to all contexts. What it overlooks is the need for methods and expectations to be correlative with their subject-matters. The concrete contexts of lived social experience can be improved, but not in the same ways, or with the same methods, or with the same lasting results as the improvements occasioned by a Pasteur or a Lister. The Deweyan hope for moving politics away from its "undeveloped" state, or moving education from its "primitive" state, looks to one model and one set of expectations when a plurality of methods and a varied set of expectations are called for. Improvements are always needed. Social reform is a continual challenge for humans. Ideals must always be compared to the social contexts claiming to instantiate them. But this is not to be confused with thinking that a Pasteur in politics will once and for all develop a technique to resolve the issues of power and exploitation so that application of a political analogue to pasteurization will keep them in check.

The fresh start view of time had such a grip on Dewey that it overshadowed a side of him that knew better. It clouded his ability to carry out one of philosophy's time-honored tasks, namely, making distinctions. It also prevented him from taking seriously enough something he knew quite well, that subject-matters and methods are correlative. Both of these, making distinctions and the correlation of subject-matters and methods, are intertwined. Human history is too complex for any single perspective to apply across the board. Distinctions between say, the history of airplane technology and that of parenting techniques need to be kept quite separate. Whereas "primitive" and "advanced" may apply successfully to the former, they are distortions at least, ethnocentric slights at worst, with regard to the latter. Specific types of approaches are required for different subjects of inquiry. Different types of inquiry, in turn, give rise to different sorts of expectations about results. This is an old lesson, taught by that pre-Galilean thinker, Aristotle.[7] In politics and morals especially, areas where the control of variables or the creation of ideal conditions are not possible, methods and expectations about results will be sui generis if they are not to be misguided or utopian. Such methods will be so different from those applicable to the physical sciences or to technological innovations that blanket historical claims such as Dewey's that our education is "primitive" or our politics "undeveloped" in comparison with scientific achievements are so misleading as to be erroneous. It is one thing to warn that constant vigilance is warranted in political philosophy because politics will always have an element of unfairness in it, because expressed ideals rarely match social instantiations, because some people are always unfairly excluded from full participation in the fruits of civilized life. But this is not the same as saying that our political philosophy today stands to the projected political philosophy of tomorrow as the Wright glider does to the latest airliner rolling out of Airbus or Boeing factories. The tools for social enhancement remain unchanged since the earliest time of philosophical reflection: historical perspective, the ability to learn from experience, listening to those who are excluded from power and privilege, projection of ideals, and attempts to formulate an accurate understanding of the human condition.

Rather than be straitjacketed by the fresh start view of history, it is better to learn from experience and realize that some questions have to be asked anew by each generation. Experience also teaches us that these questions, usually dealing with social, political, and moral questions, cannot be resolved in the way that that scientists resolved the cause of beriberi, the explanation of tides, and the helical structure of DNA. In *The Meno,* Socrates, a pre-Galilean thinker, worried about virtuous fathers who were unable to produce virtuous sons. Was Socrates' problem that he lived in the "primitive," precursor period antedating the scientific method? Are we so different from Socrates and his contemporaries that their worry has gone the way of concern about smallpox and polio? Do we no longer need ask about virtue in general or about how parents can best optimize the conditions for inculcating virtue? Are we now relieved from the task of asking the more basic question of whether phrasing the issue in terms of "virtue" is the most appropriate formulation? Experience should have taught us that the answer to these questions is "no." Issues relating to the mutual obligations of parents and children are different from those focused on by Galileo and his descendants.

At his worst, Dewey insists on painting the picture of historical development with one big brush instead of with many different brushes. He could have learned an important lesson from a major figure in the American Renaissance. Nathaniel Hawthorne was surrounded by people who believed that time had now altered decisively. The corrupt, old world, they believed, had been left behind. A New Jerusalem was being established. Although the Puritans had left behind the old world, and although their geographical situation was indeed different, Hawthorne realized the error of extending this event to the belief that moral geography had also been decisively altered. Painting with a series of fine brushes, he offered a more nuanced picture. The New Jerusalem, in many ways, was no different from the old. Adultery had not disappeared. Nor had hypocrisy, small-mindedness, the penchant for scapegoating, or the desire for revenge.

The pluralist strain within pragmatism seems to have slipped away from Dewey when the fresh start view occupied his attention. At those times he tended to long for something that should be foreign to a pluralist, *methodological monism*. Good pluralists, he seemed to forget, need not seek out one methodology to trump all others in every circumstance. One could claim that there are some areas in which the ordinary tools of common sense, experience, and philosophical reflection continue, even after the Galilean turn, to offer the best guides. These may not provide the kind of quantifiable results arrived at in the newer sciences. They might not provide the predictability and ability to control and manipulate. But they have one advantage: they are the methods most suitable to the subject area of messy, concrete human life. The new, post-Galilean methods are to be welcome as additional manners for dealing with our surroundings. They should not, however, be thought of as displacing entirely philosophical reflection based on experience. Being intelligent and being reasonable can coexist with being rational and being scientific. Different areas of concern call forth different modes of approach.

Dewey is not always careful enough in making such distinctions. "Overgeneralization," is the most charitable way to describe a blanket statement suggesting total displacement found in *The Quest for Certainty*. The new attitude, as Dewey puts it, "marks a revolution in the whole spirit of life, in the entire attitude taken toward whatever is found in existence" (LW 4:80). "Whole" and "entire" provide the key words here. For Dewey, as mentioned earlier, time might as well be divided into "B.G." and "A.G.," before Galileo and after Galileo. Dewey described the era prior to

Galileo in this way: "Aforetime man employed the results of his prior experience only to form customs that henceforth had to be blindly followed or blindly broken. Now, old experience is used to suggest aims and methods for developing a new and improved experience" (MW 12:134). Philosophy continues to be the "attempt to find an intelligent substitute for blind custom and blind impulse as guides to life and conduct" (MW 12:152).

Speaking in this overly broad way, Dewey distorts more than the past, oversimplified, nineteenth-century style, as a realm of sheer adherence to blind custom.[8] He also does a disservice to the great thinkers who, paying attention to experience, articulated many an "intelligent substitute" for blind custom. The enormity of this slight can be discerned by a short list of people who predate the scientific revolution: Plato, Aristotle, Mencius, Confucius, Cicero, the Buddha, Heraclitus, William of Ockham, Abelard, Dante, and Avicenna among others. The Dewey who could be a sensitive interpreter of the past, who drew inspiration from Greek philosophy during his years at Columbia, coexists uncomfortably with the Dewey who was willing to make Dewey's blithe, untenable pronouncements about the past. At his worst, he combined a false dilemma with a sleight of hand. The false dilemma: people in the past were trapped by the either/or of blind custom or an "intelligent substitute" for it. This would be news to the barons who forced King John to approve the Magna Carta, or to the Plebians who struggled for a shift of power with the Patricians in republican Rome. The sleight of hand: that the "intelligent substitute," while it sounds generous and open-ended, means essentially "scientific method." In a deft move, Dewey thus eliminates "intelligent substitute" as operating in pre-Modern and non-Western societies. Dewey may be forgiven the leftovers of nineteenth-century historiography sedimented into his thought. But contemporary thinkers should not follow him in this error.

As antidotes for Dewey's totalizing, distinction-free attitude we can take hints, first from Dewey himself, and then from Adorno. Discussing "individuality, equality and superiority" in an article of the same title, Dewey, now at his best, centers his analysis on an important distinction. "Superiority," and "inferiority," taken by themselves, he claims, are "meaningless words." "No one should use the words until he has asked himself and is ready to tell others: Superior and inferior *in what?*" (MW 13:296). Similarly, I would argue, when discussing human life through time, we should distinguish those aspects in which terms like "undeveloped" and "primitive" apply, and those situations in which they do not. Just as the blanket use of "superiority" and "inferiority" distorts the complexity of human life, so the blanket application of terminology indicating higher and lower development distorts the heterogeneously textured accomplishments of humans through history. Adorno, sensitive to the multiple strands within the movement of human life through time, separates an area where a progressive narrative is possible, from one where it is not: "No universal history leads from the savage to humanity, but there *is* one that leads from the slingshot to the megabomb."[9] Linguistics, once caught up in the fresh start view, was willing to speak of primitive and advanced languages. Anthropology, drawn in by the same picture of time, tended at one period to use an evolutionary model with regard to human cultures.[10] These disciplines have now abandoned such schemata in light of both their subject-matters' complexity, and the colonialist/imperialist attitudes that accompanied the older views. Deweyans need to take the same steps. It is time we admitted openly that some of Dewey's own phrasings can be irredeemably misleading in their neglect of important distinctions.

All of this is important in an anthology dealing with "passing Dewey by." For the Dewey we must pass by is the Dewey still captivated by the picture of time characterized by sharp ruptures amenable to single-label descriptions. It is also the Dewey who thinks that something called "instrumentalism," that is, the understanding of intelligence as paying attention to causes and conditions, is a new arrival on the human scene. Here is where the sleight of hand mentioned earlier causes an important confusion. "Intelligence" as paying attention to human experience in light of revising that experience has been practiced by philosophers for all time. But "intelligence" as best exemplified in the scientific method is a relative newcomer, dating from the late Renaissance. Because Dewey runs the latter together with the former, he distorts unfairly the accomplishments of the past. He can also too easily be read as suggesting, not methods of intelligence properly coordinated with subject-matters, but rather a single method applicable to all. Here, I contend, is that aspect of Dewey which most needs to be jettisoned as we move into the twenty-first century. We who come after him must be categorical. Human life is complex enough for both continuities and ruptures through time. Beware of totalizing claims. There are many methods. In practice they must be developed in correlation with their subject matters. Expectations about the nature of results must also be correlative with the conditions that set the question. There is no single method, the application of which will bring social inquiries to the model of inquiries in the physical sciences. Nor is there any need to set the problematic as if this were even a lingering ideal. Deweyans today must clearly disavow the "fresh start" reading of time along with the embrace of a purported single method that came with it.

Having gotten rid of what many people consider the centerpiece of Deweyan thought, is there anything left? Those who approach Dewey via *Reconstruction in Philosophy* and his books on logic would probably answer "no." But for those who come at Dewey from the texts with "experience" in their title, the story is different. Seeds from those texts can grow in unexpected directions once the garden is properly weeded. Passing Dewey by is not the same as constructing a Dewey bypass. We want to go explore the Deweyan landscape before emerging on the other side, a voyage that will leave some permanent impressions. Two of these are central for a fruitful philosophical savoring of things. One is lived experience. The other is mediation. Both speak to present conditions, and both help rehabilitate venerable pre-Galilean positions. The first allows a renewed appreciation for genuine philosophical irony, while the second returns correspondence to a place of respect.

LIVED EXPERIENCE AND IRONY

Art as Experience draws approvingly on Keats, who had praised the "negative capability" of Shakespeare. "Negative capability" turns out to be something positive, namely, the ability to live amidst "uncertainties," "mysteries," and "doubts." Building on such an ability, Dewey claims that there are but two philosophies. "One of them accepts life and experience in all its uncertainty, mystery, doubt, and half-knowledge and turns that experience upon itself to deepen and intensify its own qualities—to imagination and art. This is the philosophy of Shakespeare and Keats" (LW 10:39,41). It is also the philosophy of Dewey. Hamlet had chided Horatio for accepting too simplified a view of life. "There are more things in heaven and earth, Horatio, than are dreamt of in your philosophy." No one who has seriously traveled in the Deweyan territory can become a Horatio-type philosopher. Lived experience is recognized as richer, fuller, more convoluted than any rationality-obsessed simplifier would want. As William James put it, philosophers use conceptual shotguns, sending out volleys of "new vocables." Their profession demands it. But, if truth be told, the best among them realize the "hollowness and irrelevancy" of their formulations.[11]

"Hollowness" and "irrelevancy" are exaggerated terms used to make a point. If philosophers are honest, they will admit that even the best of their kin have been partial in their success and culturally conditioned in the very questions that they ask. The simplifications of abstract rationality must not be confused with the teeming richness of the lived world. Having traveled with Dewey, we know that reality is a "*denotative*" term, "a word used to designate indifferently everything that happens" (MW 10:39). The texture of events is complex, interlocked, and sometimes incompatible. Even the best of our formulations have something of the partial and tentative about them. When we act as good naturalists should, we try our best to "follow the lead of the subject matter" (MW 3:118). This philosophical hunt sometimes takes us into areas where ambiguity, vagueness, and even inconsistency characterize our prey.

The real, if I may put it dramatically, is not rational. Not, at least, perfectly rational. At the same time, the real is not "irrational," simply a surd, totally incomprehensible and always unpredictable. Both formulations derive from the same presupposition. Each assumes that the grid of rationality must either be perfectly isomorphic with existence (the real is rational) or that existence, jellylike, totally eludes the grid (the real is irrational). Other options are possible. Pythagoras's fascination with and perplexity over the number π can move us to new ground. Although π is not perfectly rational, neither is it "irrational" in the ordinary as opposed to the mathematical sense of that word. Π, for practical purposes, makes a lot of sense. We put it to wonderful use. If we think of the real on the model of π, that is, as that which, although not fully fathomable, is nonetheless within the range of comprehension and use, then we are closer to the kind of ontology acceptable to a philosophy that takes lived experience as the irreducible matrix which sets the contexts for philosophizing. If this lived experience is richer than any of our attempts at mapping it, and if its complications require of us qualifying terms like "somewhat," and "approximate," so be it.

If "somewhat" and "approximate" become focal terms, then Hegel's "the real is rational" becomes unsuitable as a safe general claim about existence. Dewey offered an alternative in 1906 when, employing a favorite term, he entitled an essay "reality as experience." This is a puzzling title.[12] It can readily be dismissed as an exuberantly misguided formulation while in the grip of absolute idealism. Such a dismissal would, however, be premature. While the actual phrasing no longer speaks to us, the grasp of things it entails can do justice to a full-blooded philosophy that wishes, as Dewey's did, to encompass both the wonders of ordinary life and the results of specialized studies.[13] "Experience" as Dewey came to use it, encompasses both what happens and the multiple ways the happenings are prehended (if I may borrow a relatively neutral Whiteheadian term).[14] It makes no prior judgments about the proper schemata to which reality must adjust itself. Reality is more than rational, reality is experience. As used by Dewey in his 1906 essay, the term has metaphysical sweep. It is a general statement about the way things are. They are interlocked and in constant interactions of multiple and varied sorts. When we speak of that which is, we are, within this metaphysics, accepting a grasp of things understood as the processes of entities exchanging information and responding to surroundings. Transactions are as basal as the events involved in the transactions. Some of these exchanges involve little more than physical contact. Others include processing of information and consequent readjustment. Some include memory, conscious reflection, and manipulation. Still others combine aesthetic and emotional prehending of situations. Such a generous, active, and multileveled appreciation of existence is the reason why those who have traveled with Dewey welcome the tangled richness of lived experience and judge eliminative philosophies to be uncongenial.[15] Reductionistic schemes of all sorts create a special problem: they cannot account for the thickness of what is prehended in ordinary experience. Such complexity becomes, almost by definition, a surd. If one accepts, on the contrary, ordinary experience as ontologically fundamental, then one is capable of accounting for the items selected as primordial by those who propose that a simpler, hidden dimension is, in a blanket way, more real, or perhaps even the only "really real." For those who accept the ontological priority of lived experience, the simpler, hidden dimensions result from being isolated and highlighted for specific purposes. They help us understand, manipulate, and utilize forces which would otherwise be unknown. As such they not only tell us about our surroundings, but they are immensely helpful in our dealings with those surroundings. There is no need, however, to transform these ultimate simples, the results of specialized inquiries, into a realm which is more real than the blooming, buzzing richness of lived experience. Within such a transformation, the world of lived experience would itself be transmuted into some inexplicable surd, an illusory tableau whose seeming obviousness becomes an intractable problem to be explained away.

Those who seek the security of ultimate simples long for a straightforward view of things that will optimize security and predictability. Pragmatists, by contrast, have learned to live with degrees of ambiguity and approximations of certitude. James, we recall, had said that our formulations are characterized by "hollowness and irrelevancy." The phrasing is rhetorically excessive, but the sentiment put forth is important. It can be restated in more balanced language as old as Socrates: all philosophical formulations are ironic. Alexander Nehemas has recently articulated two understandings of philosophical irony. One is the irony of the detached thinkers who hover above the push and pull of ordinary life, who make "an implicit claim to be superior to their victims." The second is the irony of the playful dialecticians who are quick-witted and seek to keep readers and listeners off balance by refusing explicit, straightforward statements of a position. In this way "we have no sure way of knowing the ironist's meaning: all we know is that it is not quite what we have heard."[16] The detached observer, critiquing always from the outside, and also the playful provocateur, make ample use of talents in no short supply among academics: puns, riddles, striking formulations, and the ability to undermine any constructive position almost as soon as it is offered. The vulnerability which characterizes all lovers, including the lovers of wisdom, is an unwanted accompaniment for these ironists. They prefer the more self-insulated game of *philo-nike,* love of victory (at least in the sense of attempting to be insulated from genuine criticism), over the more risky self-exposure involved with *philo-sophy.*

There is a Deweyan irony, but it is different from the two identified by Nehemas. It is linked, not to intimations of superiority, but to admissions of humility. We work out our formulations, admit their limitations, but urge them on as ways of achieving wisdom and, in turn, an enhancement of the human condition. Will these formulations be perfect? Not at all. They will be partial and flawed. But they will be constructive and bring with them the possibility of fruitful practices.[17] In turn, the limitations associated with these constructions and practices will eventually become evident. Criticism, indeed, is welcome on this view. Irony and pragmatist philosophy are correlative. But their proper meaning can only be grasped within the context of constructively seeking articulations that give us some grasp of wisdom. Whoever takes seriously the fullness of ordinary experience must accept simultaneously the limited grasp available even to the best of us. Here is an important first lesson for philosophers wishing to incorporate Dewey while going beyond him: accept reality as experience and the humble attitude of philosophical irony that goes with it.

MEDIATION AND CORRESPONDENCE

Philosophical irony is to be identified neither with skepticism nor with constructivism. It accompanies a sensible realism, one which admits that, in our transactions with things, we come to some grasp of them. As in the case of communicating with speakers of another language, the results are a combination of successes, approximations, and frustrations. The presence of the latter two need not be cause for radical doubt about whether mutual communication is possible at all. Such, however, was (and is) the great skeptical lament of decidedly un-ironic philosophers engaged in the epistemology industry. Dewey bemoaned the misguided question at the heart of this industry: "How is knowledge *überhaupt,* knowledge at large, *possible?*" (MW 3:119). The best response is to deflect the question, saying that its formulation is misconstrued. It assumes, as primordial, a radical disconnection between the knowing subject and its intended object. What could possibly have led to such an assumption? Bruno Latour, well known for his role in the sociology of science, thinks he knows. First, one makes the antipragmatist move of abstracting from the actual practices engaged in by human beings. Then, gape in awe at the resultant chasm between two polar opposites. In other words, begin by erasing "all the mediations."[18] Stuck in this amnesic state, it is not surprising "that philosophers have been unable to reach an understanding on the question of realism and relativism: they have taken the two provisional extremities for the entire chain, as if they had tried to understand how a lamp and a switch could 'correspond' to each other after cutting the wire and making the lamp 'gaze out' at the 'external' switch."[19]

Two related terms in this citation are important for my purposes, "mediations" and "chain." Dewey had complained that traditional epistemology lost itself in theories of knowledge apart from practices. Much more fruitful would be the study of specific ways in which defensible beliefs were determined.[20] Studies of this sort are being undertaken. They tend to highlight chains of intermediary instrumentalities. Philosophy has a name for these instrumentalities. They are called "mediations."

There is nothing mysterious about mediations. Latour's description of a research project in Brazil brings them into relief. The research involved determining whether the savanna was encroaching on the forest or the forest penetrating into the savanna. To make progress, many mediating steps had to be taken. Branches were marked with numbers, samples of leaves were gathered and taken back to an office where they could be classified. The area in question was divided into a grid identified by coordinates. Samples of soil, identified by location and depth, were gathered. They were sorted in a "pedocomparator," a large box containing small empty cubes, allowing careful classification of soil samples. For cataloguing soil color and sharing information with colleagues, the "pedologist" (soil scientist) relies on something called the "Munsell Code." This is a notebook which provides continua of hues separately identified and numbered. Other researchers with the same code can immediately get a visual grasp of the soil sample's color by being given its number.[21] When actual practices like these are taken into account, the seemingly mysterious ability of mind to comprehend nature dissolves into a much more pedestrian, hardly mysterious activity, that is, a set of mediating practices that allow information about what is around us to emerge.

As someone rooted in German Idealism, Dewey admitted the presence of mediations in "all knowledge" (MW 3:109).[22] Even when he spoke of *immediate* empiricism (as in the title of an important essay), Dewey took pains to emphasize that the label "immediate" did not ignore the presence of mediation. "Immediate," he pointed out, was a term applying "to anything except *knowledge*." It would be wrong to deny the "necessity of 'mediation,' or reflection, in knowledge" (MW 3:166).

Those of us building on Dewey need to take a cue from this articulation, while moving one step further. His understanding of mediation is inadequately developed and too narrowly extended. For him "mediation" is specifically limited to cognitive situations; it does not extend to all of experience. Mediation, we need to recognize, is pervasive. It goes "all the way down" as Rorty might say. Dewey's formulations erroneously run together "immediate" and "unmediated." The former signals direct, vital participation in an environment. The latter signals the absence of intermediaries which help negotiate transactions with our environment. Experience may be both "immediate" (i.e., directly participatory) and "mediated" (i.e., not free of mediations). Mediation accompanies all experience because it encompasses the habits, presuppositions, tools, and practices that mark transactions within an ambient environment.

Cultural predispositions, sedimented in language, provide the preeminent organs of mediation. They color our intermingling with things. If some areas of our lives were not shaped by cultural and linguistic factors, then it might be possible to divide areas bathed in mediations from those that are not. Such a sorting would require, at a minimum, a neutral language, one that mysteriously could get at some presumably straightforward reality quite apart from any specific mode of approaching it. Neutral languages, it is safe to say, do not exist. Nor are they in any way an ideal aspiration.[23] To say that mediation goes all the way down is simply to accept an honest appraisal of the human condition. "Mediation" means nothing more than this: our interactions with the world and each other can take place because our very being encompasses and elicits a variety of instrumentalities providing the messengers and tools of translation that allow elicitations of meaning.

Modern philosophy's longing to eliminate mediation was fueled by the Cartesian fetish for certitude and its concomitant phobia about falling into error. Pretending to achieve unmediated access requires a willful distortion of the human condition. One could either wish away, à la Descartes, our temporal and cultural situatedness, or, à la Bacon, wish away the languages we speak, the temperaments we bear, and the traditions that have shaped us. There is a kernel of truth in the Baconian and Cartesian distortions of the human situation. Mediating instrumentalities are accompanied by limitations. This is not something Deweyans need deny. They simply need to complete the story. The limitations do not amount to a veil of ignorance separating us from the subject-matters we seek to understand. Languages, natural temperaments, cultural traditions, expectations, experimental manipulations, and hopes do distort and interfere. But they also provide the means for truths to emerge. The ability praised by Keats is important in this context. "Negative capability" allows us to hold on to the idea that the same item, for example, a language, a tradition, an individual temperament, or experimental intervention, may both be a catalyst for understanding certain dimensions of reality, and an impediment concealing others.

Absolute Idealism's richest legacy was the intuition that reality could best be described as a network of interlocking processes, each of which was more than mere matter. To speak of Absolute Mind was to identify a pen-pal world of meanings everywhere, in potential correspondence with meanings anywhere. When Dewey entitled his essay "Reality as Experience," he sought to avoid speaking in terms that suggested a mind "in here" and a nature "out there." For us, embracing "mediation" in the widest sense is a good step in this direction. Certain difficulties attach themselves to the term "mediation," however. It can too readily suggest antecedently separate realms that subsequently need to be linked. Instead of growing organically out of what is ontologically primary, the label "mediation" tends to connote an imposition from without which is needed to bridge a dichotomy which itself is primary.

To block such a connotation, Dewey resorted to his title "reality as experience." Unfortunately, this title brings unwanted baggage of its own. It too readily suggests that consciousness pervades all levels of reality, a kind of pan-psychism present even prior to human life. A more suitable alternative involves rehabilitating a term much maligned by pragmatists, namely, "correspondence." Used in its hyphenated form, this is a word thick enough to characterize our world as a network of interactive exchanges, yet free enough of idealist connotations to avoid tendencies toward ascribing consciousness at every level of being. Neither the subject/object split, nor an alternative like windowless monads, is primary. The safest generic description of the way things are is to assume contexts composed of information packets corresponding with one another. Co-responding entities (which might be metaphorically identified as "messengers," the descendants of Hermes or Iris) are present everywhere. A photon, says a physicist, "is not so much the transmitter of the force per se, but rather the transmitter of a *message* of how the recipient must respond."[24] Before the universe was even a second old, the co-responding dance of quarks, electrons, neutrinos was already under way.[25] As the universe changed, the types and complexity of co-respondences blossomed into the heterogeneous wonder of which we are an integral part.

Assuming co-respondence as primordial helps in several ways. It displaces the great bifurcation which led otherwise sensible people to ask whether knowledge *überhaupt* was possible. It also allows for a loose but intact "hanging together" of important Deweyan moves. Democracy, in a world of co-respondences, is best understood as "primarily a mode of associated living, of conjoint communicated experience" (MW 9:93). Something similar could be said of an education that must be built around the social model of cooperative, shared inquiry and of philosophical search built around social intelligence. The real is not rational and single philosophers are not endowed with powers of penetrating once and for all the pattern of rationality. Reality is experience. The real is a tissue of co-respondences. Philosophers carry on, at their levels and in their ways, an activity continuous with the very tissue of existence.

We can pass Dewey by respectfully if we begin by rejecting his formulations which embrace the fresh start theory of time. Experience has taught us to be wary of an exaggerated fresh start approach. Human history is a meandering, multileveled affair. Novelty and continuity interpenetrate. By accepting a more complicated narrative about our past, we can treat Dewey the way we treat other important thinkers, not as someone we have relegated to a primitive epoch, but as an ancestor who has left a permanent deposit in his progeny. Two deposits that can be fruitfully mined have been identified by this paper. One is lived experience together with its corollary, irony. The other is mediation, with its corollary, a co-respondence theory of being. Embracing these, Deweyans can become "polytemporal"[26] thinkers. In that way, some Deweyan (as well as some Hegelian, and some pre-Galilean) elements would live on, but in a decidedly different form.

NOTES

1. The story could go on by dropping Plato further into the past as 1917 becomes the year 1 in the Bolshevik calendar. Fortunately, this idea, although floated in post-Revolutionary Russia, never really caught on. See Daniel Peris, *Storming the Heavens: The Soviet League of the Militant Godless* (Ithaca, N.Y.: Cornell University Press, 1998), 89–90.

2. Richard Rorty, *Philosophy and the Mirror of Nature* (Princeton: Princeton University Press, 1979), 12, 43.

3. This was also, incidentally, the year Shakespeare came into the world.

4. "When physics, chemistry, biology, medicine, contribute to the detection of concrete human woes and to the development of plans for remedying them and relieving the human estate, they become moral; they become part of the apparatus of moral inquiry or science" (MW 12:178).

5. Robin Marantz Henig, *A Dancing Matrix: How Science Confronts Emerging Viruses* (New York: Vintage Books, 1994), xii.

6. Johannes Fabian, *Time and the Other* (New York: Columbia University Press, 1983), 144.

7. Discussing the question of method in social inquiries, Aristotle says the following: "Our discussion will be adequate if its degree of clarity fits the subject-matter; for we should not seek the same degree of exactness in all sorts of arguments alike, any more than in the products of different crafts . . . the educated person seeks exactness in each area to the extent that the nature of the subject allows"; Aristotle, *Nicomachean Ethics,* trans. Terence Irwin (Indanapolis, Ind.: Hackett Publishing Co., 1985), 1094b 13–14; 24–25.

8. William Doty, in an essay exploring the rich religious traditions of Native Americans, traditions that have been "consistently regarded by Europeans as inferior and stupid," provides as evidence of narrow ethnocentrism (and brutal ignorance) the following citation which eerily echoes the Deweyan statement that follows. Here is Doty: "But as late as 1913—within our own generations (my father was born in New Mexico in 1914, two years after it achieved statehood!)—the Supreme Court could say about the Pueblos of the southwest that they were 'largely influenced by superstition and fetishism, and chiefly governed according to the crude customs inherited from their ancestors.'" See William G. Doty, "We Are All Relatives: The Significance of Native American Religions," *Soundings* 81 no. 3–4: 541. Here is Dewey: "Aforetime man employed the result of his prior experience only to form customs that henceforth had to be blindly followed or blindly broken. Now, old experience is used to suggest aims and methods for developing a new and improved experience" (MW 12:134).

9. Fabian, *Time and the Other,* 159.

10. Ibid., 147.

11. William James, *The Varieties of Religious Experience* (New York: Modern Library, [1902] 1994), 497.

12. See the essay "Reality as Experience" in MW 3:102–6. Assuming still a human-centered understanding of "experience," Dewey answers the objection about experience prior to the arrival of humans by speaking in emergentist terms. "We can not, however, say an earlier reality versus a later reality, because this denies the salient point of *transition towards.* Continual-transformation-in-the-direction-of-this is the fact which excludes on the basis of science (to which we have agreed to appeal) any chopping off of the non-contemporaneously experienced earlier reality from later experience" (MW 3: 103). According to Dewey, although it is true that prior to the arrival of humans we cannot, in the fullest sense, speak of "experience," we can admit its presence potentially. A less diffident way of putting the issue would be to disavow explicitly the idealist

identification of experience with "conscious" experience. Understanding "experience" more widely, as the absorption of information and subsequent response, would lead to the realization that experience exists on many levels, most of which do not depend on the presence of humans.

13. "Pragmatism is content to take its stand with science; for science finds all such events to be subject-matter of description and inquiry—just like stars and fossils, mosquitoes and malaria, circulation and vision. It also takes its stand with daily life, which finds that such things really have to be reckoned with as they occur interwoven in the texture of events" (MW 10:39).

14. Alfred N. Whitehead, *Science and the Modern World* (New York: Macmillan, 1926), 101.

15. "If experience actually presents esthetic and moral traits, then these traits may also be supposed to reach down into nature, and to testify to something that belongs to nature as truly as does the mechanical structure attributed to it in physical science" (LW 1: 13).

16. Alexander Nehemas, *The Art of Living: Socratic Reflections from Plato to Foucault* (Berkeley: University of California Press, 1998), 120.

17. Cp. "Better it is for philosophy to err in active participation in the living struggles and issues of its own age and times than to maintain an immune monastic impeccability, without relevancy and bearing in the generating ideas of its contemporary present" (MW 4:142).

18. Bruno Latour, *Pandora's Hope: Essays on the Reality of Science Studies* (Cambridge: Harvard University Press, 1999), 73.

19. Ibid.

20. "Literally, 'epistemology' means only theory of knowledge; the term *might* therefore have been employed simply as a synonym for a descriptive logic; for a theory that takes knowledge as it finds it and attempts to give the same kind of an account of it that would be given of any other natural function or occurrence. But the mere mention of what *might* have been only accentuates what is. The things that pass for epistemology all assume that knowledge is not a natural function or event, but a mystery. . . . Hence the complete divorce in contemporary thought between epistemology as theory of knowledge and logic as an account of the specific ways in which particular beliefs that are better than other alternative beliefs regarding the same matters are formed . . ." (MW 3:119).

21. Latour, *Pandora's Hope,* 58.

22. In an essay entitled "The Experimental Theory of Knowledge," Dewey admits that "there is no apprehension without some (however slight) context; no acquaintance which is not either recognition or expectation" (MW 3:108). We are not, Dewey is saying, neutral mirrors, simply receiving data haphazardly from the external world. We are engaged, interested parties who bring to inquiries certain questions, certain predisposi-

tions, and certain expectations. None of this is surprising. Lived experience can be examined in various ways. The results of specialized studies must never be confused with the totality of what is. The distance between the two can be formulated as that "between being and knowing." Such a distinction also brings with it the "recognition of mediation, that is, of art, in all knowledge" (MW 3:108,109).

23. Douglas Hofstadter's wonderful book *Le Ton beau de Marot: In Praise of the Music of Language* demolishes the pretensions of "Machine Translation," the attempts to get computer programs to translate from one natural language to another. In an idealized case, a word processing program would feature a menu containing a long list of languages, "any of which you can point at with your mouse, and at the very instant you release the mouse button, the sentence or paragraph you've highlighted on your screen snaps obediently into the language you have chosen." See Douglas Hofstadter, *Le Ton beau de Marot: In Praise of the Music of Language* (New York: Basic Books, 1997), 119. Hofstadter does not hesitate to label this "a nightmarish vision." Not only does it neglect the intertwining of form and content in language (one thinks of "full fathom five thy father lies") but it also ignores the inability of selecting *the* model language which parses the world in a perfectly objective, neutral way.

For instance, a term meaning what 'uncle' means in English could *never* be used at this hypothetically language-neutral level. Why not? Because some human languages break the world up *more finely* than this (such as Swedish, which distinguishes between a father's brother and a mother's brother, or Chinese, which carries the split-up even further), while other languages break it up *more coarsely* than this. If one really took this quest to render all content in a medium-free manner in earnest, one would come to an instant grinding halt, because *every* scheme for breaking up the world into a set of preordained categories amounts to choosing one particular expressive medium—one particular language, whether natural or artificial—as the 'objective truth.' Ibid., 120).

24. Brian Greene, *The Elegant Universe: Superstrings, Hidden Dimensions, and the Quest for the Ultimate Theory* (New York: W.W. Norton, 1999), 124.

25. "Quarks, electrons, neutrinos, and their antiparticles are born from the vacuum. But as soon as they materialize, the particles and their antiparticles encounter one another and are annihilated, turning into radiation. The packets of radiation (or photons), in their turn, disappear, giving birth to particle-antiparticle pairs. There is a constant interaction between matter, antimatter, and radiation." See Trinh Xuan Thuan, *The Secret Melody: And Man Created the Universe,* trans. Storm Dunlop (New York: Oxford University Press, 1995), 122–23.

26. For a discussion of "polytemporal" as it applies to intellectual history see the last chapter of my *John Dewey: Rethinking Our Time* (Albany: State University of New York Press, 1998), as well as "Philosophy: Postmodern or Polytemporal?" *International Philosophical Quarterly* 40, no. 3 (2000): 313–26.

SIX

(Re)construction Zone

Beware of Falling Statues

SHANNON SULLIVAN

> Truly, I advise you: go away from me and guard yourselves against [Dewey]! . . . Perhaps he has deceived you. . . . You respect me; but how if one day your respect should tumble? Take care that a falling statue does not strike you dead! You say you believe in [Dewey]? But of what importance is [Dewey]? You are my believers: but of what importance are all believers? . . . Now I bid you lose me and find yourselves; and only when you have all denied me will I return to you.[1]

I quote from Nietzsche, but as the liberties I take with the passage suggest, the words are just as appropriate coming from Dewey's mouth as they are from that of Zarathustra. Nietzsche does not declare that God is dead so that his readers will set him up as a new deity in God's place. He hopes instead that his readers have no need for a god of any type. The last thing Nietzsche wants are disciples who belong to the Church of Nietzsche, piously reciting what they think is the new Apostle's Creed that Nietzsche provides. The more one believes Nietzsche's philosophy, the more his philosophy becomes a danger to guard against. The more one solemnly respects Nietzsche's message, the more his message interferes with hearing what he has to say. If Nietzsche's followers have set him up as an idol to worship, then on the very terms of the philosophy they follow, his statue must be dashed to the ground.

I begin with Nietzsche in particular because he makes provocatively explicit what I take "passing by" to mean and what is present but relatively subtle in Dewey's work: the need for an attitude of irreverent respect toward their philosophies. We Deweyans demonstrate that we read Dewey poorly when, in response to his work, we erect his pragmatism as a statue to worship, as a creed to recite by heart. The more we earnestly believe that Dewey got it right, the more we need to be wary of our devotion to him. If we are to be true to Dewey's ideas, we at times must declare them false.

We especially need to be wary of our devotion to Dewey when it comes to matters of race. Given Dewey's insistence that philosophy be informed by the context of "real" life, it is dismaying that Dewey wrote very little about the constitutive role that race and racism play in lived experience. In his personal life, Dewey displayed concern for matters of race, as evidenced by his cofounding of the National Association for the Advancement of Colored People in 1909, but he rarely examines race or racism in a detailed fashion in his philosophical writing. This is remarkable, given how much Dewey wrote, the vast impact that race and racism had on the world during Dewey's lifetime, and the primacy Dewey gave to social, cultural, and political matters such as democracy and education, which were (and are) thoroughly raced. In some cases, Dewey needs to be passed by because we today have problems that did not exist in the first half of the twentieth century. In the case of race, however, we must pass Dewey by because he did not address adequately one of the most pressing social issues of his own time. If, as W. E. B. Du Bois claimed in 1903, "the problem of the Twentieth Century is the problem of the color line," then we cannot afford to follow Dewey on matters of race as we enter the twenty-first century because we cannot afford to ignore the color line any longer.[2]

In what follows, I critically examine Dewey's neglect of race and his implicit racism, particularly in the context of education. While my criticism is directed primarily at Dewey, it also indirectly addresses contemporary pragmatists. Perhaps in part because of Dewey's poor example, contemporary pragmatists have not paid much attention in their writings to race and racism.[3] This is problematic, since silence on issues of race has the effect of supporting the racist world in which we currently live. Fortunately for contemporary pragmatists, however, Dewey's work can help remedy the very situation to which it has contributed. Just as Zarathustra's students could use what they had learned from Zarathustra to free themselves from a slavish obedience to him, we can use some of the things we have learned from Dewey to attend to race and racism in ways that Dewey failed to do. Accordingly, in addition to criticizing Dewey on race, I demonstrate how Dewey's pragmatism contains resources to understand race and address racism by examining racial dynamics in the classroom through the Deweyan lens of "habit."

Dewey's neglect of race is not a mere instance of a gap or empty space in his work, although it is that. It is a productive lack, an omission that has significant and powerful effects. Among other things, it perpetuates what critical race theorist Charles Mills has called the conceptual and theoretical whiteness of philosophy.[4] Related to but distinct from the physiological whiteness of most academic philosophers, the conceptual whiteness of philosophy is found in the particular issues and topics that are seen as philosophically important, in what counts as a resolution to a problematic situation, and indeed in what counts as a problematic situation in the first place. To leave unexamined how race has affected and continues to affect matters of ontology, ethics, epistemology, social and political theory and practice, aesthetics, habit, and experience is to leave these topics theorized from a white perspective only. It is to theorize solely from the white center rather than also from nonwhite margins.[5] It is to fail to see how only white (male, propertied) human beings have tended to count as full persons, ethical subjects, creators of knowledge, and legitimate members of a polis; how standards of beauty privilege white physiology; how white habits of both individuals and institutions are hegemonic; and how nonwhite experience is discredited. It thus makes the social inquiry and criticism that is philosophy—and pragmatist philosophy in particular—relevant to white people only.

Even worse, the neglect of race in pragmatism contributes to a reinforcing effect in which the conceptual and theoretical whiteness of philosophy discourages black, Latino and Latina, Asian, and Native students from studying philosophy.[6] Disregard for nonwhite experiences and perspectives produces a physiologically white professoriate which tends not to concern itself with matters of race and thus perpetuates the conceptual and theoretical whiteness of philosophy, driving more nonwhite students away from philosophy, further securing its theoretical whiteness, and so on. Neglecting race, Dewey's pragmatism thus undercuts, at least partially, its own value and purpose. Rather than meliorate, it risks worsening experience. Rather than broaden and pluralize the scope of who has a voice in detecting and solving the problems of men and women, it tends to narrow it. Rather than support democracy as a way of life for all, it contributes to a racial hierarchy in which democracy is restricted to the white few.

I realize that it might seem uncharitable to criticize Dewey for his neglect of race from a perspective fifty years after his death. We today have the benefit of a relatively stronger societal concern about racism—inadequate though it still is—than Dewey had. And Dewey himself seems to call for such generosity when looking back in time to earlier cultures. As he comments on Plato and Aristotle in "An Empirical Survey of Empiricisms," Dewey makes clear that he does not think it appropriate to criticize them for not seeing the world as modern and contemporary philosophers do.[7] But Dewey's reasons for refraining from criticism in this case are significant. Dewey does not criticize Plato and Aristotle because "the account given of experience [by them] was a correct statement of the conditions of contemporary culture. The mistake involved in the philosophy of the period [instead] was in its assumption that the implications of a particular state of culture were eternal."[8] The implication of Dewey's remark is that if Plato and Aristotle *had* misunderstood the particular state of their culture (rather than taken their particular culture to be eternal), then Dewey *would* have criticized their accounts. This means that on his own terms, Dewey should be critical of his treatment of race because his particular culture was raced and racist throughout. Dewey's failure to address race and racism amounts to an inaccurate "statement of the conditions" of the culture of his day, which needs our critical correction.

Accompanying such criticism, however, should be the recognition that Dewey's pragmatism contains resources to assist going beyond it in matters of race. In my view, the most powerful of these is habit, understood as an organism's predisposition to transact with its physical, social, political, and natural worlds in particular ways. In a rare essay dedicated to race, Dewey recognized the role that habit plays in race and racism, but he provides only cursory treatment of it.[9] Dewey claims that the basis of racial prejudice is "the generic fact of prejudice," which is "the instinctive aversion to what is new and unusual, to whatever is different from what we are used to, and which thus shocks our customary habits" (MW 13:243). When the "instinctive" dislike of the strange combines with people's different physical features, languages, and religions and with political and economic tensions between nations, then racial difference and racial friction occur (MW 13:251). Eliminate the political and economic tensions, and Dewey thinks that racial friction also will disappear as people become familiar with what formerly seemed strange. Until the tensions are eased, Dewey holds that contact between different racial groups, such as that promoted by immigration, should be restricted (MW 13:254).

Given the analysis he elsewhere provides of the need for increased friction to produce social change by breaking up sedimented habits,[10] Dewey's negative attitude toward immigration because of the friction that it produces appears to be an instance of racism (or of invidious ethnocentrism). Instead of focusing on this particular issue, however, I wish here to develop the positive implications of Dewey's concept of habit for an understanding of race. On Dewey's terms, habits are that which constitute the self.[11] Because habit is transactional, in a raced and racist world, the self necessarily will be racially constituted. Race is not a veneer lacquered over a nonracial core. It composes the very beings that humans are and the particular ways by which humans engage the world. In that sense, race is ontological. Like gender, sexuality, class, and other characteristics of human beings, it is a constitutive feature of human existence and experience as they currently occur.

Let me be clear on this point: the racial ontology that I am developing by means of Dewey's notion of habit is not racial biologism, which holds that one's physiological or genetic makeup fixes one's race. Nor is it a claim that human existence must always be raced. Race as currently constituted has not always existed. Race takes different forms in different locales and situations, and at some time and place in the future, race may no longer exist. Today, however, the world is raced in a variety of sometimes settled and sometimes shifting ways, which means that as composed of transactionally constituted habits, human beings, customs, and institutions are raced in a variety of settled and shifting ways as well.

To demonstrate how habit can be used as a powerful tool for understanding the racial constitution of human life, I turn briefly to Alexis de Tocqueville's descriptions of the composition of the United States, reading them through a Deweyan lens of habit. In *Democracy in America,* the product of Toqueville's nine-month tour of the United States in the early 1830s, Toqueville notes that

> [t]he only means by which the ancients maintained slavery were fetters and death; the Americans of the South of the Union have discovered more intellectual securities for the duration of their power. They have employed their despotism and their violence against the human mind. In antiquity precautions were taken to prevent the slave from breaking his chains; at the present day measures are adapted to deprive him even of the desire for freedom.[12]

Understood as habit, slavery in the United States was not merely an external constraint imposed upon black people. It also constituted the slave's disposition to transact with the world as enslaved, as not needing or wanting freedom, as understanding his or her enslavement as appropriate and natural. Tocqueville calls this an "intellectual security" to distinguish it from the security provided by rope and chains, but this should not be taken to mean that the effects of slavery were mental only. Understood as habit, intellectual securities affected the slave's entire mode of being, as Tocqueville himself suggests when he describes slavery in terms of its influence on the slave's "manners." Tocqueville writes that "[t]he slave is a servant who never remonstrates and who submits to everything without complaint. He may sometimes assassinate his master, but he never withstands him."[13] The slave's submission could be seen in all of his or her habits—physical and emotional, as well as mental—which is to say that slavery contributed to the composition of the slave's self. Slaves thus tended not only to mentally accept their enslavement, but also to physically embody it through their bowed shoulders, their downcast eyes that would not look their master in the face, and their lack of overtly expressed anger to white people about their enslavement.

Slavery affected the habits, and thus the selves, not just of black slaves, but also of white people whether slaveholders or not. According to Tocqueville, the white Southerner learned as an infant to be a "domestic dictator." "[T]he first notion he acquires in life is that he is born to command, and the first habit which he contracts is that or ruling without resistance."[14] Tocqueville does not add that this was truer for white men than women since white women in the United States were educated into a double consciousness in which they were to obey father and husband, but also to rule over the in-house slaves and other black people with whom they came into contact. In this way, the racial habits of white men and white women in the South tended to vary. Tocqueville's point nonetheless stands that, qua white, both male and female white Southerners were encouraged to develop overt habits of domination that Northerners were not. This does not mean, however, that white Northerners were not racist. According to Tocqueville, they tended to develop racist habits of avoidance of, rather than domination over, black people.

Tocqueville claimed that the abolition of slavery would increase, rather than decrease the divisions and antagonisms between white and black people. He based his claim on the habits of white Northerners, who avoided intermingling with black people the more that legal barriers between them were removed.[15] In contrast, in the South, where legislation created significant formal separation between black and white people, "the habits of the [white] people are more tolerant and compassionate."[16] White masters could mix with black slaves during work and play to an extent because the hierarchy between them was firmly fixed. There was no danger that black slaves might be perceived or perceive themselves as similar to or equal with white people. For Northerners, however, "the white no longer distinctly perceives the barrier that separates him from the degraded race, and he shuns the Negro with the more pertinacity since he fears lest they should some day be confounded together."[17] For this reason, Tocqueville says, "[i]f I were called upon to predict the future, I should say that the abolition of slavery in the South will, in the common course of things, increase the repugnance of the white population for the blacks."[18]

Tocqueville's prediction concerning the continuation of racism after the end of slavery in the United States was devastatingly accurate. Racism and white supremacy persist, and they do so in large degree because of the enduring force of habit. Adapting Tocqueville's claims, we could say that "the abolition of slavery does not set the slave free, but merely transfers him to another master," that of racist habit.[19] What Tocqueville suggested in 1835, what Dewey failed to examine in the first half of the twentieth century, and what we Deweyans should be exploring today is the enduring legacy of slavery in personal, cultural, and institutional habits. While the details of Tocqueville's account of the habits of white Southerners and Northerners no doubt are dated in some respects and there is reason to suspect that Tocqueville was influenced by pro-slave propaganda of the time, Tocqueville's analyses continue to be valuable today because they evidence a contextual attunement to the racial composition of the self. Tocqueville is sensitive to the fact that habits might take a variety of different shapes in a raced and racist world even though his particular account of those shapes may be skewed. The general lesson that we thus can learn from reading Tocqueville through a Deweyan lens of habit is that attempts to change racist institutional and personal habits are likely to be ineffective unless they address the particular forms of habit that racism produces and the particular environments that encourage and discourage racism.

In the spirit of Toqueville's attunement to specific manifestations of racist habits, I now turn to the topic of education. While most institutions in the United States are affected by racism, I concentrate on education because it is one of the most effective ways by which habits are formed and transformed and because, for that very reason, it is central to Dewey's pragmatism. My purpose is to uncover the role that racist habits of thought play in Dewey's ideas about education and to trace how similar racist habits are at work in today's schools. Understanding the intersection of race and habit in this and similar ways is important both to an improved understanding of Dewey's pragmatism and to an improved ability to fight racism in contemporary education.

According to Dewey, education is distinct from training in that training merely makes changes to "outer action rather than in mental and emotional dispositions of behavior" and does not allow the one being educated to be "a partner in a shared activity."[20] In contrast, education remakes the self through activity with others such that both self and others come to share interests, ideas, and purposes. The remaking of the self through joint activity that characterizes education need not happen only in a classroom. It occurs whenever and wherever environmental conditions foster the growth of individuals as active participants in society. When a society becomes relatively complex, however, formal or deliberate education is needed to ensure that a society successfully perpetuates itself by communicating its values and habits to its immature members. The school thus is a special environment out of the many environments that influence members of society because it is consciously designed "with express reference to influencing the mental and moral disposition of their members" (MW 9:23).

Dewey does not discuss race in any depth when addressing education even though in 1916, when he wrote *Democracy and Education,* schools in the United States were racially segregated. He is not unique among white philosophers in this sense. As education historian Meyer Weinberg points out, "[t]he most devout defenders of the common school from Horace Mann to John Dewey held their tongues when the subject of minority—especially black—children became a public issue."[21] The omission is glaring nonetheless. While Dewey lists race, along with religious affiliation and economic status, as one of the social groups that make up the social environments that shape individuals, he largely sees these social groups as narrow constraints for the school environment to overcome, a view that implicitly deprecates people's racial and other cultural backgrounds. Dewey claims that "it is the office of the school environment to balance the various elements in the social environment, and to see that each individual gets an opportunity to escape from the limitations of the social group in which he was born, and to come into living contact with a broader environment" (MW 9:24–25). The way in which such broadening is to occur is through assimilation, in which diverse and divergent points of view become one: "[c]ommon subject matter accustoms all to a unity of outlook upon a broader horizon than is visible to the members of any group while it is isolated. The assimilative force of the American public school is eloquent testimony to the efficacy of the common and balanced appeal" (MW 9:26).

Dewey's pragmatism is racist at this point, but not, as one might think, because of the simple fact of his use of the terms "unity" and "assimilation." While these words admittedly grate on twenty-first-century postmodern ears, the larger body of Dewey's work makes clear that Dewey does not mean unity or assimilation in the sense of a melting pot in which all racial and other differences blend into uniformity. Writing the year after *Democracy and Education* was published, Dewey plainly states, "[t]he theory of the Melting Pot always gave me rather a pang. To maintain that all the constituent elements, geographical, racial and cultural, in the United States should be put in the same pot and turned into a uniform and unchanging product is distasteful."[22] The unity and assimilation to which Dewey appeals would be better described today as a building of shared interests and common ground that bridges difference and diversity. In Judith Green's words, "a closer reading [of the two terms] suggests that what [Dewey] calls for is the growth of commonalities based on *shared knowledge and experience* amidst *persisting valued differences related to group memberships,* addressed in a cooperative, reciprocal way."[23] And in Dewey's own words, his ideal is that of an "intermingling in the school of youth of different races, differing religions, and unlike customs [that] creates *for all* a new and broader environment" (MW 9:26, emphasis added).

The problem with Dewey's description of education thus is not its appeal to the idea of assimilation, understanding assimilation as a process that transactionally remakes everyone involved in it. It instead is the "mere" fact that Dewey took American public schools as eloquent testimony to such transactions when in 1916 they most definitely were not. Nor had they ever been: "[f]rom their outset the public schools [in the United States] have been racist in spirit and structure."[24] American education did not in Dewey's day engage white and nonwhite students in such a way that a new and broader environment was created for all groups. Or, rather, if, as Dewey took them to be, American public schools in 1916 were eloquent testimony to the power of assimilation to produce commonality amongst students in such a way that balance between their differences is achieved, then Dewey's use of "assimilation" cannot be generously interpreted as a product of transaction in which differences are preserved in their connection with one another. It instead must be interpreted as an implicitly (although undoubtedly unintentionally) racist call for nonwhite students to embody white ways of being.

Until the 1950s, American schools were not racially and ethnically integrated enough for much assimilation—transactional or not—to occur. Schools were racially separate and unequal from the end of the Civil War through the first half of the twentieth century. In the South, assignment to schools was based solely on race, while in the North, assignment was based on both race and one's place of residence, which led to massive geographical segregation and thus to a de facto assignment by race alone. Schools for nonwhite children suffered disproportionately from problems of overcrowding, dilapidated buildings, inadequate textbooks and other materials, and underfunding.[25]

In the relatively infrequent cases of integration before the 1950s, students of color were often treated as if they were invisible, and when they were recognized, it was often to humiliate or disparage them. In the North in the 1920s, for example, the black children who attended predominantly white schools were often "shut out" from social, cultural, athletic, and academic activities by pupils and teachers alike, sometimes going for months without the teacher's calling on them in class. Black students at mixed schools were often asked why they did not go instead to the school where they "belong."[26] Even when nonwhite students were included in predominantly white schools, such inclusion was at the price of their having to give up their particular ethnic and racial characteristics, including their native language. In the mid-1940s, teachers at in a Los Angeles school regularly enforced the view that "'the degree of social adjustment . . . [Mexican-American students] attain is dependent upon the degree to which they speak, think, dress, and act like other Americans.'"[27] As the city superintendent of schools in New York declared in 1918, Americanization was "'an appreciation of the institutions of this country and absolute forgetfulness of all obligations or connections with other countries because of descent and birth.'"[28]

The school system of Dewey's day thus tended to aim for the non-transactional assimilation of all students to white habits of life. Students of different races did not intermingle so as to create for all a transformed outlook. That is, they did not intermingle, period, in that educational institutions generally did not encourage the reciprocal influence of white and nonwhite habits. The habits of white students generally were strengthened and enforced, not changed, while the habits of nonwhite students were forced to become more like those of white people, with the pain of failure in the school system a threat if this did not happen. The school environment did not function to encourage individuals to escape from the limitations of their race because the white race was not posited as something from which students needed to be freed. It was nonwhite students who received the "opportunity" to "escape" from their race while white students received the opportunity to more fully embrace their own. Dewey's comment about social groups' being a limitation is thus not equally demeaning to all groups by claiming that all social groups were inadequate in isolation from others.[29] In the case of race, the limitations of social groups did not apply to the socially dominant group—white people—for whiteness was not considered a limitation in the educational system of the United States.

The situation has not changed much in the approximately fifty years since Dewey's death and *Brown v. the Board of Education.* But before I turn to the issue of the enforcement of white habits in contemporary education, let me explain further how Dewey's account of education privileges whiteness. Dewey did not merely neglect to relate his ideal of the "assimilative force" of schools to the concrete realities of education. He also effected the privileging of whiteness with his account of education as a civilizing process. In *Democracy and Education,* Dewey develops his theory of education by means of the contrast of "savages" and "civilized men," a contrast that is constitutive of his account and not merely illustrative of it. To be educated is to be civilized, and to be civilized is to not be savage. Civilization and savagery, and thus education and savagery, reciprocally determine each other in Dewey's work.

According to Dewey, savage communities are ones that rely upon chance environments to instill social habits into their young. In order to learn, the young share in activities with adults, as something like apprentices, but they never engage in formal education (MW 9:10, 21). For this reason, Dewey calls them "undeveloped" (MW 9:10). To his credit, Dewey argues that they are not undeveloped because their native capacities are inferior to those of a civilized person. But he makes his argument by claiming instead that they are savage because of their "backward institutions" (MW 9:41). This is significant, given the importance that Dewey places on environment. For Dewey, environment is not incidental to, but instead plays a primary role in the constitution, transformation, and education of the self, including whatever capacities one acquires (MW 9:23).

Dewey claims that the "primitive" social life of savages results in "low-grade intelligence and perhaps defective moral sense" (MW 9:41). Their social activities are such that they "limit the stimuli to mental development" and focus "imagination upon qualities that do not fructify in the mind" (MW 9:42). Sounding much like John Locke when he attempted to justify British colonization of North American land, Dewey explains that the savages are backward because they do not adequately work the land for what it is worth. Savages do not transform a large amount of nature into instrumentalities for human action, as civilization does (MW 9:42). This is because for Dewey, the civilized person is active, while the savage is passive. The savage's "adaptation involves a maximum of accepting, tolerating, putting up with things as they are, a maximum of passive acquiescence, and a minimum of active control, of subjection to use. . . . The savage is merely habituated; the civilized man has habits which transform his environment" (MW 9:52).

Dewey never uses the word "race" in connection with the term "savage," but he need not do so for his account to be raced. Because "savage" is not a racially neutral term, Dewey's discussion of savages is racially coded. Savagery represents the wild, dark non-European, in contrast with the civilized, white European. As Charles Mills explains, "[t]he Wild Man is a crucial figure in medieval thought, the domestic antipode (*within* Europe) of civilization, and is one of the conceptual antecedents of the later *extra*-European 'savages.'"[30] In the United States, "savage" was most often used to designate Native Americans, but it was sometimes also used to describe other nonwhite groups such as African-Americans. In either case, it distinguishes nonwhite sub-persons from the white European people that colonized much of the world. That Dewey probably was nonreflectively using the linguistic currency of his time does not eliminate the racist worldview contained within his usage. With his comparison of "savagery" and "civilization," Dewey marks white people as those who are fully capable of learning, of participating in education, and of directing the transformation of themselves and their world rather than passively submitting to happenstance. Given that Dewey defines intelligence as "the purposive reorganization, through action, of the material of experience," he thus effectively claims that white people possess more intelligence than Native, African-American, and other nonwhite people.[31]

That this alleged deficiency results from backward social institutions rather than native abilities does not mitigate the racism of Dewey's descriptions of Native, black, and other non-white people. It instead only strengthens the warrant for the view that they need to escape from the limitations of their social groups. If black and Native cultural environments are backward and environment shapes the self, then black and Native people need to immerse themselves in the superior environment of white culture. For all his explicit statements to the contrary, the "civilization" to which education introduces "savages" described by Dewey is not a mosaic of perspectives and habits of people of different races that equally values diverse contributions to the transactional transformation of selves. The "broadened civilization" praised by Dewey is implicitly white.

Heard in this raced and racist context, Dewey's explanation of the purpose of the school environment, while undoubtedly well intentioned, is thus somewhat ominous sounding:

> It is the business of the school environment to eliminate, so far as possible, the unworthy features of the existing environment from influence upon mental habitudes. . . . Selection aims not only at simplifying but at weeding out what is undesirable. . . . As a society becomes more enlightened, it realizes that it is responsible *not* to transmit and conserve the whole of its existing achievements, but only such as make for a better future society. The school is its chief agency for the accomplishment of this end. (MW 9:24)

Dewey is right that selective emphasis is unavoidable in the life of institutions, as well as persons. My concern therefore is not with selective emphasis as such. My concern is that the existing environment in the United States, in general, and in its schools, in particular, is often racist, and thus selective emphasis must be understood in a racial and racist context. Rather than following Dewey in asserting unproblematically that not all habits should be passed on to future generations, we must ask which habits are seen as unworthy, undesirable, and thus incapable of making a valuable contribution to future society; why are they seen as unworthy; and who has the power and ability to declare that they are unworthy. Today, as in Dewey's day, white people generally see nonwhite habits as undesirable and hold leadership positions in educational and other institutions that enable them to pass their habits of perception onto others. Failing to recognize the role that race plays in education, we (white people, in particular), like Dewey, will be prone to perpetuate racism in our well-intentioned attempts to eliminate "unworthy features of the existing environment" so as to "make for a better future society."

Racism in schools today is generally not as blatant as it was at the beginning of the twentieth century. While this is a positive development in many ways, it also has the unfortunate consequence of making racism more difficult for white people to detect and combat. (One of my black students recently remarked that he would almost rather be called a "nigger" to his face than deal with the liberal racism of the white person who espouses the abstraction that everyone is equal and cannot understand why black people feel discriminated against. The student felt that at least when he was fighting overt racism, he would not also have to fight the layers of mystification and charges of paranoia that tend to accompany liberal racism.) Chicano students today, for example, may not be told explicitly that they have to choose between being a "legitimate" student and being a Chicano—although they were still being told this through the early 1970s.[32] The implicit privileging of standards of whiteness in current educational practices in the United States is, however, just as effective in conveying the same message. These standards discourage the transactional remaking of white and nonwhite students alike and thus implicitly tell nonwhite students that they must abandon their racial and ethnic identity.

One place that whiteness can be found is in the habits of communication that college classrooms often enforce.[33] Modes of public expression in black and white communities can vary considerably, but only white, middle-to-upper-class modes of behavior tend to be utilized and viewed as appropriate in class discussions. To take just one example, for middle-to-upper-class white people, turn-taking in discussion is to be authorized by someone other than the one who wants to speak: the instructor. The polite way to engage in discussion is to raise one's hand and make one's point in the order in which the instructor recognizes students. For another student to try to speak out of turn or before a prior speaker has finished making all his or her points is to interrupt and be rude. Also, a person does not have to have anything important or on topic to say in order to take a turn; white communities are "democratic" in allowing everyone to have a turn. Finally, middle-to-upper-class white people tend to think that in discussion their points should not be made in the form of a personal argument or in an impassioned manner. In their view, to argue effectively means to calmly, dispassionately and objectively state a position without mixing it with personal opinions.

In contrast, in black communities, particularly those that are working class, people tend to value individual regulation of when turns are taken.

In a classroom, this means that rather than wait for the instructor to call on people, a person who wants to take a turn can do so anytime he or she has something relevant and valuable to say after a first point is made by another student. For a speaker to continue making subsequent points and not let others into the discussion is to antagonize them by "hogging the floor." It is also antagonizing for someone to speak merely for the sake of speaking, when they have nothing relevant or valuable say. Likewise, silence on the part of others is often seen as disrespectful during discussion of a controversial topic since if someone disagrees with a view, she or he is obliged to speak up—this is because the pursuit of truth is seen as a community enterprise that requires everyone's assistance. Finally, black people, particularly those who are working class, tend to value contributions to discussion that are made in a more passionate and personal manner. While for middle-to-upper-class white people, truth is something intrinsic to the idea itself and thus needs only a spokesperson, black people tend to take the role of advocate for an idea when they present it. Passionate belief in and feeling about an idea is not presumed by black people to interfere with discovering its truth.

I am aware of the danger of racially characterizing different habits of communication as black and white: doing so risks reinforcing common, racist stereotypes of black and white people. I am also aware of the ability of my descriptions to mislead: certainly there are exceptions to the race-based patterns sketched above, which are more complex in "real life" than any brief summary on paper can portray, and racial habits are not unchanging, eternal features of people of any color. But these dangers should not be used as an excuse to avoid the often-difficult examination of the role that race plays in the classroom—a mistake to which white people are particularly prone. I find it significant that a white person at an academic conference objected that my descriptions of race in the classroom stereotyped black people, while the black students in a class with whom I discussed the same issues agreed that these racial patterns of communication exist and thought it important to acknowledge them. It is a mistake to think that any talk of racial habits necessarily is equivalent to malicious racial stereotyping, a mistake often made by (white) people who think that the racial dynamics of a situation did not exist prior to someone's asking about them. While the danger of harmful stereotyping when talking about race is not negligible, it is more dangerous to avoid discussion of racial habits because we then leave their operation unexamined and likely misunderstood. Racial differences currently are real (although not essential) and their reality (as well as their historical contingency) needs to be recognized if racism is to be successfully fought.

My descriptions of racial habits thus should be read as an illustration of some of the ways by which habits of communication in the classroom race (and class) the space of education and therefore also the habits of those being educated, a racing of educational space that pragmatist and other educators must confront. As bell hooks has explained,

> [p]rofessors cannot empower students to embrace diversities of experience, standpoint, behavior, or style if our training has disempowered us, socialized us to cope effectively only with a single mode of interaction based on [white] middle-class values. Most progressive professors are more comfortable striving to challenge class [and race] biases through the material studied than they are with interrogating how class [and race] biases shape conduct in the classroom and transforming their pedagogical process.[34]

To the extent that turn-taking in class discussion is instructor-regulated, "democratically" allowing the person holding the floor to talk until she decides she is finished, and prioritizing dispassionate calm on the part of speakers, the classroom is one in which middle-to-upper-class white communication habits are rewarded and working-class black communication habits are penalized. Black students who do not adopt white, middle-class habits of discussion will appear to fellow students and to their instructor as rude and out-of-control. Their patterns of communication generally will not be welcomed as valid contributions to the transactional intermingling of habits. Black students who do not adopt white habits thus often will be silenced in and alienated from the class.

Another example of how black students are compelled to develop white, middle-to-upper-class habits on the penalty of doing poorly in school can be found in the different ways that black and white students tend to understand and complete assignments. In an experiment in communication conducted on poor and well-to-do black and white first-graders, students were asked to memorize the details of a story to repeat to another person.[35] The white students of both economic backgrounds and the well-to-do black students all repeated the story verbatim. In their completion of the assignment, they were literal, obedient, and uniform, reflecting the cultural norms of dominant, white society. In contrast, the poor black students completed the assignment in a more performative manner. They added "flair," including more original material in their retelling than the other groups and using their entire bodies to tell the story.

The behavior of the groups was consistent with their different race- and class-based cultural experiences. All of the white students and the black students who came from families whose parents had succeeded in the dominant (white, middle-class) culture subordinated their individuality and creativity to the task at hand, just as the dominant culture in the United

States generally requires. The poor black students came from a cultural background that emphasized oral narrative and thus valued individual performance, originality, and vitality. All the students believed they were following the instructions of listening to and repeating the story. In many schools, however, the poor black students would have failed the assignment if it had been a test. This is because the standard of good work in school often "is one in which students reproduce details correctly, avoid deviating from the norms set by the adult in charge, and repeat memorized material verbatim."[36] With such a standard, the poor black children will not succeed in school unless they give up their black habits for white ones.

Of course, it is just such an educational model that Dewey fought. Dewey calls it "pipeline" or "phonographic" education, in which knowledge is funneled from teacher to students, whose minds are like blank discs upon which a teacher writes.[37] In that Dewey argued against educational systems that prioritized rote learning and memorization and suppressed individual energies and creativity, his pragmatism helpfully challenges dominant cultural values that contribute to racism. Dewey's general lack of attention to the practical, concrete ways in which race and racism impact education and other cultural institutions nonetheless is problematic because it allows racism to flourish. The disregard of race in a racist world is not a neutral position because its effects are not neutral. It perpetuates white solipsism, which is a tunnel vision that sees nonwhite existence or experience as insignificant.[38] So that we Deweyans do not engage in white solipsism, we must go beyond Dewey on matters of race. We cannot merely invoke his ideals of pluralism, democracy, inclusion, and genuinely shared interests as important to the fight against racism. Important though they may be, as articulated by Dewey they do not explicitly or concretely address the ways that race and racism impact these ideals. Disconnected from race, the ideals effect an erasure of race that no one, white or nonwhite, can afford.

Treating Deweyan ideals as unquestionable idols interferes with efforts to understand the effects that race has on lived experience and to dismantle racism and white supremacy. Smashing Dewey's statue to the ground therefore can be a profound gesture of respect for Dewey's pragmatism. This is something that Dewey himself understood. Sounding much like Zarathustra when he paradoxically commands his students not to obey him, Dewey tells us that "[w]hat professional philosophy most needs at the present time is new and fresh imagination. Only new imagination is capable of getting away from traditional positions and schools—realism, idealism, *pragmatism,* empiricism and the rest of them."[39] Out of an irreverent respect for Dewey, pragmatists today need to get away from his treatment of race. To do so is perhaps paradoxically the best way to explore the relevance of Dewey's pragmatism to antiracist projects.[40]

NOTES

1. Friedrich Nietzsche, "Of the Bestowing Virtue," in *Thus Spoke Zarathustra: A Book for Everyone and No One,* trans. R. J. Hollingdale (New York: Penguin Books, 1969), 103, with my modifications.

2. W. E. B. DuBois, *The Souls of Black Folk* (New York: Knopf, [1903] 1976), 5.

3. Exceptions to this claim include Judith Green, *Deep Democracy: Community, Diversity, and Transformation* (Lanham, Md.: Rowman and Littlefield, 1999); Terrance MacMullan, "Impulse, Habit and Reflection: A Deweyan Method for Addressing White Racism," paper presented at the 1998 meeting of the Society of the Advancement of American Philosophy in Milwaukee, Wisc.; Gregory Pappas, "Dewey's Philosophical Approach to Racial Prejudice," *Social Theory and Practice* 22, no. 1: 47–65, and "The Latino Character of American Pragmatism, *Transactions of the Charles S. Peirce Society* 34, no. 1: 93–112; Scott L. Pratt, "The Influence of the Iroquois on Early American Philosophy," *Transactions of the Charles S. Peirce Society* 32, no. 2: 274–314; Herman J. Saatkamp, Jr., "Santayana: Hispanic-American Philosopher," *Transactions of the Charles S. Peirce Society* 34, no. 1: 51–68; John Shuford, "Four Du Boisian Contributions to Critical Race Theory," *Transactions of the Charles S. Peirce Society* 37, no. 3: 301–37; and Cornel West, *The American Evasion of Philosophy: A Genealogy of Pragmatism* (Madison: University of Wisconsin Press, 1989).

4. Charles Mills, *Blackness Visible* (Ithaca, N.Y.: Cornell University Press, 1998), 2.

5. Charlene Haddock Seigfried makes a similar point about centers and margins with respect to gender in *Pragmatism and Feminism: Reweaving the Social Fabric* (Chicago: University of Chicago Press, 1996), 268.

6. Charles Mills, "Philosophy and Race," presentation at Pennsylvania State University, University Park, Pa., October 15, 1999.

7. Dewey, "An Empirical Survey of Empiricisms," in vol. 11 of *The Later Works: 1925–1953,* ed. Jo Ann Boydston (Carbondale: Southern Illinois University Press, 1987), 75. Thanks to Bill Gavin for bringing this text to my attention.

8. Dewey, "Empirical Survey of Empiricisms," LW 11: 75.

9. Dewey, "Racial Prejudice and Friction," in vol. 13 of *The Middle Works, 1899–1924,* ed. Jo Ann Boydston (Carbondale: Southern Illinois University Press, 1983), 242–54. Hereafter cited in the text as MW 13, followed by page number.

10. John Dewey, *Human Nature and Conduct,* vol. 14 of *The Middle Works,* 90.

11. Dewey, *Human Nature and Conduct,* MW 14: 21.

12. Alexis de Tocqueville, *Democracy in America,* vol. 1 (New York: Vintage Books, 1990) 379.

13. Tocqueville, *Democracy in America,* 394.

14. Tocqueville, *Democracy in America,* 394.

15. Tocqueville, *Democracy in America,* 375.

16. Tocqueville, *Democracy in America,* 360.

17. Tocqueville, *Democracy in America,* 360.

18. Tocqueville, *Democracy in America,* 375.

19. Tocqueville, *Democracy in America,* 367. Tocqueville makes the more limited observation about the transfer of slaves from North to South when the North abolished slavery.

20. John Dewey, *Democracy and Education,* vol. 9 of *The Middle Works,* 16, 17. Hereafter cited in the text as MW 9, followed by page number.

21. Meyer Weinberg, *A Chance to Learn: The History of Race and Education in the United States* (New York: Cambridge University Press, 1977), 1.

22. John Dewey, "The Principle of Nationality," in vol. 10 of *The Middle Works,* 289.

23. Green, *Deep Democracy,* 64, emphasis in original.

24. Weinberg, *Chance to Learn,* 354.

25. Weinberg, *Chance to Learn,* 77–78.

26. Weinberg, *Chance to Learn,* 79.

27. Weinberg, *Chance to Learn,* 158.

28. Weinberg, *Chance to Learn,* 255.

29. Green makes this argument in *Deep Democracy,* 63.

30. Charles Mills, *Racial Contract* (Ithaca, N.Y.: Cornell University Press, 1997), 43.

31. As Seigfried notes, William James similarly conflates "savagery" with ignorance; see *Pragmatism and Feminism,* p. 122.

32. Weinberg, *Chance to Learn,* 149.

33. The following example of turn-taking comes from chapter 2 of Thomas Kochman, *Black and White Styles in Conflict* (Chicago: University of Chicago Press, 1981). On a similar point, see also bell hooks, *Teaching to Transgress: Education as the Practice of Freedom* (New York: Routledge, 1994), 187. Thanks to Lisa Heldke for reminding me about the relevance of hooks' work to these issues.

34. hooks, *Teaching to Transgress,* 187.

35. Susan Houston's experiment is related by Thomas Kochman in chapter 10 of *Black and White Styles in Conflict.* See Houston, "Black English," *Psychology Today* (March 1973): 45–48.

36. Kochman, *Black and White Styles in Conflict,* 155.

37. John Dewey, "Monastery, Bargain Counter, or Laboratory in Education?" in vol. 6 of *The Later Works,* 109.

38. I take the term "white solipsism" from Adrienne Rich, *On Lies, Secrets, and Silence: Selected Prose, 1966–1978,* (New York: Norton, 1979), 306.

39. John Dewey, "Review of *Collected Papers of Charles Sanders Peirce,*" in vol. 6 of *The Later Works,* 277, emphasis added.

40. A shorter version of this paper was presented at the Society for the Advancement of American Philosophy session of the 1999 Eastern American Philosophical Association meetings. Thanks to various members of the audience, Michael Eldridge, Bill Gavin, and Phillip McReynolds for their helpful comments on and suggestions for the paper.

SEVEN

Between Being and Emptiness

Toward an Eco-Ontology of Inhabitation

THOMAS M. ALEXANDER

INTRODUCTION: PHILOSOPHY AND WISDOM

Philosophy today stands in a problematic relationship to wisdom. Introductory texts still relish defining *philosophia* as "the love of wisdom."[1] But, as anyone reading on discovers, the ideal of wisdom itself is long gone. In its place is the view that philosophy provides exceedingly clever and conflicting answers to puzzles that do not particularly relate to the conduct of life or the discovery of its profoundest meanings. Most of those puzzles have to do with the problems of the justification of beliefs, putting philosophy in an auxiliary relationship to the project of knowledge. The inquiry into the nature of rational justification and the implications of holding beliefs is not something to be condemned. But it is very different to see this project as a part of the more complex whole of wisdom than as the sole end that everything else serves.[2] Philosophy today is practiced very differently from the way it traditionally was. (Perhaps we should call this modern discipline "philepistemy" rather than "philosophy.")[3] In spite of what the introductory textbooks say, most members of the established profession are not interested in the question of "wisdom." The modern practice of philosophy, like the university itself, appropriated a quasi-scientific model in which rigorous technical analysis of discrete problems isolated and concentrated upon for their own sake is believed to lead to the increase in "knowledge." A further development is the assimilation by universities and their components of models of science in service to international corporations.[4]

The search for wisdom examines what it means to live a human life that exemplifies an art of existence, a life that reflects a qualitative, emotionally nuanced insight into the human condition as it exists in the world, which requires an equally extensive and sensitive awareness of the world itself. This ideal defined the nature of philosophical discipline as understood by the ancient Greeks as well as by John Dewey. It meant living well in such a way that a distinctly human excellence is achieved through our capacity for intelligent action, that is, action that consciously realizes ends that fund existence with reflective meaning and value.[5] This goal transcends the endeavor to satisfy a given desire by negotiating the complexities and dangers of life; it involves a realization of humanity in oneself through harmony with nature. Desire is educated in accordance with a deep meaning of human existence seen in terms of nature itself. A wise human life is one that necessarily illustrates awareness of what is important in a life that is lived in awareness of the world. Wisdom is manifested in the relation of life to the world in which it is lived. This requires being aware of the possible meanings of the situations in which we find ourselves, in spite of their complexity. To understand a situation is to grasp it in terms of the possibilities is has as well as its immediate actualities. In order to interpret the actual in light of the possible, we need to see the potentialities of the present in terms of their abilities to realize a meaningful human life. Such a life realizes ideals that fulfill us and that exhibit responsibility and care for our environment—for it is the environment, cultural as well as natural, that is the ground of those ideals. In order to do this we need to be able to approach the present with a range of possible ideals of conduct. It is paramount to recognize that any endeavor to think in a Deweyan mode is to engage in the practice of philosophy as the love of wisdom, and this involves a fundamental recontextualization of the contemporary practice of philepistemy.[6]

Though the conscious goal of inquiry into wisdom was first articulated by philosophy, all cultures have cherished some ideal of wisdom. One need only compare the characters of Odysseus, Aeneas, Moses, Jesus, Confucius, the Buddha or Coyote, to grasp how diverse the ideals of wisdom have been. While all cultures stress the centrality of wisdom in human existence, it is equally clear that wisdom is capable of a plurality of idealizations. Philosophy is the conscious, critical inquiry into the idea of wisdom, but this study this must include an exploration of the range of prereflective cultural ideals of wisdom. This is especially important from a pragmatic point of view because these cultures have successfully realized meaningful human lives. The practice of philosophy, then, requires investigations into the pragmatic implementation of the desire for wisdom in the diversity of human cultures past and present. Philosophy needs experience.

The abandonment of the ideal of wisdom in modern times is one of the key events in the history of philosophy, though it passes largely unrecognized. The story of how this happened is important, having its origin in the crisis of the modern period, though it cannot be told here. The modern age, beginning with Bacon, Galileo, and Descartes, not only rejected the teleological cosmology of the Middle Ages, but put in its place the idea that the task of knowledge was to discover the facts of nature in order to control nature's power. This is what ultimately drives the debates concerning a "true method."[7] The problem of how these facts would be used was left to desire. The life of the philosopher-scientist was thus not tied to an ideal of "wisdom." Descartes's *Discourse on Method* is a revolutionary document in the way it separates the quest for knowledge from making life embody wisdom. The code of ethics it advocates is rational self-discipline combined with the art of living "like a man who walks alone and in the shadows."[8] The primary rule is to obey the customs of the country (including religious ones)—quite a contrast to the figure that speaks to us in the pages of Plato's *Apology*.[9] The culmination of this bifurcation can be found in Kant's utter separation of knowledge from morality and aesthetics.

To think *philosophically* means to critique and reconstruct these modernist assumptions in light of the question of wisdom. In contrast to philepistemy, philosophy begins with a humanist imperative: it inquires into the meaning of human existence for the sake of wisdom, that is, it puts human experience in relation to a deep existential meaning of the world. Philosophy alone does not seek wisdom: human beings everywhere do. The variety of cultures may be regarded as creative adaptations within different circumstances, but all seek to frame the possibility of a meaningful, value-rich existence. Thus philosophical method begins with inquiry into cultures and their wisdom traditions in order to discern the "shapes of wisdom." Philosophers must acquire deep and broad experience of embodied wisdom. These ideals are expressed symbolically, in social institutions, religion, mythology, and art. In contrast, then, to the modernist quest for "pure" methods that are value neutral and which aspire to mathematical formalization, philosophy must seek a broad, global literacy of human cultures. It must become aesthetically and spiritually attuned to the "shapes of wisdom" expressed in diverse cultures. This requires a flexible plurality of methods that gain their meaning in connection with their content, not apart from it. In short, philosophy primarily exists as a humanistic discipline, though it also looks beyond the human condition into the nature of nature.[10] While philepistemy will follow the fads generated by the succession of various "pure" methodologies seeking to be analogs of "the" scientific method, philosophy's first goal is cultural literacy in the worlds of human existence, past and present. Qualitative, deep, aesthetic experience rather than epistemological certainty is the first goal of philosophical inquiry. In short, philosophy must begin with broad experience of the complexity of the human and natural world. There is no method that can substitute for experience.[11] In situating human experience, nature itself must be understood. Wisdom is an art of inhabiting the world by attending to the world. Nature is the environment of our desire for wisdom, and wisdom discloses the ecology of environments.

Beyond the inquiry into the ideals of wisdom and the ecology of nature, philosophy has a critical, reconstructive role in the present. It must diagnose the deeper underlying problems of civilization so that these problems may be intelligently overcome. The world of the twenty-first century faces what may be the ultimate challenge in the survival of many species (including our own). In addition, we face the explosion of the human population, possibly beyond sustainable numbers, and the development of an intimate worldwide electronic culture of corporate consumerism. The civilization of modernism, now exported around the globe, carries with it its inherited dichotomies. These must be critiqued. Not only does this require an exploration of the negative consequences of certain assumptions, but an historical understanding of how those assumptions were generated and how they evolved. To critique the present, we must understand its historical genesis, especially in terms of the interplay of metaphysical commitments and social legitimation. Worldviews are narratives that empower.[12]

But we must go beyond critique and also articulate ideals that can successfully help reconstruct the problems of the present.[13] The ideal of wisdom we need must endeavor to comprehend and respond to the ecological aspect of nature and to facilitate communication between the diversity of the world's cultures, which must cooperate and live together now as close neighbors rather than as exotically distant lands. In this context, the conflation of the idea of "philepistemy" with philosophy becomes an extravagant luxury. Wisdom, as noted, involves a deep awareness of human life and the world in which it exists, so that the way of life is a realization of human existence as an expression of nature. The present moment calls for reconstruction at the ontological level. Philosophy is concerned with the basic ways that human experience and nature interexist. What sort of wisdom is called forth by the crisis of modernity? One that facilitates awareness of how human existence is interconnected. The quest for wisdom needs an eco-ontology.

Of all twentieth-century philosophies, the thought of John Dewey offers the most promise for an ecologically wise naturalism that also addresses the plurality of cultures. Dewey's own thought, however, was enmeshed in a number of assumptions that prevented these aspects of his thought from developing as far as they might.[14] It is not my purpose to criticize Dewey here, but to use his thought as a background, especially in sketching out the features of an ecological ontology. I attempt to develop themes so that they might contribute toward a humanistic as well as an ecological wisdom. What I present here in particular is the outline of an ontological framework that serves as a counterpart to the humanistic views I have developed in the past decade under the term of "the Human Eros." I relocate philosophical reflection as an engagement with the possibility of wisdom, searching for those ideals, and for ideals that might negotiate the impending crises we face. Ontology must be undertaken consciously within that general problematic. Contemporary wisdom must find ways of living and understanding that put us in a moral and aesthetic, as well as a cognitive balance with our environment, its inhabitants, and the global human communities that must share this planet forevermore as neighbors and fellow citizens rather than as exotic strangers.

Having already stated my conception of the philosophical enterprise, one so at variance with the way it is now predominantly practiced, I will proceed to address the "human" side of the relationship, seeing how the quest for wisdom arises from the deep impulse toward living meaningfully, which I have called "the Human Eros." Then I move toward the ontological side, outlining the aim of ontology as compassionate intelligence. In trying to articulate an eco-ontology, it is necessary to engage in a historical critique of the major ideas in the Western tradition that inhibit this development, in particular the idea of Being as identity. A possible contrast to this idea, one which at first promises to be more ecologically relevant, is located in the Buddhist doctrine of emptiness, especially as refined by Nagarjuna (ca. 200 C.E.). But this also reveals difficulties for an eco-ontological wisdom in terms of retaining an ideal of world-renunciation. I conclude by describing the elements of an intermediary position that develops the idea of natural histories as creative continuities, including some reflections on the "home" or *oikos* of philosophy as a wisdom of in-habitation. This attempt toward an "ecology of being" or "eco-ontology" is thus presented as a directive for wisdom.

THE HUMAN EROS

Before undertaking this investigation, I need to summarize the central ideas that have constituted my own efforts to think "beyond Dewey" under the humanistic thematic of what I call "The Human Eros."[15] This is primarily a claim that human beings by nature seek to experience the world as a fulfillment of meaning and value.[16] "Meaning" and "value," terms of extensive analysis and refinement in twentieth-century philosophical discussion, should be taken here in their Deweyan senses.[17] For example, these terms should be understood as they might be used in ordinary circumstances when people ask if their lives have any "meaning" or "value." Meaning and value initially belong to a continuous domain of interaction that is aesthetically undergone prior to any cognitive mediation, though this material may be mediated and refined instrumentally.[18] That is, human beings experience the world as filled with meaning or value not primarily as the result of consciously deliberative or instrumental inquiry, but as a qualitative whole of continuous interaction that has the promise of consummatory experience. It is within this whole that instrumental inquiry itself takes on significance. When human beings have experiences that give them a sense of the depth of the meaning and value of their lives, they are fulfilled.[19] Both meanings and values are directly embodied in the existential components of their experiences. These meanings and values exhibit a wide and differentiated spectrum; language can at best only crudely designate various generic parts of that continuum, which manifest themselves in the upsurge of the present in radical individuality and incommensurable freshness. One reason the arts have such power is their ability to lead us toward these experiences that are above and beyond the uses of strictly cognitive language.

To comprehend what "meaning and value" further signify, we need only think about what is involved in eradicating human life of those features so that existence itself is experienced as a negation. These involve degradation, loss of empowerment, destruction of identity, reduction of existence toward pure instrumentality—in short everything that a human being can experience which conveys "You are not human" or "Your life is meaningless and without value." History provides horrific examples of consciously undertaken endeavors whereby one group seeks to destroy the humanity of another: the Nazi and Japanese holocausts of the Second World War, the slave trade, the near genocide of Native peoples in the Americas, and so on.[20] But often this negation can be unobtrusively present in the ordinariness of everyday experience. One need not even think of the ghettos of Europe or America, the "homelands" of Africa, or barrios of the poor everywhere. One of the key features of degradation is invisibility. One is simply not seen; one's suffering is not noted.[21] Most societies require immense amounts of suffering to perpetuate their own structures, and many aspects of their codes of ethics involve training privileged members in how to avoid noticing suffering, or if it is noticed, how to interpret it as a "natural state" or "the will of God" or " the law of karma."[22] Jesus was a revolutionary in that he forced a society to notice those whom it preferred not to see; one forceful way he did this was merely by having people of different classes *eat* together.[23] The negation of the world can also be apparent in the destruction of meaningful environments for commercialized exploitation of mindless human sprawl.[24] When civilization does not creatively and wisely serve the Human Eros, but frustrates it instead, alienation, nihilism, and destructive rage are the consequences.[25]

Correlated with this primary claim about the Human Eros, namely, that all human beings desire to experience the world with meaning and value, are several other theses. One is that human experience is pervaded by "temporal quality."[26] Temporal quality is an aspect of *all* experience; it is a way human beings are in situations. The present is the outcome of a history and is oriented tensively toward a future.[27] The "present" is not a static "now," but a dramatic reconfiguration of a process that has a narrative order. In other words, the structure of time as it enters into human experience of the world is creative and dramatic. It is not a steady mathematical flow nor a sequence of self-identical moments, timeless in themselves.[28] The present is an act of reconstruction.

In addition to the priority of aesthetic wholeness in situations and the narrative form of temporal quality, the Human Eros points to the conditioning and conditioned role of community in the experience of meaning. First, communities reflect the temporal nature of care in human existence. Biologically, we need other people; that is a fact of our existence as fundamental as the need for water or oxygen. As newborns, we enter a world of preverbal care; we learn language within that world, and come to care for others as a result.[29] Meaning arises in the process of communication, and the consciousness of self and world is made possible by the imaginative extension of experience into the roles of others so that we may interpret ourselves to ourselves.[30] Human experience is a temporal flow, conditioned by care, narratively structured, pervaded by a noncognitive qualitative sense of situations, that is a dialogical process of communication in which imagination is absolutely crucial.[31] And formal methods do not lend themselves well to these issues.

Constructively, the Human Eros seeks to mediate the world in terms of building symbolic worlds that validate human existence. The Eros, unless frustrated, is essentially creative. Religions, political systems, cultural traditions articulate homes for human beings to live in; these "homes" are as vital to our existence as the environmental conditions of oxygen, food, and water. Culture is part of our human environmental being.[32] Civilizations, as noted above, are experiments of the Human Eros. They articulate worlds out of symbols that help human beings experience their world as a place for defining what a meaningful, value-rich human life is, by orienting the Human Eros toward an ideal of wisdom. Cultures provide existential environments as homes for the human spirit.[33] Most cultures concentrate on celebrating and articulating what it is to live a meaningful human life, in spite of any oppression that this may require.[34]

To study these cultures philosophically, then, involves seeing them as striving to meet a deep need to experience human life in the world as a meaningful and value-rich event. Acknowledging the Human Eros allows us to look at all cultural constructions (including philosophy itself) as symbolic experiments in life. This approach requires investigations into historical context and development. It also points to the importance of aesthetic experience and imagination as constitutive grounds of human reasoning. Our reasoning occurs within situations which have a pervasive, qualitative aspect that unifies them as frames of reference. Objects, things, actions, events—all have their being by being situated within a context. The qualitative unity of the context may be subliminal or, as in the experience of art, heightened into conscious experience. The transformative nature of situations, part of their reconstructive temporality, involves the constant use of imagination, conceived here as the ability to employ and play with alternative interpretive schemata. Intelligence is precisely this ability to see the actual in light of the possible, as well as to grasp it as an outcome of a history. In other words, imagination is a requirement of pragmatic intelligence as well as of wisdom.[35]

ONTOLOGY AS COMPASSIONATE INTELLIGENCE

The investigation into the Human Eros marks, as I said, the humanistic side of my position: human beings have a need to experience the world with meaning and value. But this is also an ontological question, not merely because it is a feature of human "being" but also because it is the *world* that can be meaningful and rich in value. It is through interpretations of being that we inhabit the world and appropriate the world in terms of its possible meanings. We need now to inhabit the world with an ecological wisdom. This wisdom must grapple with ecological issues and communicate across the diversities of cultures. The question arises *for us* historically as a question of achieving eco-ontology, since this is conducive to the sort of wisdom we need. Ontology as an inquiry is situated within the problematic of existence, and this is always historical. It seeks to understand the ways in which it means to be. Because it is undertaken in terms of the search for wisdom, it acknowledges its origin in the historical needs of the Human Eros. We undertake ontological inquiry because human beings are involved in the world.

The question of the world arises from the Human Eros, but it is addressed to the world. Reflection must be undertaken with a sense of acknowledgment of and responsibility to that which is investigated. Ontology thus begins in an attitude of genuine *caring* about the world. To look at the world merely in terms of a value-neutral epistemic field requires forcing upon us the modernist dualism—the repression of wisdom as an end and a lack of acknowledgment of the erotic origins of thought from the start. Ontological care is concern for the being of the world. Thus care has the aspects of compassion and intelligence. Because thought emerges from and operates within an affective, emotional horizon of feeling, we can designate care as compassion. Compassion aims at clarity of insight into the world in terms of seeing the present as the outcome of a process, comprehending how it is *to be affected*. The suffering of the present is discerned by clear-headed sympathy. Care also aims at clarity of insight into the possibilities of the present, and this is intelligence. Ontology may therefore be designated as a discipline of compassionate intelligence concerning the undergoing and doing of the world.

An eco-ontology, functioning reflectively within the general quest for wisdom, must think of the ends to which its concepts and distinctions aim. Ontology asks the question of the meaning of being in service to the Human Eros with care for the world. It aims at establishing a house of wisdom. In our current context, this requires the critical investigation of the historically important ideas of being and how they have successfully or unsuccessfully connected us to the world. It discerns the ways in which we suffer and act in the world. It asks, pragmatically, what are the ecological consequences of the various meanings of Being? Thus, we must undertake an inquiry into the meanings of Being in the West that may have led toward the ecological ignorance that characterizes modernity. In particular, we must look at what in the history of Western ontology has prevented looking at the world *primarily* in terms of interactive relationships, contextual reciprocities, temporal continuities, and, not least, compassion. As suggested above, this asks us to focus in particular on the ideas of identity, form, completion, and power.

But an eco-ontological approach also seeks to investigate and articulate concepts that make us more intelligent inhabitants of the planet who are more capable of communicating with each other. One important aspect of this would be developing concepts that facilitate understanding the world in terms of environmental interactions.[36]

In addition to developing ideas out of our own traditions (however resistant they may be to that end), we must also investigate the ontologies of other cultures' philosophies that may be more amenable. We need to look at the ideals of wisdom that have characterized civilizations or cultures very different from the West—which have manifested respect for the world and compassion for other beings. In other words, are there non-European ontologies that can facilitate an ecological wisdom? Though several examples are available (such as Chinese and Native American cultures), the Buddhist tradition offers the strongest contrast to the West. Buddhism developed a rigorous philosophical literature while criticizing the very ideas central to the Western ontologies of identity. A strong commitment to ontological identity was not conducive to wisdom, according to Buddhism, and was, in fact, harmful. In articulating this view, the idea of the interrelational existence of everything *(pratityasamutpada)*, or "emptiness" *(sunyata)*, became central. Also, the Buddhist emphasis on compassion *(karuna)* as a practical result of discernment or insight *(prajña)* into the fundamentals *(dharmas)* is highly important. If we are compassionate beings, capable of an affective insight into the nature of others, especially in terms of their suffering, we are more disposed toward perceiving problems and generating solutions that transcend our individual, national, and species versions of egocentrism. Thus Buddhism may be of service as an alternative in seeking an eco-ontological wisdom. In the following sections, I will contrast the Western idea of Being as perfection of form and self-identity with the Buddhist analysis of emptiness or "interbeing" in light of their service to an eco-ontological ideal of wisdom.

BEING AS IDENTITY, PROCESS AS EMPTINESS

There are three major transformations of the idea of Being in the history of the West: the Greek identification of Being with perfection of form, the Medieval identification of Being (in the primary sense) with God (infinite perfection), and the modern identification of Being with matter and physical power. These all pose problems for an eco-ontology: the reification of identity as a characteristic of substance, viewing the real as transcendent, or reducing the real to the mechanistic relations of matter and force, with the status of mind left ambiguous at best. Obviously a detailed historical analysis would be needed to do justice to this topic, and what follows here can only be a sketch.

In the Greek tradition that goes from Pythagoras and Parmenides to Plato and Aristotle, we find the coalescence of several powerful ideas defining what it means to be: form, perfection, identity, the subject of predication.[37] The Pythagorean positing of "number" *(arithmos)* as the *archê* of nature led to the idea that it is by seeing into the mathematical harmonies of the universe that one attains purification as well as truth. Number combined limit and void, expressed as harmony, and the knowledge of nature's harmonies purified the soul. But number was mainly form, and form was limit, measure. Form gave the basis for truth, that is, it perfectly accommodated rational speech, *logos*. Parmenides, seeing that the Pythagorean account of the void *(to kenon)* failed such criteria, eliminated it altogether as "What Is Not," since it neither could be nor be coherently thought or expressed. This left the primal monad, without generative duality, and this he called Being, "It Is" *(esti),* an absolute identity that alone could be the subject of true propositions.[38] In contrast to the senses, it was intellect or *nous* alone that could achieve the insight into this truth. In listing the various "signs" of Being, Parmenides states that it is: one, whole, perfect, unchanging, never not itself; it never "was" nor "will be" but always "is," a timeless present. Thus to be means to be timelessly self-identical, the object of a logical intuition that makes possible an absolute, necessary truth claim. *Nous* is precisely this insight into the true identity of something.[39] Moreover, Being is "full," without degree, one part not being "more" or "less" than another. An absolute unity has no parts. Plato and Aristotle wrestled with the extreme conclusions of this position. Plato attempted to retain the Parmenidean view of Being as the self-identical *(autos),* the source of true insight, along with the Pythagorean view of form as the basis for cosmic measure. He introduced an intermediary domain that was caught perpetually in time between Being and not-Being, an analogical realm in which nothing was ever really itself, but "like" an ideal paradigm.[40] Aristotle rejected this attempt to save nature as a kinetic mimesis of Being, and so had to defend the idea that there were logically identical subjects for predication in the world itself, rather than in Plato's world of the Forms.

What is important here is to note that what dominates throughout is the notion that a self-same identity, akin to that of numbers, constitutes the nature of a "being." The nature of process is understood in terms of achieving "fullness" or completion and definition. To be is to be perfected, formed, brought to closure, and so the subject of true identification. The implications for the West have been not only an emphasis on formal definitions in understanding something, but the corresponding belief that "what there is"—be it Platonic Form, Aristotelian *ousia,* essence, atom, soul, mind, sense datum, monad, or atomic fact—is fundamentally a self-contained, individual entity. The universe is built out of these individuals and their logical relationships.[41]

Medieval thinkers, in stressing the supremacy of an all-powerful Creator, had to relegate finitude to the derivative created world. Being in its primary sense was infinite. The ambiguity in the idea of "power" (as passive potentiality or active force) allowed the Medievals to make God infinitely powerful without making Him thereby absolutely "potential."[42] One of the revolutions achieved in the Modern period is that God's infinity was gradually ascribed to the universe itself.[43] Advances in mathematics, culminating in the calculus, made it possible to imagine a physical world capable of infinitely precise mathematical description.[44] Thus each physical body could be as perfect, absolute, and self-identical as a Platonic Form. What mathematics could not do was provide the momentum for the material bodies, and this came to be the "power"—as inscrutable as God—that was given by God to the universe at the creation.[45] As theism diminished with the rise of modern science, what was left was the idea of a universe constituted at once of an aggregate of individuals, each logically and ontologically independent, endowed with an irrational "power." Both Nietzsche's metaphysics of "the Will to Power" and the logical universe of Wittgenstein's *Tractatus* are consequences of this position.[46]

It is clear that such a worldview is inhibited from achieving an ecological interpretation of the world or aspiring toward an ecological wisdom. First, nature itself is understood as constituted of substantial individuals, internally absolute and contingently externally related. Interactive systems are derivative. Because modernism lost the passive sense of potentiality for the active sense of power, process is understood as a function of a quantity of force subsumed under formal laws of transformation. Individuals behave in accordance with the laws of their own beings, a *conatus sese conservare,* that, on the human level, leads to the view that individuals naturally act only out of self-interest determined by desire. The best hope is that this self-interest can be enlightened so that a social machine can be constructed in which these potentially conflicting desires are harmonized.[47] In short: nature is a machine, individuals are absolute, and reason exists to serve desire. When Dewey set out to articulate a genuinely ecological philosophy of nature and society, he realized that this involved a critique of the philosophical heritage of the West.[48] It is not surprising he was misunderstood at every step.

One difficulty Western philosophies have is that the deep assumptions that run through the whole tradition, such as those I have characterized, are the most difficult to discern if one does not step out of that tradition from time to time. In reflecting on the possibility of an ecological wisdom, the Buddhist worldview certainly presents itself as an impressive alternative. Not only has Buddhism developed cultural traditions of great sustaining power (and so in their own right as worthy responses to the Human Eros), it has maintained a sophisticated intellectual development for 2,500 years. Its appeal as a resource for an ecological wisdom lies in its emphasis on the ideal of compassion, its ideal of moderation as a "Middle Way," and its refusal to draw any sharp distinction between human beings and other living creatures. Its resourcefulness in dealing with the problems of psychology (especially moral psychopathology), and, perhaps most important, its rejection of "self-being" (*svabhava*—what we would call a doctrine of substance) as a desirable metaphysical possibility also recommend it.

Again, I can only briefly describe some key points very generally. The teachings of the Buddha are deeply critical of the metaphysical ideas that had been articulated by the thinkers whose views are represented in the *Upanishads,* in particular, the view that at the heart of one's inmost being *(atman)* there was nothing other than the absolute and ultimate truth *(Brahman)*.[49] The position of the *Upanishads* is somewhat different from the Parmenidean insight that there is only one ultimate, absolute Being. The goal was not logical insight, but "liberation" *(moksa)* from reincarnation.[50] The world is reduced to illusion and "magic" *(maya),* so that the ethical implication is the duty to "play one's part" selflessly as an actor.[51] The Buddha disagreed with this view. The mystical search for the absolute Self was, in the end, just an extension on a higher level of the everyday grasping after the empirical ego. It was grasping that manufactured the self, and this gave rise to suffering because the world itself was inherently an interconnected process. He thus rejected any inner absolute self *(atman)* as well as any metaphysical appeals to an Absolute *(Brahman),* and showed an intense concern for developing an ethics of daily kindness and compassion, at variance with extreme asceticism or selfless performance of karmic duty. While he retained the ideal of "liberation," this seems to mean absolute selfless peace in which one no longer suffers the "turmoil" of the world, which he called *dukkha*.[52] The Buddha articulated his "Eightfold Path" as a "Middle Way" for navigating the stream of life so that one "made it through" to *nirvana,* the selfless peace achieved by the extinction of cravings based upon illusory and indeed harmful ideas (such as being an absolute individual or self).[53]

While the ideal of compassion (or *karuna*) as well as benevolence *(metta)* was cultivated, this was not done in such a way that any idea of "self" became involved. The source of most of the turmoil and struggle in the world arose precisely because people thought of their "selves" as "real" in the sense of being substantial when, in fact, they were about as self-sufficient and permanent as soap bubbles. The "self" could be analyzed into its various momentary, transitional components (or *dharmas*).[54] The empirical ego was a function of the relational process of the world, dependent on conditions and giving rise to consequences *(karma)*. When the idea of the substantial self vanished into these transitory relationships, the source of *dukkha* itself vanished. To achieve this end, the nature of the world was characterized in such a way as to emphasize its interdependency by the technical term *pratityasamutpada* or "dependent co-arising."[55] The world is constituted as a process of interconnected relationships. There is no "self" above and beyond this process. Our identity is similar to the identity of a river, and the names given to people are basically like the names given to rivers. The famous formula for "interdependence" is: "When that is present, this comes to be; on the arising of that, this arises. When that is absent, this does not come to be; on the cessation of that, this ceases."[56] What is articulated by this expression is a "middle principle" of genetic relativity, not some absolute, underlying "cause." In other words, it is a principle of descriptive, pragmatic value. It helps us pay attention to the way we are in the world. The early Buddhist tradition, then, developed a nonsubstantialist, interrelational view of the self and world for therapeutic ends. Not only were the ideas of "self," "identity," and "substance" critiqued, they were seen as positively harmful.

Five centuries after the Buddha's death, at the apex of Buddhism in India, a series of texts were written developing this idea, which is now called *sunyata* or "emptiness."[57] The texts, written as secret discourses of the Buddha to his most advanced disciples, laid the basis for what became the Mahayana traditions of East Asia, especially the philosophically important Madhaymika or "Middle School." "Emptiness" was the term used instead of *pratityasamutpada,* because the older schools of Buddhism had come to a set of dogmatic convictions, especially about the ultimate reality of the fundamental components of the empirical self, or *dharmas*.[58] To grasp after such theoretical constructions as if *they* were the "real things" was no better than grasping after the idea of the self, be it empirical ego or *atman,* as an absolute, for this led to the same sort of egotistical action that produced and involved oneself in *dukkha*.[59]

Especially as developed by the philosopher Nagarjuna (ca. 200 C.E.), the idea of emptiness was introduced not simply as a metacategory to interpret the ontological status of the *dharmas* but it was used to deflect the tendency to reify the objects of one's theories.[60] Its purpose was to direct attention back to the practical issues of living daily in a mindful manner. In other words, it safeguarded that theory was undertaken for the sake of compassionate existence and not as a further development of the ego. The Buddha, in his advice to Kaccanya, had advocated a "middle view" between extreme metaphysical theses such as "Everything exists" and "Nothing exists."[61] Explicitly building on this, Nagarjuna argued that, just as one should avoid ideas of absolute identity, so should one avoid ideas of absolute otherness.[62] A provisional, practical sense of "identity" can be used as long as one does not fall into positing some sort of self-same substance. This is also true of "motion" or "element." These terms designate parts of the continuum of becoming. They are webs of relations rather than fixed essential identities. Hence, to see into their true nature is to see them as "empty," that is, as dynamic, relational, and vague, discerned by our practical orientation to and involvement with the world.[63] The function of the doctrine of emptiness, then, is not to present a "higher" metaphysical principle into which explanatory factors, like *dharmas,* are resolved. Its function is to help us use all conceptual distinctions practically, seeing how they contextually and dynamically apply to the process of the world, especially with reference to the issue of suffering.[64] One of the main claims made by Nagarjuna about emptiness is that it, too, is "empty."

Buddhist philosophy was useful in overcoming ordinary beliefs and the attachments they generate, but one must also overcome the philosophical concepts themselves. To achieve *prajña,* or insight into the fundamental truth of something, is to see it as "empty," as a contextualized, transitory process. Unlike *nous,* which was logical insight, *prajña* involves the compassionate disillusion of identity, for there is no self-identical subject to be "recognized," though the suffering is real enough. The "thing" is revealed in its utter clarity as both "this," "such," and "empty." The idea of emptiness was applied to all forms of dichotomized thought, including the tendency of older Buddhism to contrast the world of attachment *(samsara)* with the world of bliss *(nirvana).* Under this analysis, the old dualism collapsed: *nirvana* is nothing other than *samsara.* This does not mean that the Buddha's Third Noble Truth is rejected, that there is no *nirvana.* Rather, it is how we "handle" the world that makes the difference, especially if we see it in terms of being a *process of transformations and in relationships.* The individual being is not seen as a "substance" with a "self-identical" logical unity, but as a phase or moment of mutually interdependent relationships. The individual is seen in the intensity of its temporary uniqueness or *tathata,* "suchness." (Zen art express this idea very clearly.) By seeing into its emptiness one can respond to it with more compassion as well as understanding. *Prajña,* or the deep insight into circumstances, was supposed to give one "skillful means" *(upaya)* to alleviate the suffering of specific individuals and motivate them toward enlightenment.

The Buddhist teaching on emptiness may be contrasted at every point with the West's emphasis on substance and identity. The Buddhist ethics of egoless compassion may also be contrasted with modernism's glorification of the atomic individual driven by self-interested desire. But has it succeeded in providing the alternative basis for a genuinely ecological wisdom? In many respects, Buddhism retains the marks of its birth in India: the aim of the individual is to find liberation from the cycle of existence or *samsara,* even where *nirvana* and *samsara* are realized to be the same. While the Buddha himself advocated a "middle way" between asceticism and indulgence, in the end his was the path of renunciation. The Mahayana tradition accommodated itself further to the needs of the world (or else it would not have survived in the Confucian cultures of East Asia), but one can still see that it does not necessarily lead toward more ecologically intelligent action. To see *all* beings as suffering, not just human beings, as "Buddhas in the making," may not stimulate one to take an urgent, active role in maintaining the health or welfare of *particular* species or ecosystems as a whole. To renounce the world is not a call to engage it. The arts of the haiku, brush painting, and the tea ceremony may make one more sensitive to aspects of the world, but have not noticeably affected Japan's whaling industry. Buddhism has had difficulty articulating itself as a political philosophy.[65] In other words, while the Buddhist doctrine of emptiness offers an important and deep alternative to the Western ideas of identity, substance, and power, an eco-ontological philosophy needs to go further.

ECO-ONTOLOGY

The goal of wisdom is to guide the Human Eros toward fulfillment, that is, to secure a world that provides the conditions for an experience of a meaningful, value-rich existence. The sort of ecological wisdom proposed here includes both the ideal of living well as human beings upon the earth and the ideal of responsible, intelligent, compassionate insight as conditions for ontological reflection. We saw that the ideal of wisdom has faded in the West, while retaining its deep metaphysical commitment to an ontology of identity. In the modern period this has meant a worldview in which individuals are to be seen in external relationship to the world and each other. The existential disposition toward the world has become the control of nature's power for the sake of subjective goods determined by desire. The Buddhist tradition, by contrast, offers a challenge to this approach. Identity is due to "ignorance" and is the source of suffering. By adopting a view of the world as a conditioned and conditioning process, "things" (including selves) are seen as "empty," giving rise to an ethics of compassion and nonattachment. The danger here, in spite of the pragmatic middle path Buddhism takes, is an overemphasis on the goal of renunciation, ending up with what Dewey called an "art of acceptance" in contrast to the West's emphasis on the "art of control."[66] An ecological wisdom must be able to integrate both of these types of arts and regulate them in light of an ideal of a responsible, caring, compassionate, and creative ideal of existence. What is needed, then, is a philosophical ontology that has a view of nature as interactive, evolutionary, and nonreductionistically emergent and a view of human intelligence as aesthetic and moral as well as cognitive. The basis for such a philosophy is provided in Dewey's thought, and can be further adapted and developed toward that end.

Dewey himself advocated a humanistic or "cultural naturalism" that took a nonreductionistic, process-oriented view of the world in which various aspects of nature were understood in terms of interactive fields or situations that received various conceptual articulations by the diversity of inquiries human beings make. Human beings are involved in this process in terms of "undergoing and doing," which is both qualitatively immediate and relationally mediated. Situations are the funded outcomes of histories and contain potentialities for further development. Experience is pervaded by a qualitative aesthetic horizon and aims toward an ideal of conduct by means of an imaginative and practical reconstruction of the present. Human intelligence understands the present in terms of its actualized, historical past and discerns those potentialities in it so that an evaluation may result in conduct that experimentally seeks to realize an ideal of the good, which, on its realization, may be critically reevaluated again and again. Metaphysics has a crucial role in this enterprise as a descriptive account of the "generic traits" nature manifests in experience which allow us to connect different aspects of the world so that we can identify functional continuities and avoid setting up dysfunctional dichotomies. Metaphysics, in other words, keeps intelligence functioning for the sake of wisdom. It lays the basis for extensive, deep communication across disciplines.

Like the Buddhist doctrine of emptiness, this approach avoids reification of identity or the positing of substances. Individuals or entities exist within situations as relational, interactive phases of events. In other words, they are synchronically and diachronically situated in environments as constitutive of their being. To be is to be environed. Since events are marked by a temporal quality and so have histories, they are susceptible of being characterized with an evolutionary account of their genesis. We grasp their "whatness" not in an atemporal, identity-based essence formulable in a definitional *logos*, but in terms of an environmental-historical narrative. While the West has continually sought a core self-sameness to capture the "essence" of "things" and the Buddhist tradition has dissolved both "essences" and "things" in the arising and disappearing concatenations of the *dharmas*, an eco-ontological account will search for the "natural history" of the subject at hand. An event will be understood—always provisionally—in terms of its situational interactions that constitute its history and its contemporary potentialities. "Natural history" designates the account of how a thing comes to be within its situated contexts. This is an environmental concept, since it locates any individual within its ambit and understands it in terms of interacting with the actualities and potentialities of that ambit. To be is to be the product of a history.

History necessarily includes a narrative of how various potentialities are actualized and come to constitute the factical history of that being. We understand "what" the thing is in terms of seeing the world it comes from and how it functioned within it.[67] The event is dramatically understood in terms of actions that have a reconstructive or transformative power. This is a more integrated concept than the Buddhist view of the intrinsic "emptiness" of the *dharmas,* though, like that view, it refuses to posit a substantial underlying "self-same identity." Identity is not a useful idea when dealing with a creative process, unless it is understood in terms of the function of "identify*ing,*" in which case the realities of difference, development, and transformation are taken into account. The boundaries of the history are vague, not absolutely finite, and one may extend or limit them in various ways as one tries to understand the narrative at hand. Nevertheless the parts are (or can be) connected together with degrees of meaningfulness. (This is why multiple biographies of the same individual are not only possible but desirable). Instead of the act of dissolution of the illusory identity into the webs of relations sanctioned by Buddhism, a natural history asks for a detailed and intimate inquiry into the evolutionary ecology of the subject, and the "subject" is the creative process of transformations of potentialities into actualities. To be is to be transformative.

The idea of natural history also is helpful in dealing with the problem of teleology. Aristotle was able to pull Plato's Forms down to earth at the cost of making the species fixed.[68] Though Aristotle's doctrine of essence succumbed to the problems of the ontology of identity described above, he did describe natural organisms in terms of temporal development, using his ideas of form, matter, actuality, potentiality, and entelechy. Had this aspect of Aristotle's philosophy dominated over the theology of the Unmoved Mover, the history of Western ontology might have been different.[69] The loss of Aristotelian teleology in the modern period also had devastating consequences for the project of virtue ethics, so that one sees today struggles to overcome both Galileo and Darwin to retrieve it.[70] To understand events in terms of natural history, however, retains the Aristotelian distinctions of actuality/form and potentiality/matter without leading to either the idea of the fixity of species or identity of the individual.[71]

Actualities and potentialities are features of situations and processes. The actualities realized as the outcome of the past carry their own range of potentialities for the future. These potentialities are indeterminately articulated in radiating webs. Only a certain range of potentialities is immanent in a given situation, and from the realization of any of those, others may become immanently realizable. There is a large sedimented history that forms the predominant tendencies in the present. But the present is not entirely constituted by them. There is always a degree of random variation and creative individualization. The transformative reconstruction of the present realizes some of the situation's potentialities and not others, and so a history grows. One might compare this sort of radial evolutionary teleology with that of a conversation, whereas Aristotle's view of teleology is more like that of a linear recitation (or *mimesis*) of a previously written work. At any given moment in a conversation there is a constituting context within which remarks make sense or not; over time the conversation may range considerably, so that a remark at one time would not have been expected some time earlier. Yet, if one follows the conversation, it can be understood in terms of its history. This "conversational" or radial teleology is the pattern of evolutionary change. Natural history, rather than logical analysis (or abidharma techniques) helps us discern it.[72] To be is to have radial teleology.

If natural history indicates the facility with which eco-ontology interprets the present in terms of the past, the present must also be interpreted in terms of its future potentialities and immanent creative transformations. The dynamic fusion of the historical past and the open future in the creative present is designated by the term "continuity." Continuity is the temporal establishment of natural history. Thus eco-ontology replaces the idea of identity with that of continuity, dynamically understood. First, continuity is temporal; it is not a formal series. Second, it is creative; it is not algorithmic. Subsequent parts are not reduced to expressions of formal functions. Continuity realizes individuality-within-environment. In particular, it is exhibited in the idea of growth. It engages the present out of a past for the sake of a future. The present is the moment of transformation, and so of individuation. Creative individuation is historically temporal. This is what it means to *be* "present."[73] To be is to be continuous.

It is through acts of historical individuation that continuity is established. Continuity thus involves the ideas of spontaneity, creativity, and individuality. Each moment presents unique novelty and freshness as a fusion of past potentialities into a new actuality. Though it arises from the past, the present cannot be reduced to it. It exists as a fulfillment of the past, and so exists as its current meaning. The present itself, though, is a complex modality that intertwines the actualization of the past in the present as the fulfillment of those potentialities immediately in the past with the potentialities of the immanent future that it may become. Beyond the immanence of these potentialities is the continuum of possibilities extending toward the horizon of the future and the factical necessity of the determining past.[74] The complex intertwining of these modes in the present is, existentiality, the *agon* or moment in its dyadic push and pull and in the limited freedom of creative selection.[75] Continuity, then, is the tendency of natural process toward the establishment of a consummatory history.[76] In the context of human beings, time is the drama of the Human Eros. While emphasizing the environment and history of events, eco-ontology equally stresses the role of creativity in the present as integral to temporal continuity.[77] Individuality is the synthesis of the situation through action guided by imaginative insight into the potentialities at hand. It requires an understanding of the present as the outcome of a history in which there are tensive elements constituting the phase of undergoing. The insight into potentialities involves interpreting the present in terms of its possible meanings. The idealization of one or more of those possibilities sets an end-in-view that makes reconstructive or transformative action a way of mediating the open tensiveness toward qualitative closure. The cause for a genuine individualism, then, is all one with deeply informed knowledge of the world and its history as well as creative imagination and moral courage. When profoundly realized, this environmental individualism fulfills the Human Eros. To be is to be individual as dramatically achieved.

In achieving its history, the Human Eros must care for the world. Care is intentional: it is care *of*. To care is to understand the history and possibilities of a subject so that the subject is manifest in its meaning as beautiful. The beautiful here is not the "well-formed" or pretty. It is that which manifests the Light of suchness. The transient clarity of the world is grasped in all its affective and moral as well as its intellectual complexity. The Buddhist term *prajña* is appropriate here, for this is insight into the world in its clarity motivated by compassionate awareness that in turn enables one to select the "skillful means" *(upaya)* to respond to the world. To grasp the world in its unstable mode of undergoing *(dukkha)* is to have compassionate insight; to grasp it in terms of guiding it toward a consummatory history is to respond with intelligent Eros. One seeks to eliminate ignorance and meaningless suffering for fulfillment and the creative establishment of individuality or "creative mindfulness."

Being oriented to the world, one's own existence becomes an opening for concern. "Concern" here is understood in its Quaker sense, as that which leads one forth from the innermost depths of one's being toward that which needs one in the world.[78] The human community, the animal kingdom, the biosphere, and the geosphere itself can be grasped as objects of concern as insight discerns them. Concern may therefore be experienced for fellow human beings, animals, ecosystems. We must avoid the reification of identities but discern interactive histories of continuities. Creative transformation involves integration of the future into the meaning of the present through individuation that becomes open to the world by insight, care, and concern. Because individuality is environmental, we are called upon to care for the world by the Human Eros itself.

THE HOME *(OIKOS)* OF PHILOSOPHY—INHABITATION

Philosophy reflects our human embeddedness in the world. It offers the possibility of responsible inhabitation in pursuit of ecological wisdom. To in-habit is to have the habits that make one at home, the wisdom of the environment. Wisdom must inhabit this world, not another. Disembodied philosophy tries to live without environment. It is a disservice to its origins and is possible only through a primal act of forgetting. The initiating moment of philosophy is not just separation in reflective thought, but acknowledgment of the sources of existence. Philosophy arises in response to the tensive nature of the world within which human beings find themselves. To undertake thought without acknowledging its origin in need is to repress its own motives and to refuse acknowledgment of its grounding. Criticism is moral, involving the active disposition of curiosity and receptivity to discovery, a generosity toward the play of free possibility the world can offer. To inhabit the world is not to dominate or renounce it, but to play in it, learn from it, care for it, and realize the beauty of its meanings. "Ecology is the wisdom of being at home in the world."[79]

In the new century, philosophy is morally compelled to acknowledge its origins in the life of our species on the planet. The act of forgetfulness that allows us to drive the living systems of the planet toward extinction can no longer be accepted, even—perhaps especially—when presented at face value as "professional philosophy." Nor, in its new horizon of global existence, can North Atlantic philosophy maintain its traditional narcissism. Thought must call out to thought on a global level. Philosophy must accept the place where it lives and dwells, its home or *oikos,* which it has a responsibility to manage, as well as within which it draws its life. The possibilities of an eco-ontology to fulfill this end are numerous. It relocates the task of philosophy with the traditional project of wisdom. It engages the wisdom traditions and philosophies of other cultures. It demands that philosophy be a humanistic as well as naturalistic discipline that has a complex literacy about the cultural dimensions of human experience as well as a ecological scientific literacy about the natural world. It distrusts pure methodologies. It recognizes the origin of philosophy in the Human Eros and turns that Eros toward the problem of formulating wisdom for an ecological global community. It believes the purpose of thought is to save the world.[80]

NOTES

1. Though "the friend of wisdom" might be more accurate. Being a *philos* in ancient Greece, however, meant you would be ready to die for the honor of your friend and do nothing to disgrace it in your own deeds. To be a "friend" of wisdom in this sense meant a life of commitment to that which is noble.

2. The thought of John Dewey is thus exceptional in that it explicitly attempts to relocate the quest for knowledge back within the context

of the general issue of wisdom. See *Experience and Nature* (LW 1: 50, 305–6) as well as section IV of *Human Nature and Conduct* (MW 14).

3. Likewise we should distinguish the collective cultural wisdom that is uncritically passed along from one generation to the next as "wisdom traditions" rather than "philosophy" per se, which must have a degree of critical reflectiveness and individual responsibility in thinking. But there is no reason why philosophy, as I have described it, should ignore wisdom traditions; indeed, it should pay great attention to them. Thus I designate three partially overlapping areas: wisdom traditions, philosophy, and philepistemy. Philosophy overlaps both, though neither of them overlaps with each other. Thus philosophy involves critical self-reflection, as wisdom traditions do not, though it is concerned with wisdom, and shares with philepistemy concern over criteria for knowledge, belief, truth, meaning, etc., but not as self-contained subjects.

4. See William Reading's *The University in Ruins* (Cambridge: Harvard University Press, 1995).

5. It could be argued that the earliest Greek thinkers, the Milesians, did not exemplify this ideal (though Heraclitus and Pythagoras certainly did), undertaking speculative inquiry for its own sake. I would argue that the Milesian revolution had political overtones, challenging as it did the very basis of aristocratic government, that is, its legitimation by mythology. Philosophy began as a democratic critique.

6. Philosophy, as it was understood in the ancient world and in Medieval times, aimed at wisdom in this practical as well as theoretical sense. Moreover, it was thought impossible, then, to be able to embark upon the strictly cognitive tasks of philosophy without adopting a way of life that sought to embody an ideal of wisdom. Even Aristotle, who separated the theoretical sciences from the practical arts, accepted that a person could not be called wise who was not *eudaimon,* or "doing well." *Theoria* was undertaken because it was for him the realization of a genuine human excellence, our natural zest in understanding the universe.

7. Francis Bacon's Aphorisms in the *Novum Organon* express this eloquently: "Human knowledge and human power meet in one, for where the cause is not known the effect cannot be produced. Nature to be commanded must be obeyed, and that which in contemplation is as the cause is in operation as the rule" (*Magna Instauratio,* Aphorisms I:ii). The rendering of the formal cause as an operational rule is prophetic of the course of modern philosophy.

8. The renaissance archetype of the modern scientist-philosopher is the "magus," one who aims at mastery of nature's powers, not contemplation of its causes. See Francis A. Yates, *Giordanno Bruno and the Hermetic Tradition* (Chicago: University of Chicago Press, 1964) Besides Bruno, Paracelsus likewise becomes a key figure.

9. Descartes's *Discourse on Method* becomes a key text scripting the "code of ethics" for the modernist intellectual. *The Meditations,* likewise, is a book in ethics; truth is obtained by disciplining the will. But it is an ethics for knowledge, which itself is undertaken for power, not for realizing a better life.

10. It must be explicitly emphasized here that Dewey's frequent—and frequently misunderstood—appeals to the scientific method were contextualized for him within this larger enterprise of constructing a democratic culture that genuinely fulfilled human beings in their collective and individual lives. In other words, Dewey's "instrumentalism" refers to a *part* of his thought. See his essay "Philosophy and Civilization" (LW 5). The plurality of methods is sound Aristotelianism and can be successfully applied to a nonreductionistic study of nature.

11. As Mill said criticially of Bentham, ". . . Bentham's knowledge of human nature is bounded. It is wholly empirical, and the empiricism of one who had little experience." "Bentham," in *The Philosophy of John Stuart Mill,* ed. Marshall Cohen (New York: The Modern Library, 1961), 23.

12. Here the thought of Marx, the Critical Theorists and Foucault are extremely helpful—as is that of Dewey—in seeing how theory makes "reasonable" a certain type of social system of empowerment.

13. Thus the purely negative work of people like Adorno or Rorty must be regarded as abandoning the philosophical project in the end, leaving us with aimlessness, not wisdom.

14. While I do not accept the shallow criticisms of Dewey as an uncritical advocate of science, much less as an unthinking "optimist" or "liberal," his critique of modernism could have been stronger, his development of his ideas on civilization more extended, and his confrontation with Western metaphysics more systematic. Thus I find his aesthetics, ethics, social philosophy and metaphysics of most use.

15. For a presentation of this view see my essay, "The Human Eros," in *Philosophy and the Reconstruction of Culture: Pragmatic Essays after John Dewey,* ed. John Stuhr (Albany: State University of New York Press, 1993), 203–22.

16. See Dewey's acknowledgment of this key idea in *Experience and Nature* (LW 1: 272).

17. My own effort to spell this out is undertaken in my book *John Dewey's Theory of Art, Experience and Nature: The Horizons of Feeling* (Albany: State University of New York Press, 1987). Valuing is an integral ongoing phase of organizing situations and helps discern what features are to function as "facts" within inquiry.

18. See chapter 3 of *Experience and Nature* and Dewey's seminal essay, "Qualitative Thought" (LW 5).

19. Fulfillment need not be "happiness" in the sense of feeling good; it is a *realization* of a deep meaning *of* the world *in* human existence.

20. Elie Weisel's writings explore this idea; Viktor Frankl (see *Man's Search for Meaning*) developed his "logotherapy" in reaction to it. The thought of Ernest Becker is also in touch with this issue.

21. Ralph Ellison's *Invisible Man* is an eloquent testimony to this aspect of the negation of human existence.

22. The repression that civilizations—at least some civilizations—require is not the repression of the id, as Freud thought, but of compassion.

23. See John Dominic Crossan's major study, *Jesus: The Life of a Mediterranean Jewish Peasant* (New York: Harper Collins, 1991); and his shorter (and somewhat clearer) *Jesus: A Revolutionary Biography* (New York: Harper Collins, 1994).

24. For example, the destruction of environments essential for a species' existence, the destruction of species themselves, and the appropriation of land without thought for the sake of human suburbial migration.

25. The loss of meaningful environments and ideals of wisdom may partially explain the upsurge in random acts of impulsive violence in a society that is technologically advanced and economically thriving.

26. See *Experience and Nature* (LW 1: 72). Dewey distinguishes temporal quality from seriality. Temporal quality is the dialectic of undergoing and doing in every event that gives that event a horizon of past and future, of actuality and potentiality, in short, that which marks it as a phase of process and lends it the capacity for growth. Temporal quality is a feature of *everything* including formalized abstractions like numbers.

27. The term "tensive," originally used by Dewey, is preferable to his subsequent term "problematic."

28. In this sense, a Deweyan philosophy must acknowledge the similarity of Heidegger's analysis of *Dasein,* though significant differences remain.

29. Thus one major difference between Heidegger and Dewey is that Heidegger sees the horizon of human finitude in death whereas Dewey supplements it with the indefinite horizon of love. Though death may individualize, the ability to love and give to others (including, indeed, especially future generations) reconstitutes the individual back within both the social and the natural. Love transcends death.

30. The social-communicative genesis of the self and of consciousness is the theme of chapters 5 and 6 of *Experience and Nature* as well as George Herbert Mead's *Mind, Self, and Society*. This claim contrasts strongly with Heidegger's limited focus on the problem of individuation over against the "social" characterized as *Das Man*.

31. Thus, in the face of the "cognitive science" movement, I find studies such as those done by Robert Coles of much more significance for obtaining insight into the human situation. See especially *The Spiritual Life of Children* and *The Moral Life of Children*. Cultural anthropology, not physics, should be our ideal.

32. It should be recalled that Dewey proposed changing the title of his major work from *Experience and Nature* to *Culture and Nature,* thereby avoiding, he hoped, the subjectivist connotations of "experience."

33. See my essay, "The Technology of Desire," in *Philosophy and Technology: Philosophical Perspectives,* vol. 8, ed. Paul Durbin (Dordrecht: Kluwer Academic Publishers, 1991).

34. After all, at dinner we comment on the taste of the food rather than on the suffering of the animal that made it possible.

35. See my discussion of this in "Pragmatic Imagination," *Transactions of the Charles S. Peirce Society* 26, no. 3 (1990): 325–48. Also see Mark L. Johnson's *The Body in the Mind* (Chicago: University of Chicago Press, 1987) for a technical discussion of the nature of imagination and its employment of schemata.

36. John Dewey dominates the twentieth century as the only thinker to articulate an ecological concept of philosophy; Heidegger only did so to some extent and Wittgenstein not at all, unless his interactive descriptions of the language games of the later period could be extended as a descriptive ecology of practices. But the lack of a critical role for philosophy even in his later period makes this problematic.

37. That we are looking at a tradition is important to keep in mind: Parmenides developed his ideas from Pythagoras as Plato did from both Pythagoras and "Papa Parmenides" and Aristotle did from Plato.

38. See Parmenides, Fragment DK 8. It is my thesis that Parmenides began as a Pythagorean (as stated by Diogenes Laertius) and encountered the paradox of asserting non-Being in initially working out a cosmogony, the account of which he still gives us as the "deceitful *logos*" in the last part of his poem. The Pythagorean monad, the "seed" from which all other numbers "grew" by "inhaling" the void, could *not* grow because there was no "void" to "inhale." Thus Parmenides' One is the original Monad regarded as complete and incapable of change. The consequences of this view were fundamental for the West.

39. In Homer, *nous* explicitly is the power to see through disguises. In *Iliad* III.396 Helen perceives the true identity of Aphrodite and in *Odyssey* XIX.301, Odysseus' dog recognizes his master, that is, has direct insight into the true identity in spite of outward appearances, that is, the transformations of nineteen years of war and hardship as well as further

temporary magical disguising by Athena. To "know" in the sense of *noein* is to recognize true identity behind the appearance.

40. These problems persisted in the ideal world of the Forms, and Plato's later philosophy tries to show how "non-Being" must be introduced even there, if only in the manner of negative predication (as in the *Sophist*). But beyond that he is forced to posit a "matter" for the Forms in terms of "The Greater and the Lesser" that allows for infinite numbers, series, and all articulations of continua. See *Philebus* and Aristotle's cryptic remarks in *Metaphysics I* on Plato's later thought.

41. I do not think it is merely accidental that the civilization of the West has been characterized by intense formalism, intellectualism, and individualism.

42. The key figure here is Plotinus, whose One transcends the Forms and so is "beyond" Form, and so limitless. Because actuality was equated with form, he ascribed *dunamis,* "power" to the One.

43. This was one of the central ideas of Giordano Bruno, a heresy that cost him his life. See Alexandre Koyré's *From the Closed World to the Infinite Universe* (Baltimore: Johns Hopkins University Press, 1957).

44. Once Galileo eliminated the Euclidean belief that there were "perfect" solids, he realized that *all* bodies were capable of "perfect" geometrical expression.

45. See Newton's General Scholium in the *Principia*. Motion is introduced externally to the atoms.

46. Nietzsche, rejecting rationality, sees the task of power as culminating in creative individuality; Wittgenstein, assuming the givenness of individuals as logical subjects, makes time a mystery.

47. The insight into the essential relationship between modern material atomism and the political state is due to Hobbes; it is still fundamentally embodied in the work of John Rawls.

48. That Dewey himself realized this is made clear in the unfinished drafts for the new introduction to *Experience and Nature*. See (LW 1: Appendix 1).

49. See David Kaluphana's *A History of Buddhist Philosophy* (Honolulu: University of Hawaii Press, 1992) and Edward Conze's specialized study *Buddhist Thought in India* (Ann Arbor: University of Michigan Press, 1967).

50. A major difference between the doctrine of *Brahman* and Parmenides' Being, is that *Brahman* is totally beyond any conceptual or logical formulation, being boundless. It transcends any direct insight into the identity of something that *nous* obtains, being realized in the state of nondual, unintentional consciousness.

51. Such is the advice given to the hero Arjuna by the god Krishna in the *Bhagavad Gita*. The result is that Arjuna does pick up his bow and fight his relatives, friends, and teachers. Had the Buddha been his charioteer rather than Krishna, very different advice would have been given.

52. While often rendered as "suffering," this word embraces a broad spectrum of meanings that include "impermanence," "instability," and "lack of self-sufficiency." Thus all of the things which we would call "happy," "good," or "pleasant" are equally instances of *dukkha,* not because they are "illusory" and in fact are "painful," but because they are temporary and depend on circumstances to be realized. Thus they are not absolute. This is not a cause for pessimism; it is simply how things are.

53. The Eightfold Path was a pragmatic approach to the fact of *dukkha,* and was aimed at reducing it as a causal factor as much as possible. It consists in: Right Understanding, Right Thought (or compassion), Right Conduct, Right Speech, Right Livelihood, Right Mindfulness, and Right Concentration. See Walpola Ruhala's excellent introduction, *What the Buddha Taught* (New York: Grove, 1974).

54. The term *dharma* meant initially "that which upholds" in the sense of "duties." From that it came to mean: the "parts" or "elements" that constitute the whole, the "law" or custom governing them, and so the "teaching" of the Buddha and the Buddhist "way." The *dharmas* of the self are the "Five Heaps" or elements in continuous flux: matter, sensations (including "mind" as the faculty of thoughts), perceptions, "mental formations" (like acts of will that generate karma), and consciousness or awareness of objects.

55. See Kalupahana, *A History of Buddhist Philosophy,* chap. 4. Kalupahana notes that *pratityasamputpada* (Pali: *paticcasamuppada*) is formed from the past participle, stressing the present as the outcome of the past. This makes it closer to a radical empiricist view of causality than a substance-attribute or radical atomistic view of existence, that is, the present is its relations, including temporal relations, not a "thing" that "has" relations or an unrelated atomistic present moment. The present includes what Kaluphana calls "the obvious past and the obvious future." In contrast to an appeal to any sort of transcendent abstract principle, the Buddhist view of causality remains focused on a lucid awareness of the world as experienced. Kaluphana is aware of the deep affinity of this view with pragmatism.

56. Kalupahana, *History of Buddhist Philosophy,* 56. See *Majjhima Nikaya* I.263. As Kalupahana notes, the use in Pali here of the "locative absolute" retains the "radical empiricism" of the temporality of the relations which would be lost in formalizing the expression into a conditional

or hypothetical inference. Likewise the uses of "this" and "that" are experientially denotative rather than inferential logical subjects (i.e., individuals). And so the fallacy of denying the antecedent is not committed. See 56–57.

57. These are collectively described as the *Prajnaparamita* sutras or "Perfection of Wisdom" texts. The term *sunya,* as Edward Conze notes, comes from the Sanskrit root *SVI,* "to swell." In a worldview governed by contrariety, what can be considered to be "swollen" from the outside is also "hollow" on the inside. Likewise it may be "swollen" due to something foreign filling it up and bloating it. See Edward Conze, *Buddhism: Its Essence and Development* (New York: Harper & Row, 1975), 130–31.

58. This was rather like reductionistic tendencies in the West to resolve physical objects into ultimate bodies or minds into "ideas," "sense data," "brain states," "propositional attitudes," or whatever.

59. The sort of suffering, anger, and abuse one sees in academic departments in debates over "ideas" is an example of the sort of problem these texts addressed.

60. Nagarjuna is an extremely important and difficult thinker, the subject of widely conflicting interpretations, some of which, like Radhakrishnan's, strive to assimilate him into mainstream Indian Vedantist monism. See the brief discussion in Kalupahana's *History of Buddhist Philosophy,* chap. 16, and the essay on the Madhyamika by Douglas Daye in *Buddhism: A Modern Perspective,* ed. Charles S. Prebish (University Park: Penn State University Press, 1975). See the more extended studies by Frederick Streng, K. Venkata Ramanan, Jay L. Garfield, Kenneth Inanda, and David Kalupahana. The study by Garfield is especially clear.

61. This is of course a perfect refusal to get caught on the horns of the Parmenidean dilemma. See Kalupahana, *History of Buddhist Philosophy,* 158–59, 162. The Discourse to Kacciyana is in the *Samutta Nikaya* (2.16–17).

62. As Kalupahana notes, "this is a rejection of the rationalist solution to the problem of causality. . . . Hence Nagarjuna turns to the pragmatic definition of an event as fruit *(artha),* arguing against the rationalist that the fruit is dependently arisen, neither pre-existing as a substance nor something absolutely different, without at the same time arguing for an essentialist explanation that the fruit itself is a unique event." *History of Buddhist Philosophy,* 162.

63. See Kalupahana's *History of Buddhist Philosophy,* 163–66 and Nagarjuna's major work *Mulamadhyamakakarika,* especially chap. 15. Nagarjuna, like Zeno, offered dialectical analyses of all substantialist claims, showing that they were internally self-contradictory. "Substance" (or "self-being") cannot be conceived without "other-being," and so is not

substantial, likewise "other being" derives from "self-being." See the translations in the studies mentioned in note 60. It is important to understand that Nagarjuna did not believe he had another thesis to propound over against these. Kalupahana's interpretation is noteworthy in stressing the moderate, "middle" position of Nagarjuna as well as in bringing out his similarities to American pragmatism.

64. One is reminded of William James's statement that "Pragmatism unstiffens all our theories, limbers them up and sets each one at work." *Pragmatism,* Lecture II (Cambridge: Harvard University Press, 1974), 32.

65. The twentieth century has seen an effort to make Buddhism more political. See Christopher Queen and Sallie King, *Engaged Buddhism* (Albany: State University of New York Press, 1996).

66. See *The Quest for Certainty* (LW 4), chaps. 1 and 4. Dewey himself saw the history of the West as generating more "arts of acceptance" than "arts of control," which was a genuinely positive contribution, in his view, of the modern period.

67. This is the practice obscurely indicated by Dewey in both versions of the first chapter of *Experience and Nature* as the "empirical denotative method." It is the method of Natural History.

68. The problem was that of Parmenides: Being cannot become. Plato identified Form with Being and so put it beyond the domain of Becoming. To bring Form into the world, then, meant a compromise: indivduals come to be and die, but the species retain the eternal character of Being.

69. Indeed, his key term for *ousia,* misleadingly rendered as "essence" *(essentia)* is *to ti ên einai,* "the what it *was* going to be." The verb *ên* is significantly the imperfect tense of *einai. Essentia,* derived from the Latin verb "to be," *esse,* should have been the rendition of Aristotle's *ousia.* This term was misleadingly rendered as *sub-stantia,* "that which stands underneath."

70. The work of MacIntyre and Nussbaum being cases in point; it is of considerable note that neither really confronts how an Aristotelian ethics is possible without Aristotle's metaphysics. It is also of note that neither seems in the least cognizant of Dewey's struggle to overcome this problem.

71. Raymond Boisvert's *Dewey's Metaphysics* (New York: Fordham University Press, 1988) argues for a limited retention of the Aristotelian idea of form in Dewey, as my own book, *John Dewey's Theory of Art,* argues for a limited retention of the idea of potentiality.

72. In Buddhism, Abidharma was the disciplined analysis of the complex momentary existence of the self and world into its component *dharmas.*

73. This saves eco-ontology from the deconstructionist dismissal of being an ontology of "presence." If "presence" is understood as factical being-at-hand, it falls into the ontology of identity criticized above. But presence as pragmatically understood is creatively engaged, and so not

completely formed or actualized. The present is not only "vague," but dramatically significant, penetrated by imagination as well as reason.

74. The continuum of pure possibility I designate by the Greek term *apeiron* and the delimiting frame of the necessity of the factical past by the Greek *ananke*. The present is the "struggle" *(agon)* between them.

75. The dyadic nature of existence is discussed by C. S. Peirce in his category of Secondness. Its selective freedom is discussed by William James, most famously in "The Will to Believe."

76. This is why Dewey presents his primary example of it in terms of the aesthetic; see *Art as Experience* (LW 10), chap. 3.

77. See Dewey's highly important discussion of this in "Time and Individuality" (LW 14).

78. See Alfred North Whitehead, *Adventures of Ideas,* chap. 9, sec. 3.

79. Eugenia Gatens-Robinson in conversation.

80. I dedicate this paper to my father-in-law, E. M. Adams.

PART THREE

Don't Pass—Build!

EIGHT

On Passing Dewey By

The New Millennium and the Climate of Pluralism

SANDRA ROSENTHAL

As the old millennium draws to a close and the new one dawns, one of the notable trends that continues to dominate is the issue of pluralism both in the United States and in the world at large. In the United States, this trend is manifesting itself in the growing multiculturalism with its social, political, and economic ramifications. The dominance of the problems posed by pluralism in the move from totalitarianism to democracy throughout the former Soviet Union and its satellite countries is apparent in the tensions that have developed within many multiracial or multiethnic societies in the process of this transition. These societies house substantial ethnic and religious minorities, and the problems posed by this pluralism are developing as part and parcel of the transition to liberal democracy. The rejection of totalitarian unity and the transition to democracy and a liberated pluralism is bringing in its wake a fragmentation that is part and parcel of a tendency to stifle a sense of community embodying values held in common. The problems of cultural, national, linguistic, and religious differences are emerging as a challenge at least equal to the restoration of democracy and material well-being.

Yet, while perhaps nowhere has the entrenchment of democracy coupled with the pervasive problems of multiracial, multiethnic, multireligious life been more pronounced than in the United States, the conceptual alternatives in which American democratic theory has been couched, far from offering a pathway for resolving the dilemma of balancing the features of individual freedom and communal solidarity, too often announce their ultimate irreconcilability. This problem is starkly exhibited in Alasdair MacIntyre's view that the United States may well be founded on incompatible moral and social ideals: on the one hand, a communitarian vision of a common "telos," and on the other hand, an ideal of individualism and pluralism. Thus, he holds that "We inhabit a kind of polity whose moral order requires systematic incoherence in the form of public allegiance to mutually inconsistent sets of principles."[1] Currently we seem to be bouncing from the extreme of the "grand melting pot" to the extreme of the "grand accumulator of fragmented parts."

The inability of so-called cutting-edge political theories to deal with the problems of pluralism and democracy throughout the world is highlighted in a journal symposium published in the closing years of the twentieth century.[2] The central issue presented there—the seeming remoteness of political theory from the contemporary events surrounding it and from the changes within political life—focuses primarily on the problems created by two central trends on the political scene, democracy and pluralism, as well as the key issues of libertarianism, communitarianism, and the self-other relations with which these issues are intertwined.

The theoretical trends which have taken hold in the United States are to a large extent the fruits of foreign soil. All too often communitarians utilize the model of the Greek *polis,* which is the model of community one naturally draws upon if one is influenced by Hegel, Marx, and the German tradition. This European model of community takes for granted a cultural homogeneity which has always been foreign to the United States and which is increasingly becoming extinct in far-ranging parts of the world. Yet, many American theorists remain wedded to either the offshoots of a critique of Marxism which is now virtually dead, or a tradition of ideas growing out of German romanticism. On the other hand, there is an escape from this to a decontextualized rationality or to the radical critiques offered by deconstruction.[3]

The problems of these latter two trends have been aptly lamented in the claim that, "the 'poststructuralist' hermeneutics of suspicion" developed in France, "dissolves structure into chains of signification or patterns of representation and what you have is a form of cultural studies radicalism that thinks that all is possible in society under all conditions and at all times."[4] On the other hand, the "prestigious paradigm" of rational choice theories "is catching on like hay fire in social science departments in American universities. But this paradigm also loses social structure from sight in that it proceeds from a model of social motivation divorced from sociohistorical context and explicable in terms of decontextualized and idealized rational choice theorems."[5] There is of course also a focus on a litany of conventional historical figures, and indeed, even theorists thoroughly committed to the deconstruction of such a corpus seem drawn to it. The unfruitful nature of this situation is expressed in the observation that "people in Central Eastern Europe took to the streets and fought for the establishment of liberal parliamentary democracies . . . and tolerant societies open to individual ambition and self-unfolding." But, "after two decades of poststructuralist, post-Foucaultian, psychoanalytic, feminist, postcolonial discourse," there is a great deal of suspicion about these.[6] Moreover, many of the current approaches represent to the intellectual voices of these emerging democracies "mindless group psychology, the return of a different kind of tribalism, and the rejection of what is best in the American liberal-democratic tradition."[7]

Through all of this the voice of Dewey has remained silent in any substantive sense. He has indeed been "passed by." This silence seems strange, indeed, as Dewey's philosophy is in large part a response to American culture as an ongoing manifestation of the issues of community and pluralism embedded in American democracy, starkly polarized above in MacIntyre's claim. Dewey's thinking, whose very fiber is interwoven with the climate of American culture, has a unique paradigmatic framework for casting a novel light on all of these issues, one born of an absorption in the problems of democracy, pluralism, and community which constituted the native soil within which the climate of American culture was nurtured and which provides the source of its renewed vitality for the current intellectual scene. And, central to this is Dewey's understanding of selfhood and scientific or experimental method. The significance of the first of these for the above issues can perhaps best be highlighted by a brief sketch of the nature of the self as operative in the respective positions of the American philosopher representative of each of the above major camps within the ongoing debates, namely Rawls, MacIntyre, and Rorty.

Rational choice models, such as that offered by Rawls, focus on an autonomous, unencumbered self whose disembedded, disembodied role is to impartially take the viewpoint of the other. Alasdair MacIntyre, along with such leading figures as Charles Tayler, Michael Walzer, and Michael Sandel, has questioned both the epistemological and normative claims of liberal political theories, offering ongoing critiques of the "unencumbered self." Postmodernists such as Michel Foucault, Jacques Derrida, and Jean-Francois Lyotard and, closely akin to these though much closer to home, the neo-pragmatist Richard Rorty, have gone so far as to question both the active, autonomous subject of ethical and political considerations and the possibility of any epistemological or normative claims.

Rawls's position is rooted in the self-interest driven principles of abstract justice formed by isolated, presocial individuals operating through a veil of ignorance as to their own position in society. It emphasizes the primacy of the individual, and the social features stem primarily from the aggregate decisions of individual selves stripped of any particular attributes. While his early position[8] involves an atomism in which separate individuals are ontologically prior to their unity, he later reinterprets his position, holding that the concept of "artificial agents" deliberating in the original position does not imply any particular metaphysical conception of the self or person.[9] But this still assumes that a self, abstracted out from its concrete relations and/or roles, can be coherently thought of as a functioning self, and that such a "self" can be a decision maker. In *Political Liberalism,*[10] which some interpreters view as a "later Rawls" that nullifies criticism of the "early Rawls," he in fact maintains his previous standpoint, claiming that the original position of the decision makers, with its veil of ignorance and nonhistorical nature, is the basis for his discussion throughout the book.[11] And, his qualifications of the abstract self remain the same as those offered in "Justice as Fairness." Thus, in spite of some new twists to his position, the core criticisms of it remain. The self that decides in Rawls's position is a peculiarly atemporal self, isolated from its historical attributes, ends, and attachments.

Although in *A Theory of Justice* Rawls speaks of the formation of the principles though "our" intuitions, in "Justice as Fairness" the formation of the principles through "our" intuitions is modified to the position that there is a certain ideal implied—that of Western liberal democracies[12]—and that the core values of the agent, now called "citizen," are not derived from basic intuitions but from an overlapping consensus. But Western liberal democracies seem to embody a pluralism such that there is no considered judgment that "we" must, as Rawls claims, "look for a conception of justice that nullifies the accidents of natural endowment and the contingencies of social circumstance as counters in a quest for political and economic advantage.[13] While the formation of this frame is done from a basis of atomic self-interest-driven individualism, then, it is peculiarly nonpluralistic. Moreover, the frame which emerges from the debate is a peculiarly atemporal, rationally constructed frame imposed from above upon the contingencies of real life existence and isolated from the historically changing conditions within and among types of identities. Social structure is in some sense postulated in abstract principles and social reasoning is by and large the application of the rule to the particular case.[14]

What one has, then, are rational, decision-making, atemporal, atomic selves structuring an atemporal frame in which existential contingencies and pluralistic differences alike have been left behind for commonly agreed-to abstract principles. Rawls's position, for all its contemporary trappings, is still caught in the traditional problems of top-down reasoning and atomic individualism, both of which block the path to pluralism, especially the pluralistic openness needed in a deep-seated clash of cultures.

This ahistorical nature of the self is negated in MacIntyre's communitarian approach, which reintroduces the classical Aristotelian concepts of character, happiness, and virtue and argues for the necessity of a general "narrative" view of action in a reformulated idea of character. This character is now understood as an ongoing narrative which determines the meaning of specific actions,[15] and it is impossible to judge the intent of any act by considering it in isolation from its context or the agent's life-narrative.

MacIntyre turns to a function of societies in which individuals are subordinate to the social structure implicit in complex activities or "practices," and in which individuals should endeavor to acquire the virtues necessary to achieve the goods internal to practices.[16] He recognizes that some practices are evil, and thus while holding that practices are subordinate to the traditions by which they are transmitted, he opposes the conservative, ideological understanding of tradition. A tradition "in good order" is "partially constituted by an argument about the goods the pursuit of which gives to that tradition its particular point and purpose."[17] As he states, "The fact that the self has to find its moral identity in and through its membership in communities . . . does not entail that the self has to accept the moral limitations of the particularity of those forms of community."[18]

Yet, arguments about traditions and the limitations of community require some aspect of autonomy and some dimension of the self which outstrips social roles, a dimension of the self which remains unaccounted for in McIntyre's position. His position accommodates self-enclosed "traditions," each providing a context of rationality for working out its coherent community of civility. It does not provide for an autonomous self or creative agency which eludes reduction to roles and which engages in the ongoing reconstruction of the tradition. His communities are self-enclosed through their absorption of their pasts, rather than open to enlarging, self-transcending, future-oriented participation in a reconstructive process.

Rorty, in *Contingency, Irony and Solidarity,* argues that there is not and cannot be a reconciliation in the conflict between our private desire for self-creation and our public sense of moral duty, though this has been the aim of all "moral metaphysicians" from Plato on. He offers us an image of liberal society, an ironist utopia, which holds fast to its ideals while recognizing the incommensurability of values and its own historical contingency. In rejecting foundationalism, Rorty disallows a function for argument of principles and turns to a commitment to conversation which allows for both novelty and the inclusion of others.

But, how does this openness take place? He holds that "All that can be done to explicate 'truth', 'knowledge', 'morality', 'virtue' is to refer us back to the concrete details of the culture in which these terms grew up and developed," and that "We have to take truth and virtue as whatever emerges from the conversation of Europe." He recognizes the validity of the objection that there is something very dangerous in the idea that truth is to be characterized as "the outcome of doing more of what we are doing now," for this "we" could well be the Orwellian state.[19] To answer this line of criticism Rorty resorts to Habermas's claim that such a definition of truth works only for the outcome of undistorted conversation, and that the Orwellian state is the paradigm of distortion. But, this of course will not quite do, for as Rorty well notes, Habermas offers transcendental principles, while he himself "must remain ethno-centric and offer examples." Rorty can only say: "'undistorted' means employing *our* criteria of relevance," where "we" are the ones who view truth and justice from the direction "marked by the successive stages of European thought." "We" all share this contingent starting point for our "ungrounded conversations."[20]

The undistorted conversation which is supposed to embody novelty, openness, and inclusiveness, then, turns out to involve an ethnocentrism which encloses us within our past. This enclosure is strengthened by Rorty's view that the self is "a tissue of contingent relations, a web which stretches backward and forward through past and future time,"[21] and human life is a "reweaving of such a web."[22] For, if the self is just the web, there is no creative agency to reweave, and its present cannot redirect the course of the future. The self and its conversation are alike ultimately enclosed within its past. Rorty emphasizes the importance of increasing our sensitivity to unfamiliar sorts of people to prevent marginalizing them, to promote solidarity.[23] Yet, the question remains as to how one becomes sensitive to "unfamiliar sorts of people" if one is stifled by ethnocentrism.[24] The ability to grasp different contexts and enter into the standpoint of the other requires a creative agent that transcends the confines of ethnocentric enclosure. In spite of, or perhaps better said, because of, our supposed liberation from the illusion of any embeddedness of ourselves within a thick reality with which we meaningfully interact and upon which our experience opens, we must remain peculiarly unliberated.

Each of the above positions yields, in its own way, a self which seems unable to execute its anointed community task. For Rawls, the self is locked in a present in which it functions in isolation from its past to make decisions which ignore the contingencies of the future. And, in spite of their radically different perspectives, which color their understandings of the formation of the self by closed or ethnocentric communities, MacIntyre and Rorty alike offer an ineffectual self shut within an effectual present.

The following discussion will focus on Dewey's understanding of the self, from the perspective of which notions of an atomic self independent of its tradition and roles or a conforming self exhausted by its tradition and roles do not merely pose problems for resolving traditional tensions but represent ontological contradictions as well. Moreover, it is within the dynamics of the emergence of selfhood that the primordial embeddedness of experimental inquiry within the very nature of, indeed as constitutive of, human experience can be found.

The essentially perspectival nature of experience and knowledge goes hand in hand with Dewey's radical rejection of the spectator theory of knowledge. All knowledge and experience are infused with interpretive aspects, funded with past experience. And, all interpretation stems from a perspective, a point of view. Knowledge is not a copy of anything pregiven, but involves a creative organization of experience which directs the way we focus on experience and which is tested by its workability in directing the ongoing course of future activities. In this way, experience and knowledge, in being perspectival, are at once experimental, providing a workable organization of problematical or potentially problematical situations. Not only are perspectives real within our environment, but without them there is no environment. Further, our worldly environment incorporates a perspectival pluralism, for diverse groups or diverse individuals bring diverse perspectives in the organization of experience. The universe exists independent of our intentional activity, but our worldly environment is inseparable from our meaning or intending it in certain ways, and these ways are inherently pluralistic. However, such pluralism, when properly understood, should not lead to the view that varying groups are enclosed within self-contained, myopic, limiting frameworks or points of view, cutting off the possibility of rational dialogue, for two reasons. It will be seen, first, that perspectives by their very nature are not self-enclosed but open onto a community perspective; and, second, perspectival pluralism provides the very matrix for rational dialogue and ongoing development.

For Dewey, mind, thinking, and selfhood are emergent levels of activity of organisms within nature. Meaning emerges in the interactions among conscious organisms, in the adjustments and coordinations needed for cooperative action in the social context. In communicative interaction, individuals take the perspective of the other in the development of their conduct, and in this way there develops the common content which provides the community of meaning and social matrix for the emergence of self-consciousness. Not only can selves exist only in relationship to other selves, but no absolute line can be drawn between our own selves and the selves of others, since our own selves are there for, and in our experience only insofar as, others exist and enter into our experience. The origins and foundation of the self, like those of mind, are social or intersubjective. As Dewey notes, it is through social interaction that "the self is both formed and brought to consciousness" (LW 10: 286).

In incorporating the perspective of the other, the self comes to incorporate the standards and authority of the group; there is a passive dimension to the self. Yet, the individual responds as a unique center of activity; there is a creative dimension to the self. Any self thus incorporates, by its very nature, both the conformity of the group perspective and the creativity of its unique individual perspective. Thus, Dewey holds that the tension between conservative and liberating factors lies in the very constitution of individual selves (LW 11:133). Freedom does not lie in opposition to the restrictions of norms and authority, but in a self-direction which requires the proper dynamic interaction of these two poles within the self. Thus, "the principle of authority" must not be understood as "purely restrictive power" but as providing direction (LW 11:133). Because of this dynamic interaction constitutive of the very nature of selfhood, the perspective of the novel, "liberating" pole always opens onto a common, "conserving" perspective.

These same dynamics are operative in community. The novel perspective of the individual is an emergent because of its relation to the institutions, traditions, and patterns of life that conditioned its novel emergence, and it gains its significance in light of the new common perspectives to which it gives rise. In this continual interplay of adjustment of attitudes, aspirations, and factual perceptions between the common perspective as the condition for the novel emergent perspective and the novel emergent as it conditions the common perspective, the dynamic of community is to be found. The act of adjustment between the novel perspective and the common perspective is the essential communicative dynamic of community.

This adjustment is neither assimilation of perspectives, one to the other, nor the fusion of perspectives into an indistinguishable oneness, but can best be understood as an "accommodation" in which each creatively affects, and is affected by, the other through accepted means of mediation of some sort. Thus a community is constituted by, and develops in terms of, the ongoing communicative adjustment between the activity constitutive of the novel individual perspective and the common or group perspective, and each of these two interacting poles constitutive of community gains its meaning, significance, and enrichment through this process of accommodation or adjustment. A free society, like a free individual, requires both the influencing power of authority as embodied in institutions and traditions and the innovative power of creativity as contextually set or directed novelty. In Dewey's words, "No amount of aggregated collective action of itself constitutes a community. . . . To learn to be human is to develop through the give-and-take of communication an effective sense of being an individually distinctive member of a community; one who understands and appreciates its beliefs, desires, and methods, and who contributes to a further conversion of organic powers into human resources and values. But this transition is never finished" (LW 2:330,332).

The individual is neither an isolatable discrete element in, nor an atomic building block of, a community. Rather, the individual represents the instigation of creative adjustments within a community, adjustments which change both poles which operate within the adjustment process. There is an intimate functional reciprocity between individual and social intelligence, a reciprocity based on the continual process of adjustment. Novelty within society is initiated by individuals, but such initiation can occur only because individuals are continuous with others and with social institutions of which they are a part. "Wants, choices and purposes have their locus in single beings," but the content is not "something purely personal" (LW 2:330,332). The "along with" is part of the very life process (LW 2:249).

The ability to provide the means of mediating within the ongoing dynamics of adjustment constitutes a community of any type as a community. The very nature of community requires the openness of perspectives. And, no community is constricted by closed community perspectives. The adjustment of incompatible perspectives at any level requires not an imposition from "on high" of abstract principles but a deepening to a more fundamental level of community. As two communities recognize their openness of horizons in coming to understand the perspective of the other, there can be adjustment founded on a deeper or broader community. The demands of the human condition, in its deepest sense, can be understood as the community of communities, not in the sense that it contains many self-enclosed communities, but in the sense that it is that grounding community upon which all other communities must be founded and upon which they all open.

Thus, Dewey stresses the ideal of a world community, and holds that what would make the great community precisely a community as opposed to a mere society is "intercommunication," expressed above as the organs of accommodation which allow for the ongoing interplay of novelty and conformity (LW 2:367). The understanding of a radically diverse way of life, or way of making sense of things, is not to be found from above by imposing one's own reflective perspective upon such diversity, but rather from beneath, by penetrating through such differences to the various ways of making sense of the world as they emerge from the essential characteristics of beings fundamentally alike confronting a common reality in an ongoing process of change. Such a deepening may change conflict into community diversity, or it may lead to an emerging consensus of the wrongness of one of the conflicting positions. Such a deepening does not negate the use of intelligent inquiry, but rather opens it up, frees it from the products of its past in terms of rigidities and abstractions, and focuses it on the dynamics of concrete human existence. In this way, over the course of time, incompatible perspectives, though not proved right or wrong, are resolved by the weight of argument as reasons and practices are worked out in the ongoing course of inquiry. If such adjustments do not emerge, then community has broken down.

To understand one's own stance on any issue is to understand its inherently perspectival approach and the illuminating light which other perspectives can rightfully cast upon it. The development of the ability both to create and to respond constructively to the creation of novel perspectives, as well as to incorporate the perspective of the other, not as something totally alien, but as something sympathetically understood, is at once growth of the self. Thus to deepen and expand the horizons of community is at once to deepen and expand the horizons of the selves involved in the ongoing dynamics of adjustment. The sense of history is very much tied to Dewey's understanding of the reconstruction taking place in the present. Any novel perspective emerges from a cumulative process or history of adjustment which yields enrichment of intelligibility both of the old and of the new. By looking backward we can view the historical development within the social process, the direction of the movement. However, this looking backward is not some passive recovery of what once was but rather is a construction taking place in the present, and the past, as interpreted in the present, sets goals for the future. Thus Dewey stresses that historical materials, in their most important sense, do not signify "the past and gone and the remote," but rather a heightened perception of "elements active in present experience, elements that are seeking expansion and outlet and that demand clarification and which some phase of social life . . . brings to the focus of a selective, coherently arranged and growing experience" (LW 11:209–10).

Perspectival pluralism, though incorporating at its deepest level the endless activity of adjustment rather than convergence toward final completed truth, does not involve the stultifying self-enclosement of a relativism in terms of arbitrary conceptual schemes or an historicism in terms of present happenstance. Rather, it involves an ontologically grounded temporalism in which perspectives emerge within the context of a past which presents itself in the richness of the present and which is oriented toward an indefinite future. What is involved is not a liberation from the ontologically grounded possibilities presented by the past, a position which has been seen to house its own kind of cultural historicism, but a liberation from a restricted access to them. Our primal epistemic and ontological openness to "the other" and its demands, as understood within pragmatism, results in more pluralism, not less.

The dynamics of the experimental method, which embody "the fundamental principles of the relationship of life to its surroundings"(LW

2:106–7), are the vehicle by which the past becomes effective in the reconstruction of the present, leading to integration and fulfillment through organized movement. In this way, science is "operative art" (LW 1:269). The proper functioning of the experimental method is, for Dewey, precisely the artful functioning of experience. Indeed, in the "immediate"[25] sense of the qualitative character of *an* experience as a unified whole, or experience in its aesthetic dimension, the experimental method is embodied in its most intensified concrete unification or fusion. The sense of the qualitative character of an experience as a unified, integrated whole involves a sense of its temporal flow, its own "little history," and the dynamics of experimentalism as providing the creatively organizing and ordering movement which brings to fruition the sense of the internal integration and fulfillment of the experience. Thus Dewey notes that "scientific and artistic systems embody the same fundamental principles of the relationship of life to its surroundings," and indeed the differences between the work of the scientist and the work of the artist are "technical and specialized, rather than deep-seated" (LW 2:106–7).

It has been seen that the ability to recognize the limitation of one's own perspective and to appropriate its openness onto other perspectives is at once growth of the self. Growth of self incorporates an ever more encompassing sympathetic understanding of varied and diverse interests, thus leading to tolerance not as a sacrifice but as an enlargement of self; it involves as well the concomitant reconstruction of the institutions and practices which become incorporated within the self's conserving dimension, and at times also demands a reconstruction of the very organs of adjustment of the community which ground such reconstructive dynamics. Rationally directed change leads to growth both for the individual and the community. But for Dewey, rationality "is not a force to evoke against impulse and habit. It is the attainment of a working harmony among diverse desires" (MW 14:136–37). As he stresses, more "passions, not fewer, is the answer"(MW 14:136–37). The operation of reason cannot be isolated from the concrete human being in its entirety. Moreover, the human organism and the nature within which it is located are both rich with the qualities and values of our everyday experience, and thus experimental method as operative in the process of living must serve the qualitative fullness of human interests. In this way, rationally directed concrete growth, achieved through the expansive integration or harmonizing of novelty and continuity as guided by experimental inquiry, leads to the esthetic-moral enrichment of human experience.

The various features discussed thus far are embodied in Dewey's understanding of democracy. Dewey stresses that democracy is not a particular body of institutions or a particular form of government, but is rather the political expression of the functioning of the experimental method. Any social structure or institution can be brought into question through the use of social intelligence guided by universalizing ideals, leading to reconstructive activity which enlarges and reintegrates the situation and the selves involved, providing at once a greater degree of authentic self-expression and a greater degree of social participation. In this way, democracy provides for a society which controls its own evolution, and participation in this process is "necessary from the standpoint of both the general social welfare and the full development of human beings as individuals" (LW 11:217–18).

Dewey, then, can point out that growth itself is the only moral "end," that the moral meaning of democracy lies in its contribution to the growth of every member of society (LW 12:181,186) and that growth involves the rational resolution of conflict (MW 5:327). In this way, the moral import of democracy, for Dewey, lies in the fact that it is the ideal of community life itself.[26] Any authentic organization involves a shared value or goal, and the overreaching goal of a human society is precisely this control of its own evolution. Thus, the ultimate "goal" is growth or development, not final completion. Though Dewey refers to growth as an "end," he does not intend this in a technical sense of "end," and indeed, growth can best be understood not as an end to be attained but as a dynamic embedded in the ongoing process of life, just as the experimental method is not an end to be achieved but a dynamic embedded in the very structure of experience.

This in turn indicates that neither democracy nor the working ideal of universality can imply that differences should be eliminated or melted down, for these differences provide the necessary materials by which a society can continue to grow. Though society indeed represents social meanings and social norms, yet social development is possible only through the dynamic interrelation of this dimension with the unique, creative individual. The creative perspectives of individuals offer the liberating possibilities of new reconstructions. The liberating is also precarious. But the liberating, the precarious, the novel, occur within the context of tradition, stability, continuity, community. The demands of adjusting the old and the new, the stability of conformity and the novelty of creativity, "is inherent in, or a part of, the very texture of life" (LW 11:133).

A true community, as by its very nature incorporating an ontologically grounded temporalism and perspectival pluralism requiring ongoing growth or horizonal expansion, is far from immune to the hazardous pitfalls and wrenching clashes that provide the material out of which ever deepening and expanding horizons are constituted. But as Dewey points out,

> Life itself consists of phases in which the organism falls out of step with the march of surrounding things and then recovers unison with it. . . . And, in a growing life, the recovery is never mere return to a prior state, for it is enriched by the state of disparity and resistance through which it has successfully passed. . . . Life grows when a temporary falling out is a transition to a more extensive balance of the energies of the organism with those of the conditions under which it lives (LW 10:19–20).

When there is lacking the reorganizing and ordering capabilities of intelligence, the imaginative grasp of authentic possibilities, the vitality of motivation, or sensitivity to the "felt" dimensions of existence, all of which are needed for ongoing reconstructive horizontal expansion, then instead of growth the result is irreconcilable factionalism. The acceptance of just such a lack is what Dewey sees as the basis for the rise of totalitarian states. As he characterizes the rejection of pluralism inherent in the basic tenets of the totalitarian moral code, it incorporates the belief that if human beings "are permitted to exercise freedom of mind their policies and decisions will be so swayed by personal and class interests that the final outcome will be division, conflict and disintegration" (LW 15:177). What will solve present problems and provide the means for ongoing growth of the self and the community is human intelligence with its creativity, sensitivity, imagination, and moral awareness geared to the human condition in all of its qualitative richness.

The skills of experimental inquiry are needed not just for the adequate exploration of specific subject matter but for the possibility of the interrelated ongoing reconstruction and expansion of the self, values, and the institutions and practices of the community, including the very organs of adjudication for the communicative adjustments which make possible such ongoing reconstructions and expansions. Experimental inquiry or "the method of intelligence," as it functions to further the enrichment of the fullness of concrete human existence involves, in Dewey's words, "wide sympathy and keen sensitiveness, and persistence in the face of the disagreeable," all of which in turn allow for the "balance of interests" needed for intelligent analysis and decision (MW 12:173–74).

Dewey stresses that to have "anything that can be called a community in its pregnant sense there must be values prized in common" (LW 13:71). But he is not seeking common values as a type of common content which infringes on individualism and pluralism, which erodes freedom or melts down differences, a situation which he disparages as "a factitious sense of direct union and communal solidarity" (LW 13:176), an artificial "moral consensus" which exits through a "unity of beliefs and aims" and is "of the very essence of totalitarian states" (LW 13:157). These values prized in common are values which foster aesthetic and moral sensibility and a concomitant attunement to the other, creative intelligence, imagination, and a healthy common sense rooted in the cultivation of these qualities. These qualities promote an atmosphere in which one can develop one's values and talents, promote the development of individuals who can engage in dialogue in such a way that society can continually reconstruct itself in a manner that will lead to the ongoing thriving of individuals and communities alike through a process of participatory self-government, directed by the dynamics that direct growth in all areas of human activity—that is, the dynamics of the experimental method that are embedded in the very life process and its development within the emergence of selfhood. This synthesis of community-shared values and pluralistic freedom is precisely what Dewey sees as necessary to prevent the rise of regimes "which claim they can do for individuals what the latter cannot by any possibility do for themselves" (LW 14:93), because the inadequacy of "doing for themselves" is based on the empty character of negative freedom, of freedom without a community solidarity of "values prized in common" (LW 13:71).

Dewey's position unabashedly reflects its nourishment in the climate of American culture, yet it speaks with a unique vitality not only to the ongoing attempts to balance community and pluralism here at home but also to those engaged in emerging political situations around the world as humans struggle more and more with the issues of liberal democracy and community in the context of pluralism and diversity and the need to be open to the voice of "the other." It offers not mere descriptions of the conditions from which it emerged, but depictions of yet-to-be-realized possibilities of betterment, recognitions of what is required for any culture to achieve what it has the potential to become. Passing Dewey by is not a way to discard outmoded baggage from the past but to ignore an important road map for the future as we enter the new millennium.

NOTES

1. Alasdair MacIntyre, "Is Patriotism a Virtue?" Lindley Lecture, University of Kansas, 1984, 19–20.
2. *Political Theory* 23, no. 4 (November, 1995): 635–88.
3. See Ibid. for an examination of these trends.
4. Seyla Benhabib, "Response," Ibid., p.679.
5. Ibid.
6. Ibid., 676–77.
7. Ibid.

8. John Rawls, *A Theory of Justice* (Cambridge: Harvard University Press, 1971).

9. John Rawls, "Justice as Fairness," *Philosophy and Public Affairs* 14 (1985): 238, 239n.

10. John Rawls, *Political Liberalism* (New York: Columbia University Press, 1993).

11. Ibid.; see, for example, 22–28, 208, 242n.

12. Rawls, "Justice as Fairness," 223–51.

13. Rawls, *A Theory of Justice,* 15. In *Political Liberalism,* 147–48, Rawls holds that an overlapping consensus is quite different from what he calls a "modus vivendi," which is a compromise position between individuals or states at odds in aims or interests. However, this distinction is not relevant to the points under discussion.

14. The legislators of justice can determine whether the implementation of any given set of principles at any given time is feasible, but Rawls thinks it hard to imagine that we do not now have all the knowledge we need for the feasibility test. See *A Theory of Justice,* 137.

15. Alasdair MacIntyre, *After Virtue,* 2nd ed. (Notre Dame, Ind.: University of Notre Dame Press, 1984), see especially chap. 15.

16. Ibid., 191.

17. Ibid., 222.

18. Ibid., 221.

19. Richard Rorty, *Consequences of Pragmatism* (Minneapolis: University of Minnesota Press, 1982), 173. Rorty here creates a dialogue between the pragmatist—which he considers himself to be, and the defender of the Enlightenment or the traditional philosopher.

20. Ibid., 173–74.

21. Richard Rorty, *Contingency, Irony, and Solidarity* (Cambridge: Cambridge University Press, 1989), 41

22. Ibid., 43.

23. Ibid., xvi.

24. Rorty's focus on imagination as the vehicle of increased sensitivity to unfamiliar sorts of people does not eliminate the problem but highlights it. He speaks of the meaningless, emotive function of imagination, as opposed to literal or cognitive content with its truth-value property. (These characterizations arise in his discussion of metaphor in relation to the contingency of language (Ibid., 18), but in his discussion of the contingency of the self in the following chapter, it can be seen that what holds for metaphor holds as well for imagination (Ibid., 36). This is in a sense a new twist to the positivistic dichotomy between the cognitive or meaningful and the emotive or meaningless, a twist that now views the dichotomy from the temporal perspective of the structurally located fixity of the old versus the

utter capriciousness of a disconnected new (Ibid., 17). This capriciousness can be seen in Rorty's assertion that "the difference between genius and fantasy" is that the former represents "idiosyncrasies which just happen to catch on with other people" (Ibid., 37). Rorty's break between meaning and the meaningless, between the cognitive and the emotive, the literal and the metaphorical, is ultimately a break between past, present, and future.

25. Immediate experience, as here used, is not the experience of pure immediacy—which does not in fact exist in experience.

26. Dewey makes a distinction between democracy as a social idea and political democracy as a system of government, but notes that the two are of course connected. See *The Public and Its Problems* (LW 2:325).

NINE

Pressing Dewey's Advantage

JOSEPH MARGOLIS

I assume, of course, that the leading pragmatists of the day are Hilary Putnam and Richard Rorty, but I judge their innovations to be almost completely played out by now, without having yielded any increase in power in pragmatism's favor. In that sense they have indeed, together, prepared the ground for an improved pragmatism by isolating the most up-to-date ways of viewing "meaning," "truth," "realism," "knowledge," "philosophical reasons," and the like. Undoubtedly, a revived pragmatism must now contend with the strongest currents of late twentieth-century philosophy if it is to make its way competitively. But the unfinished business remains unfinished: our guides have brought us to the water's edge.

No one would deny that Putnam and Rorty have identified—almost singlehandedly—the main issues pragmatism must confront if it is to sustain its newfound vigor. They themselves, I'm afraid, have not fulfilled the strong expectations prompted by their considerable influence. They are, by their own admission, Deweyan in orientation, but their innovations are distinctly less compelling than are Dewey's at his most original. (That has yet to be shown.)

They have forced pragmatism to address (perhaps to revisit) a whole raft of questions, latent in Dewey's best work, raised now to the level of an explicit confrontation. These include, I would say, the following at least: Is the analysis of knowledge, reality, right conduct pointless or futile in conceptual or practical terms, now that the canons of invariance, cognitive privilege, necessity, essence, indubitability, neutrality are admitted to be no longer compelling? Or, Can there, under the conditions of flux and historicity, be a meaningful recovery limited to provisional and divergent constructions relative to our changing interests and societal practice? If the answer to the second question is yes: What kind of rigor, competence, effective constraint can still be assigned the work of philosophical analysis? In particular: What answers can be given, conformably, to the classic questions of realism, objectivity, explanatory adequacy, holism, truth, normativity, subjectivity, minds and selves, legitimation, intra- and intercultural incommensurabilities? A further, somewhat more local question insinuates itself: What did Putnam and Rorty miss or misunderstand about the enlargement or improvement of pragmatism? And, What more telling undertakings might be recommended, now that we have (if we have) the evidence of the short life of their own proposals?

Putnam admits very candidly the collapse of his official pragmatism (approximately identified as "internal realism") and Rorty has deliberately cast the entire Deweyan critique in the postmodernist mode, which has produced its own kind of conceptual cul-de-sac. By a curious twist of fate, Putnam and Rorty, absorbed in the primary contest of their very different, opposed projects, bring a plausible charge of relativism against one another and find that that same charge sticks like a tar baby to the accuser as well. The upshot is quite strange and wonderful. For the distraction proves to be far more important than their own local plans: Putnam's, to formulate a viable scientific realism, which (he realizes) should yield in a Deweyan direction; Rorty's, to displace utterly the grand canon of Western metaphysics and epistemology, which (as it turns out) cannot find a rhetoric more fundamental than Dewey's to turn against Dewey's acknowledgment of the continued pertinence of the questions postmodernism would dismiss.

The irony is that, by these reversals, Putnam and Rorty inadvertently press pragmatism (through Dewey himself) to examine more closely the heterodox options they themselves perfunctorily dismiss—for instance along relativistic and historicist lines. The fact is, these possibilities were never central to the work of the classic figures, but they have taken on a new significance among the various programs of objectivism, naturalism, materialism, holism, constructivism, postmodernism, which are now contending for a place in the philosophical sun. They therefore encourage pragmatism to air the most radical conceptual options that it may need to address if it is to define itself firmly in its second life.

Pragmatism appears to be the only currently viable American philosophical movement that is at all favorably disposed to exploring these possibilities, though it must be admitted Putnam and Rorty have given them short shrift. The fact remains that any recovery of philosophy's prospects, after we abandon the canons already mentioned, can hardly afford to ignore the challenge of defining the limits of conceptual tolerance under the potentially enabling conditions of flux and historicity.

RORTY AND THE POSTMODERNIST DISTORTION OF DEWEY'S PRAGMATISM

It's the same man, Richard Rorty, who, in a lecture that ostensibly addressed the philosophical needs of feminism, after having revitalized pragmatism two decades earlier, now fully equates pragmatism with his own brand of postmodernism.[1] Rorty's advice to the feminists has proved to be a very sly maneuver—half-right but misleading in its provocation—fortified by skimming off and deforming in the postmodernist manner some unguarded remarks of Dewey's, whom he professed to follow. Rorty's invitation to the feminists would, on an innocent reading, have suggested that absorbing the feminist claim "into *our* [the 'pragmatists'] view of moral progress" meant reconciling the two by acceptable philosophical means. But of course, for Rorty, it meant nothing of the kind!

It's the same man who opened his well-known manifesto, "The Contingency of Language," a few years before making his gesture, with the following remark, which draws on what is already familiar in James and Dewey: "Almost two hundred years ago, the idea that truth was made rather than found began to take hold of the imagination of Europe."[2] You must bear in mind that what Rorty is referring to cannot fail to include the constructivist (*not* idealist) treatment of realism that Hegel fashions in the *Phenomenology*, that makes its way by sparer and sparer means moving from Peirce to James to Dewey, but that would preclude altogether the postmodernist reading of the same remark. (Rorty, you remember, is dead set against the idea that claims are "made true.")

The clue Rorty points to regarding the classic pragmatists appeared in its leanest and most compelling form in two flawed volumes of Dewey's: *Experience and Nature* and *Logic: The Theory of Inquiry*. These plainly invite a strengthened pragmatism that Dewey never actually pursued. Hence, when, in the same essay, Rorty tips his hand to his own postmodernist use of Dewey, we are alerted at once (candidly enough) to what *he* means by a "strong" philosopher (a philosopher to compare favorably with Harold Bloom's "strong poet"). Rorty means to "misread" what Dewey meant, wherever it suits his purpose—as in giving philosophical advice to the feminists. So he says, beguilingly: "Conforming to my own precepts, I am not going to offer arguments against the vocabulary I want to replace. Instead I am going to try to make the vocabulary I favor look attractive by showing how it may be used to describe a variety of topics."[3]

This is a postmodernist maneuver in the guise of being an extension of Dewey's pragmatism. It elevates a hint into an entire method. Although Dewey would "agree" with Rorty in opposing the straightest canonical forms of "universalism" and "realism," he would have insisted that there *are* philosophically compelling reasons (still needed) for dismissing such doctrines. He would have seen no point at all in recommending their replacement without benefit of argument, and he would have affirmed that the legitimating arguments needed would not have conflicted with fair objections against the canon. Dewey would have envisioned a *third* option between the old philosophical fixities and Rorty's reckless postmodernism. In a word, Dewey never supposed his own recovery of realism was philosophically arbitrary or quixotic. He *had* his reasons, which, quite frankly, Rorty deforms in the postmodernist way.

If we take Rorty at his word—and why should we not?—then the advice he tenders the feminists belongs to the same lesson he offers in the manifesto: he thereby loses the recuperative intent of Dewey's entire doctrine; for, as a "postmodernist" (or "postphilosopher"), he means to sweep away the legitimacy and legitimating competence of philosophy itself vis-à-vis the sciences and the work of moral and political reflection.

This might have counted as Rorty's intended improvement of pragmatism. But you cannot find in Rorty's writings an actual argument to the effect that if we abandon "universalism" and "realism"—effectively, "Cartesianism" or "objectivism" or "absolutism" or "the God's-eye view"—we *will* assuredly find that there is no formulable or pertinent difference between (say) philosophy and poetry (or argument and rhetoric) or between pragmatism and postmodernism! It is true that Rorty reminds us of the hopelessness of the seventeenth- and eighteenth-century philosophies Kant and Hegel so masterfully exposed—almost in preparation for the advent of pragmatism. The reminder is still a welcome one, since so much of twentieth-century philosophy has retreated to the paradoxes of Cartesianism and so much of Anglo-American philosophy has forgotten its Hegel.[4] But the reminder conveys a more sanguine view of philosophy than Rorty would care to support.

Rorty will have none of it. By his "strong," postmodernist reading ("misprision," in Bloom's idiom),[5] he means that philosophy cannot continue in the manner practiced by the strong figures of the past, even if "universalism" and "realism" are abandoned, as they must be. I agree that we should abandon modal necessities, apodicticities, essentialisms, teleologisms, universalisms, exceptionless invariances, First Philosophies, the incontestable verities of a higher Reason; but I cannot see how it follows from conceding that, that philosophical analysis and legitimation have no further role to play. Dewey would surely have protested. Rorty's identification of pragmatism and postmodernism still seems completely willful.

BERNSTEIN'S RESPONSE

Rorty's strong dilemma: choose Cartesianism (or "realism" or objectivism) or choose postmodernism is too simple, hardly a motivated choice. On pragmatist and Hegelian grounds, the first option is a dead letter. At the very least, it cannot be resurrected without suitably answering Kant's and Hegel's objections. Hardly anyone believes that that can be done. The second is arbitrary, by deliberate default. It also risks being incoherent wherever we concede that questions of truth and evidence, however pertinent in the general run of first-order inquiries, are not really intelligible unless their legitimation is also intelligible. On this reading, when Rorty says—"I am not going to offer arguments . . ."—speaking in his postmodernist voice but not as a standard pragmatist, what he says is admittedly irrelevant, possibly even incoherent: he is *not* waiving (for the moment) the defense of his conceptions of truth and knowledge and reality and norms and natures; he is affirming (or insinuating by default) that it no longer makes sense to make any such effort! He never tells us why.

Many fail to see the Achilles' heel of Rorty's ingenuities. There is, he apparently believes, no genuine philosophy that does not make "universalist" or "essentialist" claims, but he also believes there are no viable such philosophies to consider! None could ever be convincingly defended and no other options are before us. But the argument is missing.

Responding to this stalemate, it's very much to Richard Bernstein's credit (Bernstein has been tracking Rorty for years) never to have been tempted by Rorty's postmodernism. Bernstein repeatedly criticizes Rorty's "postmodern" turn: "for Rorty [he says], contingency, historicism, and nominalism 'go all the way down.'" Charged with "self-referential inconsistency," Bernstein adds, Rorty "evades"—recommends *evading*—"the accusation of self-defeating relativism."[6] What Bernstein says here (against Rorty) is true enough and important. But we must divide the question; we must take care to consider (against Bernstein himself, against Rorty and Putnam as well) that doctrines like relativism, historicism, incommensurabilism—which are very different from nominalism, since they (but not nominalism) raise questions about the legitimacy of our evidentiary sources—*may* be coherently and defensibly formulated. At the very least, their defense should be separated from the defense of postmodernism, since they (but not postmodernism) invite legitimative briefs. In any case, Bernstein's is an objection (requiring courage) offered by one friend against another.

Bernstein correctly remarks that pragmatism "anticipated" the positive critique embedded in what (*per* Jean-François Lyotard) has come to be called "the postmodern condition"[7]: going beyond Lyotard's report, pragmatism has been pointedly "concerned with the question of how to *respond* to [postmodernism's] challenges."[8] This is a strong (though incomplete) diagnosis, which collects Bernstein's papers from the end of the '80s—although his book *(The New Constellation)* was published as late as 1992. It identifies an important lacuna in the analytic narrative.

The trouble with Bernstein's treatment of the pragmatist "response" he favors is that the best he can offer is a form of *pluralism* that he neither justifies nor shows us how to justify (for instance, in separating pluralism and relativism in a principled way). Bernstein's proffer is completely unsupported, though hardly for postmodernist reasons. It is perhaps no more than a telling piece of evidence of the profound impasse the whole of Western philosophy had come to at the end of the twentieth century. On that reading, the impasse Rorty obliged pragmatism to address in the '90s is itself a legible emblem of the larger impasse of the whole of Western philosophy. You begin to see the importance of strengthening pragmatism's hand beyond its original concerns. You must bear in mind that Rorty and Putnam *are,* however puzzlingly, pluralists of a sort (of very different sorts) *and* that each, even more insistently than Bernstein (but no more convincingly), rejects relativism and fends off any and all efforts to be tagged as a relativist.

There's an irony there. Bernstein is right to remark that, for Rorty, "contingency, historicism, and nominalism 'go all the way down'"; but he fails to see the full import of this part of Rorty's thesis. Contingency and historicism *do* indeed "go all the way down"—I won't bother with nominalism, it's irrelevant here and untenable in any case. But since Rorty embraces radical contingency and historicism, I say he cannot escape relativism; and since he also insists he is not a relativist, he has no further option but to declare himself a postmodernist, that is, a conceptual anarchist in philosophical matters who can in good conscience deny the need to answer the original charge. (It does not appear on the postmodernist's screen!)

I take the maneuver to be incoherent on the following grounds: that first-order inquiries cannot abandon questions of truth and evidence; that such questions make no sense without a second-order legitimation of our epistemic concepts; and that the distinction between first- and second-order matters is itself a second-order matter.[9] (This triad of distinctions helps to explain what is missing in Rorty's strong disjunction between the universalisms and realisms he abjures and the postmodernism he would have us adopt.) Besides, what is the point of declaring that one is a nominalist or a historicist or an opponent of invariant or necessary regularities, or a postmodernist for that matter, if saying so is *not* a *claim* of any sort?

Dewey also embraces radical contingency; he might have adopted historicism, which Mead barely begins to explore, but he does not do so.

What he admits, however, does already implicate *some* concession in relativism's direction, which he nowhere pursues. For his part, Bernstein, who expressly opposes relativism—in fact, offers a form of "pluralism" (not otherwise specified) as the missing third option between objectivism and relativism[10]—risks falling in with the old "objectivists" since he opposes a contingency that goes "all the way down"; *or* risks opposing Dewey (whom he claims to follow) *or* risks being unable to distinguish between his own thesis and Rorty's (which he takes to be self-refuting). In effect, Bernstein stalemates his own solution. What I am signaling here is just *how* the dispute between Putnam and Rorty, the insertion of Bernstein's inchoate third option, and Dewey's own adherence to radical contingency oblige us to consider whether and to what extent pragmatism entails, or is reconcilable with, one or another form of relativism—and how that affects, for instance, the quarrels about truth and realism.

Bernstein is the unwitting litmus of the entire affair. If you look carefully at his *The New Constellation,* you will find that it is even less confident about the prospects of pluralism than the earlier and more important book, *Beyond Objectivism and Relativism* (1983). In the earlier book, reading Rorty and Putnam more conventionally as pragmatists (though with strenuous caveats in Rorty's case and no actual discussion of Putnam's alternative), Bernstein appears to be preparing the ground for something akin to Putnam's conception of pluralism as a third option between the unacceptable extremes of objectivism and relativism. The narrative is not altogether easy to follow. Bear with me, please: I shall have to hop from one source to another to put the account in a clear light.

PUTNAM'S ALTERNATIVE

In *Reason, Truth and History* (1981), the classic locus of Putnam's "internal realism"—Putnam's most sustained statement of what, *later,* came to be regarded (on his allowance) as his own version of pragmatism but, at the beginning of the '80s, was still formulated as a strong (perhaps the strongest) version of (a kind of scientific) realism he found he could still support—Putnam announced that his "aim" was "to break the strangle hold which a number of dichotomies appear to have on the thinking of both philosophers and laymen. Chief among these [he notes] is the dichotomy between objective and subjective views of truth and reason."[11]

He plainly thinks of the division between the objectivists and the subjectivists as a division chiefly between Anglo-American analytic and continental philosophies, but he also associates Thomas Kuhn and Paul Feyerabend (whom Bernstein considers) together with Michel Foucault (and the French poststructuralists in general) in terms of the subjectivist or relativist alternative. In "Two Philosophical Perspectives," the central essay of the *Reason, Truth and History* volume, Putnam goes a step further to contrast "metaphysical realism" and "the *internalist* perspective" (or, simply, what he calls "internal realism"). In effect, he offers a glimpse of his third option between metaphysical realism (or "absolutism" or "Cartesianism") and relativism.

In the first perspective, "the world [says Putnam] consists of some fixed totality of mind-independent objects. There is exactly one true and complete description of 'the way the world is.' Truth involves some sort of correspondence relation between words or thought-signs and external things and sets of things." This effectively captures what Bernstein understands by the term "objectivism"—a doctrine he of course opposes.

In the other perspective, the most important consideration proves to be this: that "*What objects does the world consist of?* is a question that it only makes sense to ask *within* a theory or description. Many 'internalist' philosophers, though not all, [Putnam observes,] hold further that there is more than one 'true' theory or description of the world. 'Truth', in an internalist view, is some sort of (idealized) rational acceptability—some sort of ideal coherence of our beliefs with each other and with our experience *as these experiences are themselves represented in our belief system*—and not correspondence with mind-independent or discourse-independent 'states of affairs.'"[12] The thesis is broadly Kantian in Putnam's hands; more Hegelian in Bernstein's. Ultimately, it proves to take a pragmatist form in both, though Putnam eventually treats this same thesis as open to an unacceptable idealist reading.

About these options, you must bear in mind: (1) that Putnam's "internal realist" doctrine was not originally meant to capture his "pragmatism"—the use of the label was forced on him by fair-minded commentators, and he has allowed the slippage as a reasonable reading;[13] (2) that Putnam has now abandoned the ("pragmatist") internalism developed from the position just cited, largely on the grounds of having been fatally seduced by William James's "idealism" and subjective representationalism[14]—although it is not yet clear what, apart from his recovering a strong sense of realism ("natural realism," as he now names the thesis, under the influence of John McDowell), actually constitutes his present position; (3) that Putnam had been (and still is) a *pluralist* in the sense already remarked; (4) that he realized he had to defend *the realist sense of his pluralism* against Rorty's charge of relativism, by introducing at the very end of the book—fatally, it now seems—the arbitrary notion of a necessary (or rationally compelling) *Grenzbegriff* of truth and reason that would offset the possibility that *his own pluralism was in effect a closet rel-*

ativism;[15] (5) that Rorty took this weakness in Putnam's attempted defense to confirm his own postmodernist critique;[16] (6) that Donald Davidson may have been drawn to improvise his own counterpart "realist" reading of the correspondence and coherence theories of truth—perhaps not yet under Rorty's full influence—which was explicitly directed (at least in part) against what he took to be Putnam's untenable alternative;[17] (7) that Davidson has now acknowledged, in commenting on Rorty's own philosophy (which he is unwilling to accept in its postmodernist form), the "blunder" (his own word) of his own attempt to join correspondence and coherence in the form of a *theory* of truth—in particular, Davidson has distanced himself from Rorty's inaccurate attribution (and untenable advocacy) of the postmodernist treatment of truth;[18] (8) that Rorty has now relented (somewhat unreliably) under Davidson's criticism, but still means to recover the validity of his own postmodernist account of truth—which appears to be an odd mélange of his postmodernism and Davidson's "naturalizing" (the stance of "A Coherence Theory of Truth and Knowledge");[19] (9) that Rorty's deliberate "misprision" of the views of other philosophers has begun to unravel—most notably, among recent respondents (that is, among respondents who are still alive), most notably Quine;[20] and (10) that we also have protests by many hands—against Rorty—in the name of ensuring an accurate interpretion of Dewey and Wittgenstein and Heidegger!

THE ROAD TOWARD RELATIVISM

Apart from the relative force of Putnam's and Bernstein's respective analyses, their positions on the extreme options are very similar. In *Reason, Truth and History,* Putnam rejects as completely untenable the strong—"Cartesian" or "objectivist" or "God's-Eye"—disjunction between the "objective" and the "subjective." At the time of writing, Putnam was not entirely clear about the full implications of his own view. More recently, in the Gifford Lectures (1990), published as *Renewing Philosophy* (1992), Putnam featured the choice between "the absolute conception of the world" (which he associated, for expository reasons, with the view of Bernard Williams) and what he now characterizes more explicitly as "relativism" (a doctrine he associates, in the English-language tradition with Williams again, and, more revealingly, with Rorty and French philosophy, for example with Jacques Derrida).

He notes for instance: "My own philosophical evolution has been from a view like Bernard Williams's to a view much more like John Dewey's," by which he means to mark the acceptable middle ground between absolutism and relativism and to distance his own pragmatism from Rorty's. He means to feature Dewey's pluralism: that is, the rejection of "a final theory," an insistence on the inseparability of theoretical and practical reason, and an acknowledgment of the essential epistemic inseparability of the subjective and the objective (by means of which, for instance, idealism may be effectively evaded).

In fact, Putnam says: "In this book *[Renewing Philosophy]* I want to explain and, to the extent possible in the space available, to justify this change in my philosophical attitude."[21] Hence, by the beginning of the '90s, Putnam is clearly aware that his own version of scientific realism has had to yield in the direction of a pragmatized realism (à la Dewey), *which invites the relativist charge he wishes to evade.* He now offers a tripartite choice between "absolutism," "relativism," and a Deweyan-like pluralism—which comes very close to the general lines of Bernstein's contrast between objectivism and relativism and the preference for a pluralism (between the two) that (in Bernstein) owes as much to Kuhn, Jürgen Habermas, Hans-Georg Gadamer, and Hannah Arendt as it does to Dewey.

The important difference between Bernstein's and Putnam's accounts, quite frankly, is that Bernstein's is primarily a reportorial summary, whereas Putnam's is based on an original attempt to solve the puzzle they share: Bernstein cannot really claim to offer a solution (beyond a sketch of what would be needed if it could be secured); and Putnam has now made the attempt, which, in his own opinion, has failed.[22]

Putnam would probably claim to have succeeded in recovering a defensible "realism" nevertheless—largely through John McDowell's rejection of an "interface" between cognizer and cognized.[23] But the fact remains that McDowell has nothing to say beyond countering Putnam's unnecessary Cartesian demons or Davidson's excessively spare version of realism; in particular, he has nothing to say about the detailed epistemological issues a pragmatist would need to explore. (Putnam needs to look elsewhere.) In effect, there is no satisfactory attempt in McDowell, Putnam, Bernstein, Rorty, or Davidson to meet the threat of relativism or historicism! But, of course, under constructivist conditions, eschewing privilege, every viable realism must yield some in the pragmatist direction—and, yielding there, must address the "relativist menace."

It's here, then, that we may expect to recover the thread of the earlier contrast between Putnam and Rorty. For Rorty is a pluralist of the postmodernist stripe—which, I suggest, signifies that his notion cannot fail to devolve into a form of relativism if viewed in terms of a legitimating rationale (which of course Rorty refuses). By contrast, Putnam (in the context of *Renewing Philosophy*) is a pluralist of the pragmatist or Deweyan sort—which, I claim, signifies that his pluralism also devolves into a form of relativism. (Always supposing, that is, that relativism can be formulated in a coherent and defensible way. Putnam, Rorty, Bernstein, and Davidson judge this to be impossible of course. But none of them offers a compelling argument.) The fact is, none of the principal discussants has ever conducted a genuinely open canvass of relativism's possibilities *or,* for that matter, of whether any tenable realism (in effect, constructivist views that would include Dewey's, Putnam's, possibly Rorty's, Bernstein's, but not Davidson's) *could* responsibly avoid the relativist option.[24]

I believe we cannot convincingly preclude relativism as a viable constructivism, *and* no known version of a constructive realism (short of transcendentalism) has ever succeeded in excluding it.[25] In short, there is no way to avoid the question whether and to what extent Dewey's realism is or is not compatible with one or another form of constructivism, relativism, incommensurabilism, historicism, or similar possibilities.[26] There, at least, you have a glimpse of pragmatism's likely future.

RELATIVISM IN RORTY AND PUTNAM

The discussion of relativism between Rorty and Putnam is a curious affair. Each is a decisive critic of the other: each, to my mind, shows compellingly that the other *is* a relativist (of an unacceptable sort) and each is caught in a formal or pragmatic paradox. The strange thing is that neither ever demonstrates that a viable relativism is impossible—or, indeed, that a reasonable extension of Deweyan realism is not already committed to a relativistic treatment of realism! In truth, the analysis of what relativism must entail is extraordinarily primitive in both Rorty and Putnam and never moves beyond the self-inflicted paradox of Plato's *Theaetetus.*[27] The point is: we must bring the diagnosis of late pragmatism and pragmatism's untapped prospects more clearly into line with one another, if we are ever to benefit from the unexpected second life that the running exchange between Rorty and Putanm has now made possible.

Already in *Experience and Nature,* in 1929, Dewey had demonstrated the coherence of a constructive realism committed to the flux. That is clearly the earliest site of a viable realism in English-language philosophy that is at once the equal of the strongest forms of realism the analytic tradition can boast and the only version that invites a closer study of what a fluxive constructivism might either entail or accommodate.

For their part, Putnam and Rorty are understandably obsessed with the relativism issue. *Renewing Philosophy* confirms how central the question had become for Putnam. The reason is plain. Putnam had set himself the task of formulating a viable realism that escaped the paradoxes of the "Cartesian" vision of the "One True Theory." He treated the matter autobiographically, as if to exorcise his early commitment to the absolutist pretensions of a scientific realism within the unity of science program. He pursued the matter down to the point where it became clear that his own best prospects required adopting something close to Dewey's realist reading of pragmatism, which happened to converge rather nicely with McDowell's correction of his (Putnam's) own first preference of a Jamesian model.

In the meantime, Rorty sensed the fatal weakness of Putnam's internal realism as early as *Reason, Truth and History*—in Putnam's false step intended to combat the relativism implicit in Rorty's postmodernism, which now began to threaten Putnam's own ability to withstand Rorty's attack on all bona fide efforts to support a proper realism. That attack was linked, in Putnam's mind, to the self-referential paradoxes of Protagorean relativism. Under the circumstances, precisely because he would not (or could not) yield to relativism or historicism or (indeed) incommensurabilism, Putnam defined relativism more and more tendentiously and adjusted his own position to a kind of shadow version of Cartesian realism, under the protection of McDowell's "correction."

Rorty could care less about these niceties, since, from his point of view, relativism *was* incoherent (more or less for the reasons Putnam provides). Moreover, postmodernism is not (he insists) a form of relativism at all, since it abandons (as, in a way, relativism does not) all canonical attempts to validate realism itself. This is precisely what Rorty hoped to tempt Putnam into accepting, when he affirmed that "pragmatists should be ethnocentrists rather than relativists."[28] The fact remains that Rorty does venture an argument of sorts to justify his resisting encumbering postmodernism with a relativistic charge, but he does not explain whether or why the effort is needed.

Rorty rests his case rather cleverly on Putnam's having construed truth in terms of "idealized rational acceptability," which, separated from correspondentist presumptions (which both Putnam and Rorty—and, also, Davidson—take to be "absurd" or illicit),[29] undermines Putnam's attempts to vindicate a reasonably full-blown realism. That is one way of putting the failure of the *Grenzbegriff* maneuver.

But, of course, contrary to what Rorty suggests, postmodernism *is* parasitic on the absolutist model of realism which it rejects, since it is the collapse of every *such* program that (on the argument) "forces" or "invites" us to adopt the postmodernist stance. That is precisely what Putnam means by treating Rorty as an arch-relativist.[30] But what if there *were* a third option between absolutism and postmodernism, and what if that option *were* a form of pragmatism (or pragmatist realism), which, in accord with Dewey's advocacy of radical contingency, entailed or was continuous with, or could accommodate, one or another form of relativism (shown, independently, to be coherent)? We would then, by a single stroke, have defeated Rorty, Putnam, Bernstein, Davidson, and McDowell! I myself have no doubt at all that relativism can be defended. Putnam believes that there *are* (but has yet to show) ways of securing a viable realism that yields nothing to postmodernism. But the evidence remains that he is caught between his *Grenzbegriff* (which is the vestige of his scientific realism *or* scientism) and relativism (which he insists is incoherent). In that case, Putnam cannot escape.

Rorty's question, however, is the right one: What could possibly vindicate "idealized rational acceptability," if we cannot rely on privilege or correspondence, *except* "ethnocentric solidarity?" The question goes back to Rorty's important 1984 paper, "Solidarity or Objectivity?" which he himself says was a response to Putnam's relativist charge against his own postmodernism—in the closing pages of *Reason, Truth and History* (which involve of course the *Grenzbegriff* maneuver).[31]

In a curious way, the different forms of philosophical failure evinced in Putnam's and Rorty's pragmatisms are neatly matched: in Putnam's, by refusing to distinguish between a responsible relativism and an irresponsible postmodernism; in Rorty's, by construing relativism as a hopeless maneuver legible only against the backdrop of canonical philosophy, which (Rorty claims) is not true of postmodernism. Both views may be struck down by simply acknowledging that Deweyan pragmatism *is* a constructive form of realism hospitable to relativism! (That still needs to be shown.)

You may glimpse something of Rorty's deliberately slow-paced, almost imperceptible retrieval of *philosophical argument* (that is, legitimative, second-order argument) in the opening essay (addressing relativism once again) of his recent book, *Philosophy and Social Hope:*

> we who are accused of relativism [should, Rorty advises,] stop using the distinctions between finding and making, objective and subjective. We should not let ourselves be described as subjectivists, and perhaps calling ourselves "social constructivists" is too misleading. For we cannot formulate our point in terms of a distinction between what is outside and what is inside us. . . . We anti-Platonists cannot permit ourselves to be called "relativists," since that description begs the central question. The central question is about the utility of the vocabulary which we inherited from Plato and Aristotle.
>
> Our opponents like to suggest that to abandon that vocabulary is to abandon rationality. . . . But of course we go on to [say] that being an irrationalist in *that* sense is not to be incapable of argument. We irrationalists do not foam at the mouth

> and behave like animals. We simply refuse to talk in a certain way, the Platonic way. The views we hope to persuade people to accept cannot be stated in Platonic terminology. So our efforts at persuasion must take the form of gradual inculcation of new ways of speaking, rather than of straightforward argument within old ways of speaking.[32]

I draw three findings from all this: first, Rorty is surely inching his way toward formulating a "new" form of philosophical argument, opposed to "the Platonic way," that *might* legitimate the position he now advances in his own postmodernist voice; second, he has invented out of whole cloth (without accompanying argument), apparently *from* the resources of postmodernism, an entirely new vision that might, in time, support philosophical "argument"—but that ignores the plain fact that Dewey *had* constructed such a conception (as have many others within the "Hegelian" clan) but never found himself drawn to anything like Rorty's postmodernism; and, third, the new adjustment belies the "advice" (and the rationale for that advice, already remarked) which Rorty had offered the feminists, who, well beyond his own postmodernism, saw precisely how a constructivist view of politics could be fashioned and saw how (at least implicitly) such a politics would be inseparable from a constructivist view of realism.

In the passage just cited, you cannot fail to see that, although Rorty holds that the very formulation of relativism presupposes (agonistically) the language of the "Platonists," he neglects to admit that the same is true of postmodernism. The entire argument collapses, therefore, like a house of cards. It does so simply because it merely pretends to be introducing a "reasonable" form of "persuasion" (without philosophical argument), where we lack any clear idea, *beyond Dewey,* as to what the important problems *are* in terms of which the facilitating mode of argument may actually be specified. Not to put too fine a point on it, the trouble is that what Rorty *says* is not yet within our grasp *is* comfortably caught in Dewey's!

DEWEY'S CONSTRUCTIVE REALISM

Putnam and Rorty have excellent arguments against one another. Each is able to show that the other's program is profoundly defective, and each regards the damning evidence as sufficient to confirm that the other is a relativist. These arguments are, however, a little lame, as lame in fact as the sense of relativism they share. For neither is open to the possibility that relativism may take a coherent form, may avoid the self-referential paradox of (say) the charge brought against Protagoras in Plato's *Theaetetus*. Neither considers the possibility that relativism may enhance the conceptual resources of the pragmatism they claim to share. There is a perseverating quality there, since both profess to have abandoned all a priori fixities and prejudices.

What Rorty means by the charge (against Putnam) is that Putnam fails in the defense of his "internal realism," except of course by means of the deus ex machina of his *Grenzbegriff*, which reliably rules out the threat of relativism at the start. What Putnam means by the charge (against Rorty) is that Rorty offers no justification for his refusal to provide reasons in support of the adequacy or pertinence of "ethnocentric solidarity" (which, otherwise, seems to mean no more than that "anything goes"). Both charges are reasonably compelling. Each, therefore, is able to score points against the other; but neither—the one as a pragmatic realist, the other as a pragmatic postmodernist—vindicates his own doctrine or even bothers to consider whether it may indeed require some reconciliation between relativism and something akin to Dewey's conjunction of pragmatism and realism.

The matter is more important than either seems to realize, since what they share, in describing themselves as Deweyan pragmatists, is Dewey's constructivist approach to truth and reality. In assessing the prospects of Dewey's attenuated summary of the Hegelian critique of Kant and Descartes—applied now to the salient puzzles of late twentieth-century philosophy—we find ourselves obliged to consider the implications of any constructive realism shorn of all the forms of epistemic privilege and pitted against the pretensions of scientific realism and other strong attempts to recover something akin to Cartesian realism.

If (1) Putnam cannot recover a realism stronger than Dewey's, if (2) McDowell (say) does not recognize the need to broach the deeper epistemic questions that Dewey had already formulated (in particular, the sense in which theoretical reason is a form of practical reason emerging within "problematic situations") and, beyond Dewey, subject to historical drift, if (3) no contemporary realism has been able to bypass Dewey's "Hegelian" solution (sketched in *Experience and Nature*)[33] or something like it, if (4) Rorty cannot make his postmodernist subversion of realist inquiry appear intellectually credible, then we must ask ourselves whether a viable extension of Dewey's position might not need to concede an inning to one or another relativist option. The irony is that this seemingly slim question might never have arisen had it not been for Putnam's and Rorty's running dispute. For now we see that even if we abandon their particular projects, pragmatism would still be obliged to confront the matter of avoiding the Cartesian-like recovery of realism favored in late analytic philosophy.

Take a closer look at the failure—and the meaning of the failure—of Putnam's and Rorty's actual undertakings. The most telling clues are within our grasp. They may be drawn from Putnam's and Rorty's own texts by way of featuring what each neglects. Each fails to perceive the deep lacuna within his own doctrine, which, once exposed, confirms that not only pragmatism but any viable realism along constructivist lines can hardly disallow one or another moderate form of relativism. How far the concession may be pressed is not the issue here.

If relativism may take a coherent form, then it may be brought to bear on the question of a viable realism; and then we should have to consider the compatibility of realism and relativism. That would mark at once a decisive turn in an ancient quarrel. For the history of that dispute, notably in the interval spanning Hegel and Dewey, has already reconciled realism with a number of important preparatory concessions: (1) with the abandonment of cognitive privilege, (2) with the denial of the necessary invariance of what is real, (3) with the insuperable symbiosis of the subjective and the objective, and, as a consequence, (4) with constructivism and the artifactual standing of our discursive categories.

If, in addition, we conceded something akin to Dewey's analysis of a "problematic situation"—favoring *savoir-faire* (practical know-how yielding an acceptable measure of success) over *savoir* (nondistorting cognitive faculties addressed to the real world) and drawing the realist import of our cognitive powers from precognitive (animal) impasses—we should have to concede as well the reconcilability of realism (5) with relativism. That would signify the most extraordinary declension of the entire realist idea.

My own prognosis is that we are led to all this by tracing the path from Descartes to Kant to Hegel to Dewey and, now, more opportunistically, through Putnam and Rorty. If more is required—I am sure more can be elicited—then, by admitting the Hegelian theme of the historicity of thought, which the pragmatists oddly neglected (except, incipiently, for Mead), we should have to concede that realism was reconcilable (6) with historicism as well. In any event, we begin to see how far pragmatism may be coherently extended: we see how easily Putnam and Rorty may be eclipsed, how much they remain tethered to vestiges of the absolutist arguments they profess to have discarded. Putnam's *Grenzbegriff,* Rorty's "solidarity," both behave suspiciously like the last defenses of a calling they would deny.

I cannot undertake, here, the demonstration that relativism *can* be coherently formulated so as to be brought to bear on the realist issue. (I have done so elsewhere—many times.) But, for the sake of closure, I now say that Rorty's "ethnocentric solidarity" *is* an inchoate form of relativism, which he may yet confess if he approaches the recovery of philosophical argument. In any case, there is no way in which one's ethnic home can be relevantly identified in a way that would preclude relativism; and Rorty himself has urged that we should pick and choose our home "society" as we please.

By contrast, once Putnam denies any principled disjunction between the subjective and the objective, which Rorty is prepared to endorse as well, whatever realist proposals we thereafter favor could never vindicate anything as strong as Putnam's *Grenzbegriff;* but if we lacked such a regulative principle, then if Putnam continued to oppose objectivism (or abolutism), he would not be able to distinguish in principle between his position and a moderate relativism.

Rorty holds that "relativist" is an epithet usually attributed to philosophers who "do not accept the Greek distinction ['Platonism' in Rorty's vocabulary] between the way things are in themselves and the relation which they have to other things, and in particular to human needs and interests" *applied by those* committed to the "Greek distinction."[34] Since Rorty himself "eschew[s] the distinction," he insists that, though he has been called a relativist, he is not one (nor, by the same argument, is Dewey): "we pragmatists," he says, "never call *ourselves* relativists. . . . [W]e define ourselves in negative terms."[35] (But what does that matter if others call "us" relativists or if we "define ourselves in negative terms"? Does "pragmatist" signify a defensible policy?)

I grant Rorty's point: it's entirely harmless. But I cannot see its philosophical payoff, since it appears that Rorty *is* bent on recovering (if he can) a mode of "argument" (other than the "Greek") that would suit his deep opposition to all "dualisms" (which, as he says, he shares with Dewey). *Some* affirmation seems to be forthcoming. What, otherwise, would be the point of *applying his distaste for dualisms to science and morality and art?* He must mean to avoid sheer anarchy and arbitrariness. But if so, then nothing he says in disparaging relativism carries any weight at all.

The ultimate weakness of Rorty's "postmodernism" comes to this: he claims the benefits of "unforced agreement," "consensus," "solidarity"—notably, for instance, for whatever science has accomplished—but he refuses to sketch any grounds at all for thinking that those would-be benefits *are* "unforced" or reasonably defended:

> To say that unforced agreement is enough [for science, for pragmatism, for rationality, for distinguishing between the objective and the subjective] raises the specter of relativism [Rorty admits]. "Unforced agreement among whom? Us? The Nazis? Any arbitrary cohort or group?" The answer, of course, is "us." This necessarily ethnocentric answer simply says that we must

> work by our own lights. Beliefs suggested by another culture must be tested by trying to weave them together with beliefs we already have. . . . [T]he only sense in which science is exemplary is that it is a model of human solidarity.[36]

In what sense *is* science a "model"? In what sense *is* it the fruit of "unforced agreement"? These questions point to the unearned advantages of Rorty's refusal to explain just *what* it is he is preferring and why. The very success of science is now used as a blackmail argument to distract us from the arbitrariness of his refusal to answer. The fact remains that there *is* no principled demarcation between "us" and "another culture." Quine had already made the point in the strongest terms (in *Word and Object*): there is, he says, no principled distinction between the inter- and the intra-linguistic (or -societal); and of course Rorty could not, on his own stand, admit such a division.

By constrast, when he agrees with Putnam's pronouncement—namely, "To say, as [Bernard] Williams sometimes does, that convergence to one big picture of knowledge [absolutism] is required by the very concept of knowledge is sheer dogmatism. . . . It is indeed the case [Putnam continues] that ethical knowledge cannot claim absoluteness; but that is because the notion of absoluteness [in ethical as in scientific matters] is incoherent"—*Rorty* exposes not only his own dogmatism (perhaps inadvertently) but the fatal flaw in *Putnam's* internal realism as well.[37] For if, in Putnam's view, "the metaphysical notion of 'all objects' has no sense," then, *in principle,* Putnam can no longer assure us that when we are describing what purports to be "the same situation," our alternative descriptions of *"it"* will or must converge (moderately, without reaching the absolutist goal, perhaps in accord with our trusty *Grenzbegriff*) instead of assuming incommensurable forms à la Kuhn and Feyerabend.

If we concede that incommensurabilism, like relativism, can be coherently formulated, then Putnam's internal realism—whether "scientific" or "ethical"—must depend on a (suppressed) absolutist longing that cannot count on more than pluralist approximations:

> In *The Many Faces of Realism* [Putnam reminds us] I described in detail a case in which the same situation, in a perfectly commonsensical sense of "the same situation," can be described as involving entirely different numbers and kinds of objects (colored "atoms" alone, versus colored atoms plus "aggregates" of atoms). . . . How many objects are there "really" in such a world? I suggest that *either way of describing it is equally "true."* The idea that "object" has some sense which is independent of how we are counting objects and what we are counting as an "object" in a given situation is an illusion.[38]

Putnam neglects to explain just how the *"it,"* "the same situation," is ever freed from the same conceptual or theorizing encumbrance that affects the alternative parsings he admits. Without explaining that, he cannot distinguish between his pluralism and a relativistic or even incommensurabilist reading of his doctrine.

The truth is, Putnam's pluralism is never more than a "logical" or "terminological" pluralism (that may be interpreted in ontological terms): it never advances epistemic credentials by which it could be contrasted with a coherent relativism or incommensurabilism. Putnam never shows us that alternative "pluralisms" *cannot* be epistemically justified *on* incommensurable grounds; he only shows us that *if* we have already determined *what* to count as real in a given context, we can if we wish, parse *that* part of the world by other ways of counting entities. But that's not the important issue.

This explains the sense in which Rorty and Putnam fail to provide any reason for not thinking that pragmatism must, in all likelihood, yield to some benign form of relativism (always assuming that a coherent relativism is indeed formulable). Dewey need not have resisted any such concession, and its defense would go a great distance toward demonstrating that straightforward philosophical arguments can indeed be recovered without falling back to the dilemma posited by absolutism and postmodernism. That is in fact no more than the minimal mark of the gains that span the work that runs from Descartes to Kant to Hegel to Dewey and beyond.

What it signifies, *au fond,* is pragmatism's unfinished business. Through the sheer vitality of their running exhange, Rorty and Putnam rescued pragmatism from near oblivion, almost as a by-product of their quarrels. They invented, without perhaps meaning to, a more fundamental contest between pragmatism and analytic naturalism than could be drawn from the work of the classic pragmatists alone. But, in the process, they exhausted their own resources, and they now appear to be searching for a defensible perch of their own, without bothering any longer to define what pragmatism should now mean.

As it turns out, pragmatism has always had deeper linkages with the post-Kantian tradition than the "analysts" had been concerned to fathom. In particular, admitting all the stalemates on the realism issue that late twentieth-century American philosophy has spawned, it begins to sound sensible to bring the relativist and historicist "menace" into the open, without prejudice, so as to test the best prospects for a pragmatist recovery of realism. We are now at a point where that very tired conviction, the one that insists that relativism is incoherent or incompatible with a realism robust enough to accommodate the best work of the sciences may not be as difficult or as awkward to defeat as it once appeared to be. In any event, we cannot drop the realism question merely because Putnam and Rorty have failed to gain the advantage for themselves. We must appreciate the reason for their obsession with the relativist threat, as well as the prospect that, in approaching its resolution, the new century will have made its own efforts to bring contemporary philosophy into accord once again with the most persistent quarrels of the ancient world. The open-ended inquiries of the original pragmatists now signify as well the unfinished reconciliation of Anglo-American and continental European philosophical practice.

NOTES

1. See Richard Rorty, "Feminism and Pragmatism," in *Philosophical Papers,* vol. 3 (Cambridge: Cambridge University Press, 1998), 207–8 and chap. 3.

2. Richard Rorty, "The Contingency of Language," in *Contingency, Irony, and Solidarity* (Cambridge: Cambridge University Press, 1989), 1.

3. Rorty, "Contingency of Language," 9.

4. See, for example, Michael Devitt, *Realism and Truth,* 2nd ed. (Princeton: Princeton University Press, 1991).

5. See Harold Bloom, *A Map of Misreading* (Oxford: Oxford University Press, 1975), chap. 1.

6. Richard J. Bernstein, *The New Constellation: The Ethical-Political Horizons of Modernity/Postmodernity* (Cambridge: MIT Press, 1992), 267, 270.

7. See Jean-François Lyotard, *The Postmodern Condition: A Report in Knowledge,* trans. Geoff Bennington and Brian Massumi (Minneapolis: University of Minnesota Press, 1984).

8. Bernstein, *New Constellation,* 324.

9. See, further, Joseph Margolis, *Historied Thought, Constructed World: A Conceptual Primer for the Turn of the Millennium* (Berkeley: University of California Press, 1995).

10. See Richard J. Bernstein, *Beyond Objectivism and Relativism: Science, Hermeneutics, and Praxis* (Philadelphia: University of Pennsylvania Press, 1983).

11. Hilary Putnam, *Reason, Truth and History* (Cambridge: Cambridge University Press, 1981), p. ix.

12. Putnam, *Reason, Truth and History,* 49–50.

13. See, for instance, Hilary Putnam, "Sense, Nonsense, and the Senses: An Inquiry into the Powers of the Human Mind," *Journal of Philosophy,* 91 (1994), Lecture I: 182n36, 183n40.

14. See Putnam, "Sense, Nonsense, and the Senses," Lecture I.

15. See Putnam, *Reason, Truth and History,* 214–16.

16. See Richard Rorty, "Hilary Putnam and the Relativist Menace," in *Philosophical Papers,* vol. 3 (Cambridge: Cambridge University Press, 1998).

17. See Donald Davidson, "A Coherence Theory of Truth and Knowledge," in *Truth and Interpretation: Perspectives on the Philosophy of Donald Davidson,* ed. Ernest Lepore (Oxford: Basil Blackwell, 1986).

18. See Donald Davidson, "Afterthoughts, 1987," added to a reprinting of "A Coherence Theory of Truth and Knowledge," in *Reading Rorty: Critical Responses to Philosophy and the Mirror of Nature (and Beyond),* ed. Alan R. Malachowski (Oxford: Basil Blackwell, 1990). On Rorty's reading of Davidson on truth, see Richard Rorty, "Pragmatism, Davidson, and Truth," in *Truth and Interpretation: Perspectives on the Philosophy of Donald Davidson;* and Richard Rorty, "Is Truth a Goal of Inquiry? Donald Davidson versus Crispin Wright," in *Philosophical Papers,* vol. 3 (Cambridge: Cambridge University Press, 1995).

19. See Rorty, "Pragmatism, Davidson, and Truth," also, "Hilary Putnam and the Relativist Menace."

20. See W. V. Quine, "Let Me Accentuate the Positive," in *Reading Rorty.*

21. Hilary Putnam, "The Prospects of Artificial Intelligence," in *Renewing Philosophy* (Cambridge: Harvard University Press, 1992), 3.

22. Compare Bernstein, *Beyond Objectivism and Relativism;* and Putnam, "Sense, Nonsense, and the Senses."

23. See John McDowell, *Mind and World* (Cambridge: Harvard University Press, 1994, 1996).

24. See Margolis, *Historied Thought, Constructed World.*

25. See Rorty, "Hilary Putnam and the Relativist Menace."

26. See Joseph Margolis, "John Dewey: The Metaphysics of Existence," first presented at the Catholic University of America, Washington, D.C., October 13, 2000 (publication pending).

27. See, for instance, Hilary Putnam, "Wittgenstein on Reference and Relativism," in *Renewing Philosophy.* See also Myles Burnyeat, "Protagoras and Self-Refutation in Plato's *Theaetetus,*" *Philosophical Review* 85 (1976).

28. Rorty, "Hilary Putnam and the Relativist Menace," 52.

29. See Davidson, "Coherence Theory of Truth and Knowledge," 307.

30. See Hilary Putnam, "The Craving for Objectivity," in *Realism with a Human Face,* ed. James Conant (Cambridge: Harvard University Press, 1990).

31. See Richard Rorty, "Solidarity or Objectivity?" in *Philosophical Papers,* vol. 1 (Cambridge: Cambridge University Press, 1991); also, "Hilary Putnam and the Relativist Menace," 51n26.

32. Richard Rorty, "Relativism: Finding and Making," in *Philosophy and Social Hope* (London: Penguin, 1999), xviii–xix.

33. For a fuller account, see Joseph Margolis, "The Benign Antinomy of a Constructed Realism," for presentation at a conference: "The Future of Realism in the American Tradition of Pragmatic Naturalism," State University of New York at Buffalo, Buffalo, New York, October 20–22, 2000 (publication pending).

34. Rorty, *Philosophy and Social Hope,* xvi.

35. Rorty, *Philosophy and Social Hope,* xvi.

36. Richard Rorty, "Science as Solidarity," in *Philosophical Papers,* vol. 1 (Cambridge: Cambridge University Press, 1991), 38–39.

37. The remark is cited in Rorty, "Hilary Putnam and the Relativist Menace," 44. Putnam has made the point in many places. Here, it is taken from Hilary Putnam, "Objectivity and the Science/Ethics Distinction," in *Realism with a Human Face,* 171.

38. Hilary Putnam, "Irrealism and Deconstruction," in *Renewing Philosophy,* 120.

TEN

Improving Life

JOHN LACHS

In an otherwise astonishingly abstract and tedious essay, Harry Frankfurt argues for the interesting thesis that the unidirectional relation between means and ends is insupportable.[1] He points out that Aristotle, the father of the Western tradition of thought concerning means and ends, maintained that means are valuable only for their tendency to bring about desirable ends, while ends are valuable in and of themselves. The relation is asymmetrical because means derive their value from the ends to which they lead, but ends gain no benefit from the relationship.

Frankfurt argues, by contrast, that even if ends do not profit from having certain means necessary for their attainment, people do. For the actions in which one must engage to bring about certain ends endow one's existence with meaning by providing purposive activity that is complex and "radiates extensively within the person's life."[2] So just as means have instrumental value because they lead to certain ends, ends have instrumental value because they require certain activities as means. Further, ends have "final" value because we care about them and they are worth having on their own account, and means have final value because they are worth having as necessary constituents of a meaningful life.

This point appears remarkably similar to Dewey's idea of what is sometimes called "means-end integrated actions."[3] According to that view, human actions are at their best when each one of them is both means and end, that is, useful for what it produces and enjoyable for what it is. Is this "coalescence" (LW 10:202) of instrumental and consummatory value what Frankfurt has in mind? If it is, Dewey has at last made his much-awaited appearance in the precincts of analytic philosophy. Unfortunately, however, his arrival continues to be delayed. Frankfurt's ideas are different from

Dewey's for at least two reasons. First, he speaks of ends acquiring instrumental value because they require certain means that have final value. The means obtain such intrinsic value, however, only because of their relationship to a meaningful life. Frankfurt says that the means are necessary for, but do not constitute, such a life. This indicates that the means lack intrinsic value, after all. They simply serve as means to two desirable ends instead of one: they are useful for obtaining both the specific final goods at which they aim and also a meaningful life of purposive activity.

Frankfurt could amend his view, I suppose, and say that the connection between means and meaningful life is more intimate than he initially implied, for such a life is constituted by purposive activity rather than being merely brought about by it. But this still keeps him a distance away from Dewey. The hallmark of what Dewey calls an "external means" is substitutability.[4] Working as a waiter is an external means to earning the money necessary for life, for nothing about earning a living specifically requires it. This is but another way of saying that working as, say, a taxi driver can easily and adequately replace it. Similarly, what we need for meaningful life is not this or that specific purposive activity, but only some purposive exertion or other. So means acquire final value not for what they are but for the sort of thing they represent. This is at odds with Dewey's commitment to the value of individual activities and events, and also with what we treasure and how we treasure it in everyday life.

The second difference between Frankfurt's and Dewey's views is closely connected to the first. Frankfurt is satisfied to talk in generalities about the order of meaningful lives, suggesting that some activities acquire intrinsic value for contributing to such lives. With characteristic common sense and commitment to the denotative method, Dewey avoids speaking of such totalizing abstractions, restricting his account of the coincidence of means and ends to specific activity-sequences. Instead of arguing that nibbling one's lover's ears contributes to something as nebulous as a meaningful life, he points out that such small bites are both intrinsically delightful and truly helpful in getting where one wants to go. This strikes me as a far more interesting and promising approach to the improvement of life than anything Frankfurt has to offer.

How far can Dewey's ideal of means-end integrated actions take us in the quest to improve human life? I examined this question once before, but there is more to say than I had a chance to develop there.[5] Here, I first explain why this topic and Dewey's response to it are of great significance. Then I outline historically important alternative approaches. Finally, I examine Dewey's proposal in detail and evaluate it against the background of these alternatives.

Since the beginning of the historical record, humans have enjoyed the pursuit and possession of valued experiences. Unfortunately, the pursuit was often painful and the possession disappointing. But even when the enjoyment was deemed worth its cost, it could be attained only at considerable labor or sacrifice or pain. The Bible testifies to this element of the human condition and identifies it as a consequence of original sin. God's punishment of Adam and Eve's transgression condemns women to bearing children in pain and all of us to earning our daily bread by the sweat of our brows. The situation has not changed much since those early days. Although life today is immeasurably easier than it must have been thousands of years ago, we still face having to delay gratification, having to do much that we don't care for, and having to submit to the discipline of enduring painful means to obtain satisfying ends.

Perhaps the first systematic response to this lamentable condition was the establishment of class structure, shifting all onerous activity to large groups of unfortunate slaves or laborers. This allowed the tribal chief or king or lord to devote his time to the enjoyment of the goods of the world. Hegel describes this strategy well in the master-slave dialectic, noting the struggle by which the lord attains control over the lives of his slaves.[6] The result is that the slaves work the ground to produce the necessities of life, while the lord retains for himself the negation, that is, the "consumption and enjoyment, of things."[7] Whether the lord ends up bored, dependent on his slaves, or desperately in search of a challenge, it remains true that he does not have to do much he does not want to do, and lives with far fewer demands on him for unpleasant exertions. Since his happy self-indulgence is gained at the cost of great misery to others, this procedure solves the problem only for a few, while it exacerbates it for everyone else.

Another strategy to deal with unavoidable misery, as Hegel aptly points out, is the slave's. He has no opportunity to shift the burden of the painful cost of delight unto others and thus no choice but to face endless labor with equanimity. The Stoic solution is to accept whatever comes one's way without complaint and to do what one must as though one wanted to. "Do not seek events to happen as you want them to," Epictetus, himself a slave, says, "but instead want them to happen as they do happen, and your life will go well."[8] Such control over desires or refusal to acknowledge the unpleasantness of the unpleasant can presumably be attained by anyone. But its cost is too high, requiring the extinction of natural human preferences and feelings. Indifference to the painful quickly turns into indifference to all things, exacting loss of the joys of life as the price of subduing its pains. If the lord lives at the expense of others, Stoics hardly live at all: they despair of our ability to improve the human lot, abandon all hope, and satisfy themselves with changes to their attitudes even when the drive for objective changes would succeed.

Aristotle's famous distinction between processes and activities is a highbrow variant of the class-structure strategy. Processes involve the usual separation between potentially painful means and desirable ends. Their hallmark is that their ends are external to the means used to attain them, and the ends can be attained only with effort and over a period of time. In activities, by contrast, means and ends coalesce or else means simply drop out. Each activity is pursued for its own sake and we can engage in it directly, without having to perform any antecedent acts. This means that activities involve no instrumentalities at all. They are ends-in-themselves that require neither preparation nor time for their performance: they are instant accomplishments and hence transcendent moments of delight.

The way to eliminate the painful labor of life, then, is to concentrate on those experiences that are possible without it. Such experiences tend to point away from the material underpinnings of life, consisting mainly of the higher achievements of what Aristotle calls "intellectual virtue." Thinking and seeing and contemplative enjoyment are activities in the required sense: to do them, he says, is to have done them,[9] meaning that, in them, doing and deed, process and product, are indissolubly one. Small wonder then that the life of the philosopher is second only to God's. Thinkers know how to engage in activities and thereby to liberate themselves from the dissatisfactions and drudgeries of life. Free of the incomplete acts to which we are condemned in the temporal world, philosophers can live, at least for a few moments, in the eternal.

Aristotle's plan for bettering life is not as harsh as the plan described by Hegel's lord, but it is just as elitist. The difference is that class divisions rest on discrepancies of power, whereas Aristotle's strategy relies on divergences of taste and training. But, in reality, a division of labor underlies Aristotle's proposal as well. The material needs of life don't disappear while we contemplate; only when they are met, in fact, can we enjoy the leisure necessary for thought. So the shift from processes to activities does not solve the problem of unavoidably painful instrumentalities. It redistributes the pain to those who must produce the goods of the world and to those times in the lives of the educated when they are not busy contemplating.

A variant of the Stoic slave's strategy has for long enjoyed popularity among morally serious people. The approach is reminiscent of Kant and is, in at least one version, powerfully supported by the promises of religion. Instead of recommending indifference to joy and suffering alike, this strategy isolates necessary but undesirable labor and designates its performance a matter of moral obligation. Calling it duty removes such misery from the realm of what we could expect to like; that what we ought to do should be no fun is unsurprising and irrelevant. Kant sums it up neatly by asserting that morality has nothing to do with happiness. Its austere edicts derive from reason and bind us to obedience through respect for a law we impose on ourselves. Whether we like it or not is never to the point; it would not only be hopeless, but also wrong to try to change the course of things in such a way that duty becomes less onerous or, God forbid, something we can happily embrace.

Self-development, for example, is a duty we must not avoid.[10] Boring teachers, endless practice, and painful self-control must be endured without complaint. That we experience them as torture testifies to the fact that they do us good; they could surely not be as beneficial if they were fun. Pain, therefore, is a natural, inevitable, and wholesome signal that we take our obligations seriously. In the *Critique of Practical Reason,* Kant goes a step further and converts the traditional promises of Christianity into philosophical support for the view that we must overlook the painful instrumentalities of life. For those who put up with them and do what duty demands are entitled to heavenly rewards.[11] Over the infinity of our immortal lives, God will adjust happiness to match virtue and thereby compensate the upright for their pains. Evidently, this does not erase the suffering in this world, but it holds out the hope that things might go better in the next.

A central characteristic of modernity is the unwillingness to leave it to God to set things right. For the last five hundred years, Western civilization has been in the business of showing God how He might take a more active role in bringing improvements to the world. What I will call "the technological strategy" consists in identifying undesirable features of reality and launching intelligent efforts to change or to eliminate them. This has been a hugely successful enterprise, enabling us to extend human life, defeat disease after disease, and make daily existence vastly more comfortable than earlier generations could have imagined. Many of the pains previously thought unavoidable no longer plague us. Machines have taken over much undesirable labor and resort hotels testify that social life is organized so that at least some people can enjoy stretches of time as an uninterrupted series of ends.

Intelligent industrial and commercial activity has been so effective in dealing with human problems that we hear more and more sanguine appraisals of its ultimate promise. Various forecasts predict an end to wars, the expansion of life expectancy to a hundred and fifty years, the elimination of hunger and all disease, and mastery over both depression and aggression. Manipulation of the genetic material of the species is supposed to enable us to create problem-free individuals whom we can clone into societies of happy and responsible people. Distinctions of class, race, and gender will disappear as we educate or breed prejudice out of people. Everything unpleasant will be recognized as unnecessary or at least as unworthy of humans, to be accomplished by metallic or silicon machines. Utopia, in brief, is just around the corner, offering ever greater benefits at diminishing cost.

The promise of such unclouded days is curiously at odds with the reality of industrial and commercial life. No matter how much better off they are than prior generations, people today do not seem any happier. The incidence of mental illness is increasing, and suicide, especially among healthy young persons, is a baffling and distressingly common phenomenon. Even the best adjusted find themselves engulfed in a whirl of immediately pressing but otherwise meaningless activities. Our work days are filled with busy preparations for consummations that are fleeting or that never come. Most important, the tedious labor we used to have to expend to secure the necessities of life directly has been replaced by an equally tedious but different service to huge institutions.

This last point is crucial. We do not have to go hunting each day; we do not even have to fertilize the garden and kill and clean a chicken for lunch. But we do have to go to work and serve in whatever ways our employers direct. Many of these activities are of little interest to us and carry no intrinsic reward. They involve pushing paper and attending meetings on issues of momentous indifference, or moving physical objects from one place to another, or attending to things that are difficult to see as anything but insignificant. No matter how many external means we succeed in eliminating, others no better rush in to take their place. The servant of modern corporations may enjoy fewer satisfying ends-in-themselves than did the hunters and farmers of old.

This brief look at historical alternatives highlights the importance of Dewey's idea of means-end integrated actions. His view promises permanent improvements to the human condition. Instead of solving the problem of how to dispense with undesirable labor for a few people only, as do class-structure arrangements, Dewey offers a strategy that is universally or at least generally applicable. Instead of proposing a subjective, attitudinal adjustment, as do the Stoics, or a trick of reclassification, as does Kant, he presents a way of objectively reconstructing our relations to our activities. Although he strongly favors intelligent improvements in the material conditions of life, he has no difficulty in seeing through the excessive optimism of the devotees of technology to the travail that underlies the achievements of civilization.[12]

Dewey's view of means-end integrated actions consists of the following three general ideas:

1. Each event and action has an intrinsic quality that can be enjoyed;
2. Each event and action is connected to others by means of causal or sequential relations;

3. Events and actions can be arranged in sequences so intimate that their earlier and later phases are united.

Although Dewey was deeply indebted to Hegel, he learned from Peirce not to be satisfied with mediation or thirdness alone. Peirce's category of firsts reminded Dewey that there is an inexpressible immediacy in all of experience. The enjoyment or suffering of the qualities of what happens is the outcome of paying attention to them for what they are, independently of the relations connecting them to other events. I am satisfied that experiences have such qualities and that, in a stance of immediacy, it is possible to enjoy many of them. I am by no means sure, however, that all of them can be enjoyed rather than suffered, but I will wait to discuss that issue until Dewey's position is clear.

Dewey's second claim also strikes me as unproblematically correct. What he calls "the sequential order"[13] consists of naturally connected events, that is, of processes or natural histories. These orderly connections make it possible for us to achieve some measure of control over the environment. I may note, for example, that sunflower seeds falling on the ground tend to germinate and grow into new plants. I can exploit this connection and place sunflower seeds where I want the plants for decoration or maximum yield. The procedure works equally well in situations in which we wish to prevent a natural process from prevailing. I may notice, for instance, that rain soaks my head when I am outside, but not when I have a roof over my head. I can then design a small roof, called an umbrella, to carry with me to prevent nature from having its way. Such useful interventions presuppose no special theory of the nature of causation: all we need to do is observe sequences and find the time or the place to direct, abort, or redirect them.[14]

The first idea affirms the possibility that each experience can be enjoyed as an end; the second points to the fact that every event is instrumental in bringing others into existence. Important as these claims are for Dewey's view, the characteristic feature of his theory is the third idea, addressing the way earlier and later events must be connected in order for a sequence of actions to be means-end integrated. In general terms, the relation needs to be one of unity. Dewey seems to have identified two different sorts of unity that may obtain between means that are not external and the ends to which they lead. The weaker condition for escaping the status of being an external means requires that means be enjoyable as ends-in-themselves and that ends be useful for further attainments. This suggests that such processes must exhibit unity at least in the sense that their elements are similar in being both useful and intrinsically valuable. This condition, if met, would be adequate to eliminate the drudgery of life by rendering means inherently and not only instrumentally valuable.

The stronger condition for a means being "intrinsic" demands an internal relation between means and ends. According to it, sharing final and instrumental value is inadequate for means-end integrated actions. There must also be a more intimate connection which takes one of two forms: either the means must be a part of the end or the end must be a completion of the means. Dewey explains the first version of the relation with great rhetorical power, returning to it again and again. He attacks the view that means are antecedents that must disappear before our desires are fulfilled. On the contrary, he says, they are vital ingredients of what will come about, in just the way flour is both a means to and an element in the bread we bake. He uses a variety of other illustrations to make sure his point is clear: he notes that sound institutions are both means to an orderly society and elements of it (LW 1: 275–76), bricks and mortar are both necessary instruments and valued components of houses (LW 1:201), and paints are means to the pictures they constitute (LW 1:275).

The second version of the relation is a little more difficult to explain than the first. Dewey suggests that means and ends must be related in such a way that the means foreshadow the ends and the ends complete the means. An example may make this relation clearer. Baking an apple pie is an activity united by the identity of purpose and outcome. When all goes well, my objective and the eventual object produced are the same, and the entire process is directed by what I want to attain. I may begin by looking for apples to peel, rejecting squash and carrots; I buy pie shells instead of cheese pizza; I place the unbaked pie in the oven rather than in the disposal. Dewey insists that such intimately interconnected processes occur in nature even without human intervention. He has in mind sequences the ends of which are fulfillments and not merely cessations (LW 1:201). The mating of animals and the creation of islands as a result of volcanic activity may be instances of such fulfillments, though the question of whether they are or not is irrelevant to what Dewey wants to say about means and ends and, accordingly, does not need to be decided here.

In perfect accord with his method, Dewey developed the weaker and the two versions of the stronger account of how means and ends may be unified by observation of experiential sequences. He may not have realized that he was dealing with three independent requirements for means-end integrated actions or he may have thought that any one of the three involves or entails the others. I see no obvious or simple connections among them. One could subscribe to the demand that all elements of an experiential sequence be both means and ends while rejecting the idea that means must be parts of ends or ends fulfillments of means. Similarly, even if a means is eventually incorporated in its end, it need not be an end on its own account when experienced as an early element of a process. However this may be, meeting three criteria, even if interconnected, is a heavier burden than Dewey needs to bear. For this reason, I will examine them one at a time, and credit Dewey with a significant advance if even a single one of them can be generalized enough to help us improve human experience.

What sort of generalization do we seek? We want to see if by using Dewey's criteria of nonexternal means we can convert displeasing experiences into ones that satisfy. Such conversions cannot be matters of adjusting attitudes alone. They require reconstructions of experience and possibly even significant institutional changes, albeit none that is utopian. Such a test of Dewey's ideas is clearly in line with his meliorism and expresses in concrete terms his commitment to philosophy as the critic of social practices.

The idea that ends are fulfillments of purposive processes is, among the three requirements, the one most expressive of Dewey's commitments. His notion of purposive process connects to his ideas about meaning and intelligent control. Viewing ends as completions of human efforts, therefore, amounts to placing them in the context of our desires to bring about outcomes favorable to life. Careful attention to the conditions of what we do enables us to achieve the consequences we want, and outcome controlled by our own actions is what Dewey calls "meaning" (LW 1:277). He adds that "The characteristic human need is for possession and appreciation of the meaning of things" (LW 1:272).

For ends to be fulfillments of means, they must be meaningful and therefore humanly constructed outcomes. Dewey's idea is that anything so constructed involves effort and victory, and he finds it impossible to believe that such successful activities could fail to be joyous. His prescription, then, is to make the employment of means intelligent so that we can take delight in the effective exercise of human powers. This is thoughtful observation of what pleases us and generally good advice. As early a student of human nature as Aristotle remarked that unimpeded activity directed upon worthy objects is naturally accompanied by pleasure.[15] The joy of possessing the end spreads to the means used to attain it and is reinforced by the exhilaration of experiencing our power. What we have to do to carry the day is then not an alien necessity, but an affirmation of what we want and who we are.

The obvious problem is how we can experience means-end sequences as self-controlled exercises of our power. Clearly, most of the ends we enjoy are fulfillments resulting from our intelligent efforts, if "we" and "our" are taken to mean "human" or "social" or "institutional." "We" manufacture airplanes and fly them all over the globe. "We" build skyscrapers and fill them with corporations that bring goods from the far corners of the world to satisfy our cravings. "We" create systems of communication that enable us to know what happens in Australia or in outer space. Modern life is full of stunning institutional achievements of which we, if we manage to identify ourselves with the human race, can be genuinely proud.

The difficulty resides in the relation of the we to the I. Normally, the grander the fulfillment, the more people are required to secure it. Participants in such social acts must be organized in chains of mediation,[16] with a clear division of labor between those who plan, those who execute the plans, and those who enjoy or suffer the consequences. An astonishing level of ignorance pervades these chains: though everyone is busy contributing to the ultimate result, very few understand how what they do is integrated into the larger whole. This means that even the people whose direct agency attains the end find it difficult to see the achievement as their own. They are only familiar with their own small fragment of the means; the control of consequences is not in their hands.

We find, therefore, that agents in our highly mediated society experience themselves as instruments of causes they do not adopt and may not even approve. Contributing but an insignificant ounce of power to the megawatts needed for large-scale social acts, they cannot adopt the end as the fulfillment of anything they know about or labor to achieve. Their alienation is an outcome of the magnitude of institutional acts and the multitude of people required to carry them out. For this reason, it is very difficult to overcome. Eliminating large-scale mediated chains sacrifices the attainments of industrial civilization. Quite apart from Dewey's abhorrence of psychological manipulation, the last hundred years provide ample evidence that increasing social-mindedness or identifying the I with the we in peacetime cannot be achieved for long by propaganda.

How could individuals come to see the ends they help attain as meaningful fulfillments of their own efforts? Three conditions would have to be met: (1) They would have to understand the social acts in which they participate much better than they do now. (2) They would have to be partners in the decisions to undertake such acts. (3) They would also have to share equitably in the benefits such acts generate. This is but another way of saying that our society would have to be organized to provide effective and universal education, openness in institutional, social, and governmental decision making, participatory democracy in all human interactions, and social justice for all. Human life would, indeed, be immeasurably better if we lived under such circumstances. But no one can seriously contemplate such developments outside the realm of dreamy utopia.

Is the other, simpler form of Dewey's strong criterion for nonexternal means applicable to much of human experience? The wide range of Dewey's examples suggests that means that both generate their ends and become parts of them constitute the rule and not the exception. Flour certainly is both instrumental to and an ingredient in bread, bricks are necessary for houses and are also parts of them, and colors are required for paintings and also constitute them. If this relation obtained generally in experience, means and ends would be at least partly identical, the recognition of which would tend to transfer to means some of our enjoyment of ends. Instead of viewing means as oppressive necessities, we could welcome them as early, incomplete appearances of what we hope to achieve.

Unfortunately, as convincing as Dewey's examples may seem, they all share a common, limiting feature. The means he selects for attention consist of enduring physical and social objects. Bricks are not used up when we build a house and flour does not pass out of existence when we convert it into bread. The cultural objects he identifies tend also to persist: a "good political constitution, honest police-system, and competent judiciary" (LW 1:275–76) are continuous patterns of activity. These examples overlook all the elements of means subject to the destructive power of time. Bricks must be carried to the masons, and they must fit them in the wall hour after tedious hour. Flour must be mixed and kneaded at night by a baker who would much sooner be home sleeping with his wife. The integrity of institutions is achieved by the agonized self-control of those who could abuse it, and must be safeguarded by painful vigilance.

All of these activities disappear with the doing, and most of them involve undesirable labor. None of these elements of means can be retained and raised to glory as parts of what in the end satisfies. They torture us with their boredom, their repetitiousness, and their unavoidable pain, filling our days with what no one wants and no one can escape. The long, uncomfortable journey does not end up as part of the fun of visiting distant places. A sonata beautifully played does not incorporate years of youth lost in involuntary practice. The starving person's anguished search for food is best forgotten when the meal begins. Even if some elements of means survive and reach fulfillment in their ends, most of them do not; they remain as the bitter costs of getting what we want.

That leaves us, alas, only with Dewey's weak criterion of means-end integrated actions. This conception presents means and end as a continuous process each part of which is useful, on account of its relations to other events, and enjoyable, because of its intrinsic qualities. Dewey thinks so highly of this coalescence of means and ends that he employs it to explicate the nature of the esthetic. His point is that artistic creativity aims to produce works each element of which is delightful and yet leads seamlessly to the rest. Symphonies are like this and our lives can be lived this way, as well, if we do not permit enjoyment and utility to be separated.

The Enlightenment dream was to make life rational. Dewey adds to it the nineteenth-century hope of making it a work of art, as well. This creates a grand ideal that we can, here and there, approximate for a time. There are activities every element of which is rich in consequences and rewarding to experience. The play of children comes to mind, as does the sexual play of adults; sports qualify, as do good conversations. I have discussed this at greater length elsewhere and I continue to think that having such experiences suffuse one's life would make for an exceptionally satisfying existence.

The problem for those of us wishing to improve life is that some of our experiences are already means-end integrated actions and it is not clear how the bulk of those that are not can be reconstructed on that pattern. Giving a cat a pill, having a rattle found and fixed in the car, and preparing one's tax forms are just not joyous activities, and there is nothing we can do to make them so. One can bribe oneself with rewards for undertaking such tasks, and if one is gullible, one can make oneself believe that they are fun. Such psychological manipulation, however, is not what Dewey has in mind. His idea is that every experience has a quality intrinsic to it that, if we focus on it properly, can be a source of joy.

There is no denying that careful attention to the details of things elevates the human spirit. Intricacy of pattern and richness of involution still the human mind with grateful amazement at the actual. But such resolute focus requires leisure and peace of mind; interest in the utility of the perception tends to negate concentration on the immediate. Many qualities, moreover, are not agreeable to experience. Attention to the distinctive features of agony, of foul smells, and of human failure is not rewarding, and it is best to move through such deserts without looking long and hard.

We can, of course, imagine the world without deserts, but that is utopian. For Dewey, rightly, the issue is how to make incremental changes, improvements that in the end add up. And that is just where the notion of means-end integrated actions is supposed to help, but does not help enough.

But how much is enough? In spite of occasional statements that demand and promise more, Dewey is satisfied with modest progress in the affairs of life. Perhaps no one should hope for more. Difficult problems have no grand solutions; it may be wise to settle for ideals that leave us a little better off here and there. Combined with the power of technology to relieve us of the worst suffering and of the most inhuman labor, Dewey's idea of means-end integrated actions may help us achieve some, though by no means all, of the little improvements of which the human frame is capable. Not wishing for utopia, or even for universal improvement, is a sign of maturity. Yet it is a sad sign: relinquishing the hope for more decisive and more permanent betterment of our condition leaves a living wound in the human soul.

NOTES

1. Harry Frankfurt, "On the Usefulness of Final Ends," *Iyyun* 41 (January 1992): 4.

2. Ibid., 15.

3. John Lachs, "Aristotle and Dewey on the Rat Race," in *Philosophy and the Reconstruction of Culture: Pragmatic Essays After Dewey,* ed. John J. Stuhr (Albany: State University of New York Press, 1993), 97–109. Hereafter referred to as "Rat Race."

4. Lachs, "Rat Race," 201.

5. Lachs, "Rat Race."

6. G. W. F. Hegel, *Phenomenology of Spirit,* trans. A. V. Miller (Oxford: Oxford University Press, 1977), 111–19.

7. Ibid., 116.

8. Epictetus, *The Handbook* (Indianapolis, Ind.: Hackett Publishing Co., 1983), 13.

9. Aristotle, *Nicomachean Ethics,* trans. Terance Irwin (Indianapolis, Ind.: Hackett Publishing Co., 1985), 273–75.

10. Immanuel Kant, *Foundations of the Metaphysics of Morals,* in *Critique of Practical Reason and Other Writings in Moral Philosophy,* trans. Lewis White Beck (Chicago: University of Chicago Press, 1949), 82.

11. Ibid., 225–34.

12. A good example of Dewey's critique of modern institutional life may be found in *Experience and Nature* (LW 1:271–77).

13. Ibid., 66.

14. Dewey presents a good discussion of his idea of natural histories in *Experience and Nature* (LW1: 69–99).

15. Aristotle, *Nicomachean Ethics,* 275.

16. I discuss chains of mediation and the resultant alienation in *Intermediate Man* (Indianapolis, Ind.: Hackett Publishing Co., 1981.)

ELEVEN

In the Wake of Darwin

VINCENT COLAPIETRO

INTRODUCTION: LIVING IN THE WAKE OF DARWIN

Momentous occasions call for deliberate recollection.[1] In the winter and spring of 1909, Columbia University sponsored a series of lectures on "Charles Darwin and His Influence on Science" as a way of marking the publication of *Origin of Species* fifty years earlier. One of John Dewey's most famous essays grew out of his contribution to this series. In "The Influence of Darwinism on Philosophy," he was quick to point out that the crisis precipitated by Darwin's book was "primarily within science itself" (MW 4:4).[2] This crisis was rooted in an irresolvable conflict between our inherited conception of human knowledge and the dramatic results of evolving practices of experimental inquiry. The advances of scientific investigation demanded the abandonment of classical ontology and traditional epistemology. In particular, *Origin of Species* marked the end of the eternal (MW 14:3,6). The forms of all things are reckoned to be historical and thus mutable. Everything whatsoever is transient[3] and everything alive is mortal. What are we to make of life in light of an unblinking acceptance of transience, mutability, and mortality? How are we to understand it and, indeed, to live it in the wake of Darwin?[4]

Dewey's essay itself concludes by noting that "the greatest dissolvent in contemporary thought of old questions, the greatest precipitant of new methods, new intentions, new problems, is the one effected by the scientific revolution that founds its climax in the *Origin of Species*" (MW 4:14). It may indeed be that "intellectual progress usually occurs through sheer abandonment of questions together with both of the alternatives they assume."[5] But human wisdom might also demand addressing traditional questions from a truly novel angle, including those concerning death and how to face this and other losses.[6] To address traditional questions even in radically innovative ways implies that these questions are legitimate. Our resolute refusal to abandon some traditional questions is not incompatible with the realization that, very often, the most responsible course of philosophical inquiry involves asking new questions, not addressing old ones in new ways. In any event, the question of what makes life significant and, thus, tragedies bearable, precisely when one takes the biological frame of human existence to define the limits of our lives, is at once a traditional and timely philosophical question.[7] Of course, what gives point and even urgency to this question is that occasionally our lives threaten to become unbearable because our losses, frustrations, and humiliations threaten to become unbearable. Hence, the question of how our lives are to be lived luminously is of a piece with the question of how losses are to be borne lightly or, if this is impossible or inappropriate, gracefully. What makes life significant must be what makes its defeats, deficiencies, and tragedies bearable.[8] The dumb pluck of the human animal is certainly part of this story,[9] but so is the symbolic articulation of human loss in the form of ritual, myth, and memoir.[10]

A sign of humanity is the refusal simply to abandon our dead: our concern for human life extends to our treatment of lifeless humans. The specific rituals by which human communities care for the corpses of their members are complex and various, but the totality of these rites attests to the exigency of confronting human loss in a humanizing way.[11] The individual who is no longer alive is still human, this lifeless body is yet an integral member of some particular communities (if these communities have any semblance of humanity).[12]

"The influence of Darwin upon philosophy resides," according to Dewey, "in his having conquered the phenomena of life for the principle of transition" (MW 4:7). Life in the biological no less than the experiential sense is *in the transitions.*[13] The intellectual revolution inaugurated by Charles Darwin was in fact encapsulated in the very title of his book: species, the forms of biological existence and indeed all else, are not eternal but historical (MW 4: 4). They come to be and cease to be. A world of such transitions is, thus, inevitably one of extinction, the emergence of novel forms being entangled with the elimination of once regnant species.

The psychoanalytic theorist Adam Phillips notes that: "The world of continuous change—the daunting new world that both Darwin and Freud both report back from—is a world of continuous loss."[14] But he immediately adds that neither thinker in his confrontation with transience, loss, and mortality is stricken by grief; both exhibit or (to use Phillips's own telling word) "*perform* in their writings an intrigued resilience, neither bumptiously optimistic nor complacently gloomy."[15] If nature is (as William James suggests in *A Pluralistic Universe*) a name for excess,[16] it is thereby a way of indicating myriad and inevitable losses, ones exceeding the possibility of imagining their number or depth. "Both Darwin and Freud were fascinated by losses that could be survived—or even seen to be sources of inspiration—and by what survived, as evidence, of lives that had been lived. It was to these formative scenes of loss that they returned again and again in their writings."[17] But so too did Dewey. Human experience is, among other things, a tangled record[18] of having survived countless losses and, in doing so, of having acquired "an intrigued resilience" to make good present and future losses.

For Dewey, the influence of Darwin marked the irreparable loss of the classical outlook in which the very forms of being were taken to be eternally fixed.[19] In his own undramatic manner, Dewey returned again and again to the formative scenes of our definitive losses[20]—the losses that define us, for example, as modern rather than medieval—in order to show how such losses might be not so much merely borne as vibrantly celebrated, but celebrated in a manner embodying our respect (in some instances, even our intense reverence and abiding love) for what has been lost. Dewey's attitude toward Plato's dialogues is exemplary of how the process of working through the definitive losses of the most central parts of our once definitive heritage can be a complex and interminable process.[21] Dewey returned to Plato, again and again, deriving pleasure as well as insight from his rereadings of the dialogues; moreover, his reenactment of reading these texts bears the marks of a ritual.[22]

The only possibility of bringing "to consciousness America's own needs and its own implicit principle of successful action" (MW 10:47) is by *working through* a historically extensive cultural inheritance (going back at least as far as Plato), not by trying to jettison this heritage once and for all. (Here, as in other important respects, pragmatism stands in marked opposition to Cartesianism.) For Dewey, philosophy was integral to the task of making good our losses—for instance, our loss of the Athenian *polis;* of the medieval *ecclesia;* of our centering faith in an unseen order vouching that at least some of our most cherished ideals and objects are destined to survive the absolute annihilation of the material universe;[23] of the Jeffersonian ideal of agrarian democracy; and of the unbounded optimism of Enlightenment rationalism. Making good these losses involves both extracting their abidingly relevant promise and resisting their subtly deadening lure. It involves that most intriguing form of "intrigued resilience" for it involves marrying promiscuity to fidelity! What Phillips discerns in Darwin and Freud can also be seen in Dewey: "they describe, or implicitly prescribe the intelligence . . . of certain kinds of promiscuity—in the individual constructing his dreams, or in the successful species exploiting its niche—but without asking us to give up on history, and therefore on loyalties and allegiances from the past."[24] For Dewey no less than for Darwin and Freud, the past is never the sort of the thing that could ever be simply abandoned or jettisoned: "it can only be variously reconstructed and experienced."[25] Just because life *is* in the transitions and more decisively there than anywhere else, whither we go is of a piece with whence we came. This does not justify being fixated on the past, but rather suggests the only way of liberating ourselves from the fixations and infantilisms[26] woven into the very fabric of our psyches, cultural and personal.

For example, my fidelity to Plato might require falling in love with any number of other authors. My love of my own culture might invite or even demand partaking of other cultures. Our defining loyalties and attachments are not utterly plastic or malleable, but they in the excess of their vitality *are* expansive and ramifying. Some attachments and loyalties are betrayed when they are allowed to preclude other attachments and loyalties. They are (to use Phillips's term) promiscuous; and, as the origin of this word suggests, this means that they prompt us to go forth among and mix with others.

John Dewey self-consciously wrote in the wake of Charles Darwin (as did, of course, Charles Peirce, William James, Josiah Royce, and George Herbert Mead).[27] He did so most obviously in the sense of philosophically traveling in the wake of the H. M. S. Beagle and *its* aftermath, hence in the sense of intellectually moving along—and beyond—a course partly defined by a route to faraway, strange islands. In physically traveling to the Galapagos Islands, the grandson intellectually positioned himself to inherit the ideas of his grandfather: the strange flora and fauna on these islands helped to make plausible the equally strange hypothesis of Erasmus Darwin. But, in its turn, this hypothesis worked to render implausible, even incredible, some of the most central tenets of Western culture. This heresy appears to have been destined to become orthodoxy, at least among a significant segment of the educated population here and in countless other places.[28]

To travel in the wake of a ship implies of course that one is traveling behind this vessel. To take part in the wake of one who has died is, for some of the cultures with which I am familiar, not only to stay with the deceased person but also to stay awake during a time of transition: the body should be accompanied by one or more persons until it is interned or cremated. In its origin, a wake is a time of wakefulness. One is called upon to be awake, thus mindful or attentive, alert and solicitous. In assisting the transition of the body of the other, one is in effect facilitating one's own transition of living at a loss, of detaching oneself in certain ways so that one might remain attached to this particular person in a manner embodying a simultaneous acknowledgment of inseverable attachment and irrevocable loss. One possibility is to conceive mourning as the process (or, in Freud's lexicon, work) of simultaneously loosening the tie to one to whom we are inseparably bound and attaching ourselves to one from whom we are forever distanced.[29] It is often, though not necessarily, a process of attachment by means of detachment; for sometimes it might simply be a process of letting go.

We live and thus are invited to reflect and question in the wake of Darwin. This means that we are part of a ritual of passage: we are called upon to be mindful of how the Darwinian outlook itself is caught up in a process of transforming itself into something other than itself. There is no self-transcendence without self-transformation; in turn, there is no self-transformation without self-annihilation. But living in the wake of Darwin also means that we are looking forward to a movement ahead of us: the future beckons us in a way that makes us feel that we are behind ourselves, that our present is part of a past quickly receding behind us and, simultaneously, part of a future subtly eluding us still. The continuous reverberating impact of the Darwinian perspective upon our cultural psyche has proven to be an effective means of turning our cultural inheritance against itself, for the sake of intensifying experience. The task is not so much to go forward as to go on,[30] when the very capacities enabling us to go on can, in altered circumstances, spell extinction rather than survival, immutable fixations rather than flexible adaptations.[31]

ON THE OCCASION OF LOSS

Our going on is frequently a going forth without others with whom we have traveled an immeasurable distance. This going forth is hardly ever a process of simply leaving behind or passing by these others. It is ordinarily an incredibly complex process of letting go *and* carrying forward; only thus do we position ourselves to move on. Whatever the character of this process, we *customarily* find it necessary to mark, formally and communally, just this necessity to go forth in the absence of some intimate other. Upon the deaths of James, Mead, and Tufts, Dewey himself publicly marked the loss of his friends.[32] Upon Dewey's own death, John Herman Randall, Jr., undertook this task. But the loss of a friend or acquaintance is but one form of loss with which we are compelled to deal, however obliquely or unconsciously. The loss of one's childhood faith or one's unquestioned patriotism points to other forms of significant loss. In this section, accordingly, I will examine the way Randall marked the occasion of Dewey's death and, from his memorial reflections, extract a central but unacknowledged feature of Dewey's philosophical life. We can discern, at the center of this life, a nuanced response to the irreparable loss of what is arguably the classical tradition of Western thought. In other words, the manner in which Randall came to terms with his loss of Dewey as a friend and colleague helps us to see the manner in which Dewey himself came to terms with the loss of the illusion of a universe in which meaning is divinely ordained and, hence, antecedently secured. Since mourning is a process of working through potentially devastating loss, we might interpret Dewey's ceaseless engagement with the intersecting traditions of Western culture as the process of working through the loss of a humanly sustaining culture. In coming to terms with the loss of Dewey, Randall was reminded of what was startling about his teacher, colleague, and friend: for all of his emphasis on experimentalism, Dewey was in a certain respect a traditionalist. In coming to terms with the loss of a humanly sustaining culture, Dewey became aware that letting go is crucial for going on. But he also appears to have been aware that letting go is also a way of carrying on what never can be simply thrown aside or left behind.

The "capacity to experience ambivalence is," in Hanna Segal's judgment, " a fundamental achievement, a major step in development."[33] She notes: "In melancholia the work of mourning is impeded by an ambivalence towards the object, an ambivalence that continues in relation to this object even after it has been internalized. . . ."[34] Put positively, this work is facilitated by the achievement of ambivalence. Such an achievement demands owning up to one's ambivalence, "accepting it, and working through it."[35] Aggression is certainly not absent from this process; but it becomes tempered and tutored insofar it is shaped by a resolute effort to come to specific and nuanced terms with what has been lost. These observations apply not to Randall vis-à-vis the death of Dewey but rather to Dewey himself vis-à-vis the historical loss of sustaining traditions and a humanizing culture. Central to the argument of this paper is that Dewey's attitude toward tradition reveals an achievement of ambivalence, only made possible by working through the loss of what had been humanly nourishing. Traditionalists are disposed to see only Dewey's aggression toward the antecedently established (i.e., the traditionally consolidated and historically instituted). Many of his defenders are, in turn, only appreciative of Dewey's ability to twist himself free from the past. Modern societies are defined in opposition to traditional societies; hence, modernity means by implication living beyond the reach of traditional authority and outside the confines of traditional roles. But Dewey realized that the modern epoch is in its own way a time of traditional societies. Traditions have not been—

and, indeed, could never be—simply abolished. They have imploded in ways calling for reconstruction, not only at quite specific levels but also at the more general one of understanding traditions in light of their historicity (thus, in light of their mutability, contingency, and partiality). Modern societies are no more posttraditional than are traditional societies unqualifiedly prescientific. Our species is the unintended experiment in which experimental improvisations are among its defining activities. Members of "primitive" societies are experimentalists along with those in "civilized" ones. Simple oppositions must be opposed, crude dualisms deconstructed. One of the most insistent champions of modernity (above all, of the distinctively modern practices of democratic polity and experimental investigation) is best understood when his subtle recovery of tradition and, allied to this, his unheralded achievement of ambivalence, are brought into focus. His carrying on the work of philosophy was, at once, a letting go and a carrying forward of an indispensable historical inheritance. Randall enables us to discern this facet of Dewey, whereas Dewey exhibits in his painstaking involvement with intertwined histories a process little appreciated by even his most insightful expositors and defenders.

In response to John Dewey's death in 1952, John Herman Randall, Jr., took the alternate expressions "traditional critic" or "critical traditionalist" to be good words[36] by which to identify his colleague and friend's philosophical role.[37] He wanted his "teacher" and friend to be remembered in this light. Moreover, in introducing *Nature and Historical Experience* (1958), a work comparable in depth and scope to Dewey's own *Experience and Nature* (1925), Randall noted that: "My teachers are no longer among the living. . . . What I have learned from them is presumably *not* what they intended to teach. Doubtless John Dewey did not set out to impress me with the overwhelming importance of tradition."[38] Yet what Randall learned from Dewey was precisely the importance of tradition.[39] One of the ways in which Dewey conveyed a sense of this importance was quite explicitly, in passages such as the one quoted by Randall in his memorial tribute to his institutional colleague and philosophical companion: "If a philosopher ignores traditions—the classic tradition of Greece and the Middle Ages, the tradition of eighteenth-century rationalism, the tradition of German idealism, the religious and philosophic traditions of Europe—his thought becomes thin and empty."[40] The thinness and vacuity of Dewey's own philosophy is an illusion cast by ignoring how much Dewey revered the traditions in which his own concerns and tasks were rooted.[41]

Dewey was of course a philosophical pluralist even more than he was a philosophical traditionalist. This pluralism pervaded *his* traditionalism, for his appreciation of the importance of tradition was marked by sensitivity to the plurality of traditions (a sensitivity in evidence in the passage quoted by Randall). His pluralism was of a piece with his skepticism toward what is often dubbed traditionalism, for such traditionalism tends to privilege one tradition over all others (thereby exhibiting its provincialism and often its ethnocentrism).[42] While he had no doubt about the importance of tradition, he had deep, abiding doubts about our propensity to use the singular form of this word. To recall once again Dewey's own words here: "I am highly skeptical of all arguments that assume there is but one available tradition. We have at our disposal many traditions" (LW 11:117). His list of the traditions uppermost in his mind when defending *A Common Faith* is instructive: "there is the great tradition of autonomous literature, of music, of painting, of all the fine arts, in each of which, moreover, there are many significant traditions. There is the tradition of democracy; there is the tradition of experimental science, which if not thoroughly established is yet far from embryonic" (LW 11:117). Of course, Dewey was acquainted with Eastern as well as Western religious, intellectual, and cultural traditions. He astutely observed shortly before his death that neither the East nor the West is a block, so discussions of how to synthesize East and West are fundamentally misguided. Just as there is a plurality *of* traditions, there is ordinarily an irreducible pluralism within any truly vital tradition (a point made about the arts in the passage just quoted). What ought to have been too obvious to merit assertion, let alone emphasis, was felt by Dewey to be nonetheless habitually overlooked (and who among the readers of this essay has not encountered so many and so facile global characterizations of Western culture, Enlightenment rationality, and European modernity that Dewey's recollection of a commonplace appears even today to be necessary?):

> There are great and fundamental differences in the East just as there are in the West. The cultural matrix of China, Indonesia, Japan, India, and Asiatic Russia is not a single "block" affair. Nor is the cultural matrix of the West. The differences between Latin and French and Germanic cultures on the continent of Europe, and the differences between these and the culture of England on the one hand and the culture of the United States on the other (not to mention Canadian and Latin American differences), are extremely important for understanding the West. (LW 17:35)

The stress is on specificity as well as plurality: it is imperative to discern the specific ways in which various traditions intersect and, in their intersection, support, undermine, and in other respects influence one another.

But Dewey's characteristic emphasis should not blunt our appreciation of his equally characteristic awareness of the ineluctable presence of our traditional inheritances in any recognizable field of human endeavor. Of course the fields to which Dewey was himself most devoted were philosophy, politics, education, and more generally culture. He knew all too well how appeals to tradition could be used to block the road of inquiry. He often expressed the need "to break through the imprisoning crust of traditions and customs," far less often thematized than the task of maintaining and enhancing our traditions (LW 15:17). But, for an experimental traditionalist of a Deweyan stripe, this largely goes without saying. *Of course,* traditions, conventions, and institutions must be conserved. But their conservation will often require at critical junctures reconstruction. The reconstruction of (say) philosophy is the conservation of a tradition of reflection, interpretation, and critique, though one responsive to the driving forces of an ongoing history (economic, technological, scientific, and other kinds of forces). Reconstruction is more than conservation, but not less. Dewey was decidedly no romantic (the most typical form of romanticism in his day, as in ours, often taking the form of anticonventionalism and antitraditionalism): "To view institutions as enemies of freedom, and all conventions as slaveries, is to deny *the only means* by which positive freedom can be secured" (MW 14:115, emphasis added). Conventions and customs, traditions and institutions, are necessary for carrying any human impulse to "any happy conclusion." Thus, a "romantic return to nature and a freedom within the individual without regard to the existing environment finds its terminus in chaos" (MW 14:115). There must be regard for the existing environment, cultural as well as natural. The traditionalist is a conservative, one self-consciously devoted to the task of conserving the natural and cultural matrix in which human flourishing alone emerges and evolves. Natural piety and cultural piety are thus of a piece, since on the one hand human culture is a unique configuration within the natural world and on the other hand the natural world is the womb whence human cultures have sprung.[43] Gratitude and loyalty are traits of piety.

> There is sound sense in the old pagan notion that gratitude is the root of all virtue. Loyalty to whatever in the established (or existing) environment makes a life of excellence possible is the beginning of all progress. The best we can accomplish for posterity is to transmit unimpaired and with some increment of meaning the environment that makes it possible to maintain the habits of decent and refined life. (MW 14:19)

This passage from *Human Nature and Conduct* needs to be juxtaposed to a text from *Experience and Nature,* one more famous though not more revelatory of Dewey's philosophical temperament. "Let us admit the case of the conservative; if we once start thinking no one can guarantee where we shall come out, except that many objects, ends and institutions are surely doomed" (LW 1:172). Thought is inherently dangerous and unpredictably so; for every "thinker puts some portion of an apparently stable world in peril and no one can wholly predict what will emerge in its place" (LW 1:172). The traditionalist is a conservative because s/he is committed to the conservation of those traditions in and through which the viable forms of human striving are alone possible. The thinker appears dangerous to traditionalists and conservatives precisely because that figure *is* dangerous ("Let us admit the case of the conservative": once thought is unfettered, some parts of our world are in peril). But the task of thought requires traditions of reflection upon which thinkers inescapably, even if unwittingly, draw. The studied ignorance of these intellectual traditions insures that thought will be "thin and empty"; only a self-conscious and thus self-critical engagement with our complex intellectual inheritance fosters a sustainable form of intellectual autonomy. The adolescent gestures of romantic rebellion are one thing, the measured critiques of mature reflection quite another. While the gestures of the romantic are in the service of an oppositional identity, the criticisms of adults are informed by the self-imposed task of generativity.[44] The deeds of such adults eloquently proclaim the felt need to carry on, without any assurance that their efforts will be an instance of carrying forward;[45] they in effect say that we, the adults, owe it to our inheritance—that is, to our ancestors, to those who have brought us forth from nothingness—to bequeath to our children at least as well as we have received. We must carry on by carrying over whatever might be useful to those whom we ourselves have brought forth from nothingness. Our responsibility to them entails a responsibility for the world, in particular, for the natural environment and intergenerational institutions (that is, traditional practices), the conjunction of which make up the human habitat (LW 9:40–57). So, let us admit the case of the conservative—and, in almost the same breath, acknowledge the task of conservation, of imposing on ourselves the work of preserving and (if possible) enhancing the conventions, traditions, and institutions in and through which reflection, interpretation, and critique acquire shape and point, maintain and reconstruct themselves (maintain themselves *by* reconstructing themselves).

Though Dewey often used the words *tradition, convention,* and *custom* in a pejorative sense (perhaps less frequently than we are inclined to suppose), he also used them in an honorific way. The unqualified rebellion against (say) conventional modes of human conduct is the mark of romanticism and thus of immaturity: "Not convention but stupid and rigid convention is the foe" (MW 14:115). Nor is there any way of countering the crippling or disfiguring effects of such conventions except by recourse to other conventions: "a convention can be reorganized and made mobile only by using some other custom for giving leverage to an impulse" (LW 9:40–57). In another context, he notes "no one would deny that personal mental growth is furthered in any branch of human undertaking by contact with *the accumulated and sifted experience of others* in that line" (LW 2:56, emphasis added). He generalizes, in the manner of Socrates, from the example of carpentry, suggesting, "the customs, methods, and *working* standards of the calling constitute a 'tradition'" (LW 2:57). Initiation into these customs, methods, and standards—in a word, into this tradition—is the sole means "by which the powers of learners are released and directed" (LW 2:57). Such initiation is in substance, even if not in name, an apprenticeship. In the course of making these points, Dewey asks his readers to imagine an apprentice carpenter who works for an intellectually constrained and hence pedagogically constraining master: "a master carpenter who believes in only one kind of house with a fixed design, and his aim is not only to teach his apprentice to make just that one kind of house, but to accept it with all his soul, heart, and mind as the only kind of house that should ever be built" (LW 2:57)! Dewey refuses to identify this manner of practice (even presumably if it is intergenerationally sanctioned) as a tradition. Rather he insists that: "Here is a case where tradition is not enhancing and liberating, but is restrictive and enslaving" (LW 2: 57–58). If such a carpenter has pupils, they are not so much pupils as "disciples" and s/he is not so much a more experienced coworker as a "master." "Tradition is," Dewey concludes, "no longer tradition but a fixed and absolute convention" (LW 2:58). The implication here seems to be that the only constellation of methods, customs, and standards worthy of the name *tradition* is a set of flexible and relative conventions (conventions relative to the evolving norms and ideals of the experimental and thus alterable activity under discussion). This is, to be sure, an honorific sense of tradition. Dewey's inclination occasionally to use *tradition* in this sense suggests that one of his "pupils" knew something crucial about this "master." The appeal to experience in its most mature and effective form cannot avoid being an appeal to our communal and indeed historical experience (our "accumulated and sifted experience"); and any such appeal is a moment in the process of participating in a practice such as carpentry or childrearing, representing a political unit or conducting a scientific experiment, sustaining a philosophical inquiry or celebrating an erotic friendship. It is a means by which the process is directed or, better, redirected by one or more of the participants in this practice, in an effort to better realize the immanent, constitutive goals of that practice.

"There is no thinking which does not present itself on the background of tradition, and tradition has an intellectual quality that differentiates it from blind custom" (LW 6:12). Traditions are inherently intellectual in quality and ubiquitous in influence; a completely blind tradition is an anomaly, rather than the paradigm, of our intergenerationally refined practices, just as most instances of coming to feel the dead weight of tradition are signs of rigor mortis. The wings of tradition by which we are borne aloft are ordinarily not felt, at least insofar as they so effectively bear our weight that we feel weightless. (To a degree rarely noticed or appreciated, our flights of thought ride upon inherited symbols and personal appropriations of traditional exemplars.) In contrast, the dead weight of tradition *is* felt when it constrains or obstructs the spontaneous flow of our activity. Dewey was reluctant to give the name *tradition* to such constraints and obstructions; he often tended to reserve it for those inherited yet internalized factors and forces that facilitate and even liberate the spontaneous flow of our *sustained* exertions (apart from these factors and forces our exertions would become readily frustrated and hence checked or dissipated).

In light of countless passages insisting upon these or related points, and in light of an ongoing philosophical exchange with Dewey, Randall concluded that Dewey was "neither the mere traditionalist, blind to the new world and to our intellectual resources[,] . . . or the mere contemporary experimentalist, confining his bibliography largely to his own writings."[46] Rather Dewey "was what may be called an 'experimental traditionalist' or a 'traditional experimentalist.'"[47] Of these two expressions, Randall preferred the characterization of Dewey as an "experimental traditionalist" because, in his judgment, Dewey's most promising contribution to philosophical inquiry "is not to be found in those places where he exhibits himself primarily as the critic of a too narrow tradition" but to be encountered at those junctures where Dewey "extends and broadens the classic tradition by setting it in the context of the wider experience of modern knowledge."[48] Note that Randall is referring to Dewey's efforts to situate the classic tradition of Western philosophy in the encompassing *experience* of modern knowledge, not simply in the theoretical context of experimental science. We have undergone and are yet undergoing the consequences of our own experiments, including our cultural experiment to recast the most authoritative forms of human knowledge into self-consciously experimental practices. The historical experiment of recasting human knowledge as a fallible undertaking, as never anything more than a patchwork of guesses, drives us toward an ever more unblinking acceptance of the transience of our most cherished ideals and also toward an ever more inclusive acknowledgment of the fallibility of even our most authoritative judgments (at least those about substantive, rather than purely formal, matters). The patterns of our inquiry, no less than the objects, processes, and relationships disclosed by these inquiries, are not fixed forms. They are never more than evolving forms, accordingly never more than transient affairs. But this emphasis on transience and mutability anticipates too quickly the central themes to be sounded in the second half of this essay, even before our opening themes of tradition and generativity have been returned to their origin—Randall's memorial words regarding Dewey's philosophical character.

For these were words of memorial uttered shortly after Dewey had died at the age of ninety-two. The occasion of this characterization partly defines the function of these expressions: Randall was here reenacting a ritual of recollection, observing the custom to mark, at the time of a person's death, some of the most salient features and significant accomplishments of that person's singular history. On numerous occasions, Dewey himself had assumed the responsibility of marking the loss of persons who were both colleagues and friends (or, at least, acquaintances).

It is instructive to recall, if only briefly, several of Dewey's own reenactments of this ritual, paying especially close attention to what is implicit in his observances regarding inescapable transience and irrevocable loss. Unbearable losses must be borne; unimaginable tragedies must not only be endured but also revisited, thus reenvisioned. Is it always, or ever, possible to make good our losses? Might not the very attempt to make a particular loss good be obscene?

On such an occasion, it is imperative to find the most fitting words with which to evoke a nuanced sense of a unique loss, the death of *this* man at this time and in this place. The struggle to find fitting words is part of the task of coming to terms with the loss itself: indeed, to come to terms with our losses ordinarily entails groping for terms in which the shape and significance of the losses might be articulately experienced, not just dumbly endured. While experience generally drives toward expression,[49] our experiences of transience and loss severely challenge our capacity to give articulate form to our actual experience. This struggle is a phase in our rituals of mourning, the *work* of our grieving,[50] for such rituals ordinarily allow the experience of loss to be expressed (not only endured) silently and inarticulately. The absence of words and the presence of tears are, for most of us, integral to working through such experiences. Of course, grief is felt and experienced; but grieving is enacted and reenacted as well as shunned and circumvented.[51] There is of course nothing unusual in the felt need to mark, in a public and otherwise appropriate manner, the loss of such a friend and colleague, who was also a figure of national importance and international note. To speak well of one who has just died is an integral part of our mourning rituals. There is, however, an unusual note struck in Randall's particular characterization of Dewey's intellectual role. Moreover, there is a noteworthy absence, or at least dearth, of virtually any philosophical treatment of these crucial rituals. This is perhaps truer of the classical American pragmatists than of philosophers working out of other intellectual traditions. It is therefore necessary to address the indispensable work that our mourning rituals facilitate. Dewey engaged in, but did not reflect upon, the traditional ritual of communal recollection so often integral to our efforts to confront the death of a person. In response to the loss of such philosophical allies and personal friends as William James, George Herbert Mead, and James Hayden Tufts, John Dewey's simple yet eloquent words of recollection were uttered. Especially in the case of those with whom he was intimate (e.g., Tufts and Mead), the personal is avoided because, if it were recalled on this occasion, the grief would be overwhelming. Even so, we have specific examples of Dewey engaged in the traditional practice of the funeral oration.

One of the most moving passages in the entirety of Dewey's vast corpus (the concluding sentences of *Human Nature and Conduct*) nonetheless betrays an inadequate understanding of the crucial significance of traditional rituals for transacting the most momentous transitions in human existence.[52] In this text he claims that:

> Within the flickering inconsequential acts of separate selves dwells a sense of the whole that claims and dignifies them. In its presence we put off mortality and live in the universal. The life of the community in which we live and have our being is the fit symbol of this relationship. The acts in which we express our perception of the ties that bind us to others are its only rites and ceremonies.[53]

But the acts by which we acknowledge our ties to those who constitute this community include the acts by which we acknowledge our loss of those to whom we are yet tied and moreover to whom we so often vow our memory. We are bound to those who are torn from us or who have more gently departed; and we need to mark in a communal and ceremonial manner our ties, perhaps above all, to those from whom we have been severed by death.[54] The birth of a human is a communal affair, as is the death of such a being. As such, human birth and death demand appropriate forms of communal recognition.

On the occasion of Dewey's death (that is, the loss of his "teacher" and friend), Randall was moved to recall Dewey's unique life in a commensurately unique manner. On the occasion of the deaths of first James, then Mead, and still later Tufts, Dewey himself felt moved to recall these unique lives in an equally appropriate manner. Let us recollect his words of recollection and, having done so, reflect upon the nature of the process of working through grief that such words try to facilitate. Here it will also be illuminating to remember the words of Jane Addams upon the death of Gordon Dewey.[55]

In focusing upon the process of *working* through the tragic experience of irreparable loss, I intend both to supplement Dewey and answer Cavell. But I also hope to set the stage for the enactment of a brief tragicomedy, a play called "In the Wake of Darwin." There is a wide range of quite important rituals between the arts devoted to propitiating supernatural powers and those ordained toward directing natural forces. Within this range we find the arts or rituals of symbolic acknowledgment; and among these we find our rites of mourning, of trying to come to terms with *this* loss.

The triumph of Darwin marks a loss to which a variety of responses is possible, *from* a gleeful and perhaps even spiteful "Good riddance!" *to* a lugubrious and even pathological stance of refusing to accept life on these terms (as we often hear individuals confess that "If *this* is all there is, then my life is worthless)."[56] Dewey's own response was neither jauntily irreverent nor even remotely lugubrious, but one exemplifying a praiseworthy form of human resilience in which the work of bearing loss is one with the work of carrying on,[57] of conducting and consummating our everyday experiences in a manner intensified and deepened by a vivid sense of our communal attachments, including our attachments to those no longer living.[58] It may be, however, that the work of mourning cannot always or immediately take the form of work in its most straightforward sense; it may be that mourning is a distinctive form of human work deserving formal recognition in its own right.

CARRYING ON: DIALECTIC OF LETTING GO AND CARRYING FORWARD

The inspiration for this collection of essays was the spur of one of Nietzsche's texts (in fact, a text in which the metaphor of spur itself occurs). In the penultimate section of Part I ("On Free Death") of *Thus Spoke Zarathustra,* the central figure announces that: "I show you the death that consummates—a spur and promise to the survivors. He that consummates his life dies his death victoriously, surrounded by those who hope and promise. Thus one should learn to die. . . ."[59]

Nietzsche went mad and in effect died all too soon. In contrast, Dewey lived a very long life, writing until almost the very end; he was, if anything, pathologically stable! Moreover, Dewey in a quiet and private manner bore the loss of his childhood faith and his early optimism, even more tragically bore the devastating losses of two of his very young children,[60] by apparently working through his sense of loss mostly by simply working (by reading, writing, reflecting, and conversing). Work in the ordinary sense might of course serve various and even contradictory goals. One of its functions is that of enabling a person to bear what so often feels like an unbearable loss. So here again we are led back to the topic of mourning.

Did Dewey live too long and thus die too late? Or was his manner of living truly a consummation of life (in Nietzsche's as well as his own sense), making of it a spur and a promise to those who survived him (or even those who simply came after him), especially those survivors who were or eventually became intimately and definitively attached to Dewey? Was his death one in which "the oaths of the living" were and can yet be hallowed?[61] Yes, but ironically only if our oaths *to* the dead, including Dewey himself, are better honored than this philosopher of experience ever managed to do. At the center of our oaths to the dead is the vow that they will not die before we ourselves do: they *will* live in and through us. Our resolve to remember them is the heart of our oath to them. And, so, again we are prompted to return to the topic of mourning.

Cavell helpfully recalls that Freud speaks of mourning as work (a process of working through our grief not so much that we might get beyond loss but that we might carry on with our lives, by transforming our losses into life). But then he pointedly asks: "Does the writing of Dewey or James help us understand this idea of work?"[62] He argues that, whereas some of Emerson's essays help us to understand the character and importance of mourning precisely as a unique kind of human *work,* the writings of Dewey and James are unhelpful in this regard. Hence, in treating Emerson as essentially a forerunner of pragmatism, we are likely to render inaudible the distinctive voice of those Emersonian essays,[63] a voice articulating (allegedly) an appreciation of mourning as "a path to human objectivity with the world, to separating the world from ourselves, from our private interests in it."[64] Cavell uses a psychoanalytic term to express the process by which the Emersonian voice, in its irreducible difference from other American authors, is lost: "*To repress* Emerson's difference is to deny that American is as transcendental as it is pragmatist, that it is in struggle with itself, at a level not articulated by what we understand by the political."[65]

Following Freud and Cavell, we should broaden and deepen our understanding of work. And we should do so in such a way that the ritual labor, the symbolic action, of working through grief is accorded in our philosophical accounts of human experience the truly pivotal place it occupies in our actual experience. But, following Dewey and Mead, we also need to expand and deepen our understanding of the political.

The spur and promise of Dewey's life and writings drive me to address anew the multiple senses of work and power, to probe the complex relationships between a wide array of psychoanalytic phenomena on the one hand and the ordinary sense of political action on the other. In tracing out the trajectories of Dewey's insights, but also in filling in the lacunae in his philosophical explorations,[66] we cannot leave unsaid or unexplored what so often for Dewey went without saying or questioning. Dewey was convinced that: "Man continues to live because he is a living creature, not because reason convinces him of the certainty or probability of future satisfactions and achievements. He is instinct with activities that carry him on" (MW 14:199–200). Of course, some individuals are unable to carry the weight of their own experience: they are weighed down to the level of depression, barely able to drag themselves through life, sometimes not at all able to carry on. The narrator in Bharati Mukherkee's *Jasmine* notes, in reference to professors she had met when working as an au pair: "They had things they wanted me to translate, paintings they wanted me to decipher. They were very democratic that way. *For them,* experience leads to knowledge, or else it is wasted. *For me,* experience must be forgotten, or it will kill me."[67] Any adequate account of human experience must take into account the forceful testimony of this fictional character. Humans ordinarily do exhibit "the dumb pluck of the animal" (MW 14:200). Endurance, hope, curiosity, irrepressible curiosity, and spontaneous exertion seem to belong to humans by their structure or constitution, not by their thought or resolve.[68] But the human animal *does* all too often collapse under the weight of its own lived experience: life proves too much to bear, loss too great, too overwhelming, to accept or in some cases acknowledge. The question of how we acquire the capacity to bear our losses, of how symbolic articulations and communal rituals are necessary to sustain the dumb pluck of the human animal, ought to be explored.

In the wake of Darwin, and with the help of Dewey, we have been guided and goaded into fashioning viable notions of human experience and the natural world, that is, in refashioning our classical heritage and more recent traditions in such a way that this complex bequest more fully meets the defining exigencies of our historical moment. Mutability, contingency, transience, and finitude are not only acknowledged to be irreducible traits of the natural world but also definitive aspects of the ultimate context in which human existence emerges and evolves.

In the wake of Freud, and following the example of Cavell, however, the specific mutabilities constitutive of an individual life and the structural exigencies of our most critical transitions need to be not only acknowledged but also investigated. Ritual, myth, and memoir are not only to be acknowledged as historically important ways of articulating the substance and discerning the texture of our lived experience, but also as indispensable resources for the ever pressing human need to give arresting symbolic expression to our fleeting experiences.

Dewey very near the end of his life disparaged the way philosophers, especially those who make a show of their commitment to experience, tend to discourse about experience (LW 1:367–68). In their theoretical accounts, philosophers tend to make the focal object of an ordinary experience (for example, a chair) less than it is; in contrast, such an object in the experience of ordinary persons in their everyday circumstances is, most often, "a good deal more than a chair." For such a person "lays hold of a wide spatial context, such as the room where the chair is, and a spread of its history, including the chair's period, price paid for it, consequences, public as well as personal, which flow from its use as household furniture, and so on" (LW 1:368).[69] For these and other reasons, Dewey concludes that: "I would rather take the behavior of the dog of Odysseus upon his master's return as an example of the sort of thing experience is for the philosopher than trust to such statements [as those in which the abstracted results of reflective analysis—such as isolated qualities—are taken to be experientially primitive]" (LW 1:368). Cigars and handkerchiefs are hardly ever, in our experience, simple data or even constellations of such data. "A physiologist may for his special purpose reduce Othello's perception of a handkerchief to simple elements of color under certain conditions of light and shapes seen under certain angular conditions of vision. But the actual experience was charged with history and prophecy; full of love, jealousy and villainy, past human relationships and moving fatally to tragic destiny" (LW 1:368).

The pragmatic reconstruction of human experience[70] is, and ever must be, a work in progress. Dewey did not desire "disciples" but those individuals who by their joint participation in the ongoing work of some worthwhile undertaking are learners (LW 2:58). That is, he desired coworkers and, since his work was philosophical, co-inquirers. We bear the loss of grandparents, parents, and others by carrying on some part of their work or embodying some of their attitudes. But, for me, to carry on the work of this intellectual grandparent means attending more carefully than he ever did to the *work* of bearing our losses.

It seems especially fitting that the editor of this volume is one whose forebears hail from Ireland. For Darwin's wake can only be an Irish wake, one in which celebration and even rowdiness are as integral to the occasion as are an articulated sense of loss and a dumb numbness of being. Often the end of a life is, in some respects, an occasion for celebrating, both that life and our own: such celebration is integral to the work of grief and, accordingly, pivotal to the conduct of our experience (to how we bear and, in order to bear, how we appropriate, acknowledge, reenvision, and refashion the stuff of our experience). "What Emerson calls for is," according to Cavell, "something we do not want to hear, something about the necessity of patience or suffering in allowing ourselves to change. What discipline will call for this if philosophy does not?"[71] But what Dewey calls for is, in truth, a form of humility close to what Emerson is calling for—the gentle rather than begrudging acceptance of the task of allowing ourselves to wait and even to suffer, in order to carry on (MW 14:200). Dewey's deeply personal grief was not publicly expressed,[72] nor did he philosophically investigate the central experience of irreparable loss. If I take this to be not a cause for tears but an inducement to join Dewey in articulating an experientially comprehensive and rooted account of our lived experience, I will betray myself to some as just another "Dewey-eyed pragmatist" (in John Patrick Diggins's caustic phrase). My task is, however, not simply to join Dewey in the cooperative activity of philosophical reflection but to join him to Freud, Marx, Nietzsche, and others who were self-consciously working out the implications of the influence of Darwinism on culture; and I am doing so in a way that accords loss as well as transience the centrality both actually have in our experience. This hardly seems naïve or sentimental; but, then, in my own experience of reading Dewey, I have rarely encountered a naïve, and never a sentimental, thinker, but only a spur to think through experience in its irreducibly complex, thorny, and frequently dark character.

NOTES

1. It is crucial to remember that many of the most important forms of remembrance are, no matter how deeply personal, irreducibly communal. See Paul Connerton, *How Societies Remember* (Cambridge: Cambridge University Press, 1989). In *The Need of Strangers* (New York: Viking Penguin, 1985), Michael Ignatieff suggests: "We need words to keep us human. Being human is an accomplishment like playing an instrument. It takes practice. . . . Without a public language to help us find our own words, our needs will dry up in silence. . . . Without the light of language, we risk becoming strangers to our better selves" (141–42). We need not only words but also other communal modes of articulating the definitive and significant experiences by which we have become who we are. Communal rituals of recollection are as crucial as communal rituals of

mourning for conserving and deepening our humanity. This paper itself undertakes the work of memory, in particular, the task of recalling how a central figure in an intellectual community commemorated the publication of Darwin's *Origin of Species* and, later, how another member of this same community marked the loss of the one who years earlier had marked the epochal achievement of Darwin's scientific discovery. John Dewey's commemorative appraisal of Charles Darwin is, thus, joined to the way John Herman Randall, Jr., marked the death of John Dewey. Both were not only deliberate but also communal recollections of momentous occasions.

2. By implication, the crisis is *not* primarily between science and religion. This point is explicit in Dewey's text.

3. It is instructive to compare Sigmund Freud's "On Transience" (1916) with such writings by Dewey as "Nature and Its Good: A Conversation" (1909) and "Time and Individuality" (1940). Freud's short essay can be found in the *Standard Edition of the Complete Psychological Works of Sigmund Freud,* edited by James Strachey. "Nature and Its Good" was reprinted in *The Middle Works of John Dewey,* vol. 4, 15–30; "Time and Individuality" was reprinted in *The Later Works of John Dewey,* vol. 14, 98–114.

4. In *Darwin's Worms: On Life Stories and Death Stories* (New York: Basic Books, 1999), Adam Phillips suggests: "Both Darwin and Freud were fascinated by losses that could be survived—or even seen to be sources of inspiration—and by what survived, as evidence, of lives that had been lived. It was to these formative scenes of loss that they returned again and again in their writings. What could be made of what hadn't yet disappeared—the fossil record, or the half-remembered dream, species of birds or childhood memories—was their inspiration. It was the transience of things, the impermanence of natural phenomena, that fed them their best lines. Life was about what could be done with what was left, with what still happened to be there" (116–17). The same might just as truly be said of Dewey.

5. Ibid. Additionally, the opening paragraph of Dewey's famous "The Need for a Recovery of Philosophy" bears directly on this theme:

> Intellectual advance occurs in two ways. At times increase of knowledge is organized around old conceptions. . . . At other times, the increase of knowledge demands qualitative rather than quantitative change; alteration, not addition. Men's minds grow cold to their former intellectual concerns; ideas that were burning fade; interests that were urgent seem remote. Men face in another direction; their older perplexities are unreal; considerations passed over as negligible loom up. Former problems may not be solved, but they no longer press for solution. (MW 10:3)

As an example of abandoning the alternatives traditionally assumed to be the only possible ones, consider the existence or (Peirce would insist) the reality of God. Either a supernatural being exists and therefore such traditional religious *attitudes* as reverence, awe, mystery, piety, and fidelity are crucial for human existence and, moreover, traditional religious rituals are indispensable for giving human shape to human lives; or God does not exist and hence such attitudes and rituals are merely useless vestiges of our superstitious past (or worse, disfiguring attitudes and stupefying practices). A robust naturalism of the distinctive character advocated by John Dewey and John Herman Randall, Jr., however, tries to show the still significant role of religious attitudes in the radically altered world of modern life. Of course, the shape of this world is due decisively to the influence of Darwin. In the wake of Darwin, virtually everything has to be rethought and re-envisioned; perhaps much needs to be jettisoned. More likely, most of our inheritance has to be refashioned to accord with a sensibility in which finitude, transience, mutability, and contingency are given their experiential and cosmological due.

6. Anticipated losses might be more intensely felt than actually experienced losses. One can imagine that a friend's death brings home to someone that individual's own death, so much so that hours and even days are consumed by the intensely personal, anxious realization of that person's mortality.

7. See, for example, William James, "Is Life Worth Living?" in *The Will to Believe and Other Essays in Popular Philosophy* (New York: Dover Publications, 1956), 32–62, and "What Makes a Life Significant," in *The Writings of William James: A Comprehensive Edition,* ed. John J. McDermott (Chicago: University of Chicago Press, 1977), 645–60. See also John Dewey, *Experience and Nature* (LW 1).

8. The role of art here ought not to be overlooked. Loss is somatically borne. See Joy A. Mayo, "Dark Elegy: The Mourning Works of Suse Lowenstein," *Sculpture Review* 44 (winter 1996): 29. The sculptures of Suse Lowenstein make this manifest, especially in reference to the initial shock of traumatic loss. She lost her son in the 1988 terrorist bombing of Pan AM Flight 103. She came to terms with this loss partly by sculpting the naked bodies of other women who had also lost loved ones as a result of this crash, at the moment of their loss: "Each woman is asked [by the sculptor] to go back to that moment in their lives. 'When that moment comes, it is fascinating to me because the women not only emotionally, but also physically, fall back into a unique position,' she [Lowenstein] says. 'Some rage and scream, many curl up in a ball, while others are just very quiet'" (Mayo, 29). Also see Maya Lin, *Boundaries* (New York: Simon & Schuster, 2000) and "Making the Memorial," *New*

York Review of Books 47, no. 17 (November 2, 2000): 33–35. In this article, the architect responsible for the Vietnam Veterans Memorial in Washington, D.C., recalls that she felt memorials should be "honest about the reality of war, about the loss of life in war, and about remembering those who served and especially those who died" (33). "I imagined," she goes on to say, "taking a knife and cutting into the earth, opening it up, an initial violence and pain that in time would heal. The grass would grow back, but the initial cut would remain a pure flat surface in the earth. . . . The need for the names to be on the memorial would become the memorial; there was no need to embellish the design further. The people and their names would allow everyone to respond and remember" (Ibid.). Such a memorial embodies a ritual of recollection and mourning. Such rituals can, however, be improvised. See Marshall Stella, "Missing" [How a Grief Ritual Is Born], *New York Times Magazine,* October 7, 2001, 48–51. The revisions of my essay are being made in the wake of September 11, 2001. Thus, it seems especially pertinent to include such references.

9. John Dewey, *Human Nature and Conduct* (MW 14). Man "is instinct with activities that carry him on. Individuals here and there cave in, and most individuals sag, withdraw and seek refuge at this and that point. But man as man still has the dumb pluck of the animal. He has endurance, hope, curiosity, eagerness, love of action. These traits belong to him by structure, not by taking thought" (MW 14:200).

10. See John E. Smith, *Experience and God* (New York: Fordham University Press, 1995), 12–13, 23, 41ff; also Patricia Hampl, *I Could Tell You Stories: Sojourns in the Land of Memory* (New York: W. W. Norton, 1999).

11. For an example, see Francine du Plessix Gray, "The Work of Mourning," *American Scholar* (summer 2000): 8–9. Regarding the more general theme of humanizing our experience, see John J. McDermott, *The Culture of Experience: Philosophical Essays in the American Grain* (New York: New York University Press, 1976), chap. 1 ("To Be Human Is to Humanize").

12. One of the most poignant passages in William James's writings is his distinctive formulation of a Spencerian argument in support of materialism: "Matter is indeed infinitely and incredibly refined [not in the least 'gross']. To anyone who has ever looked on the fact of a dead child or parent the mere fact that matter *could* have taken for a time that precious form, ought to make matter sacred ever after. It makes no difference what the *principle* of life may be, material or immaterial, matter at any rate cooperates, lends itself to all life's purposes. That beloved incarnation was among matter's possibilities" (1907 [1975] 50).

13. In his *Essays in Radical Empiricism* (New York: E. P. Dutton, 1971), William James asserted: "Life is in the transitions as much as in the terms connected; often, indeed, it seems to be there more emphatically, as if our spurts and sallies forward were the real firing line of the battle, were like the thin line of flame advancing across the dry autumnal field which the farmer proceeds to burn" (46–47).

14. Phillips, *Darwin's Worms*, 132. I take it to be significant that Phillips uses an epigram from William James's *A Pluralistic Universe* ("Nature is but a name for excess") to open the Prologue to *Darwin's Worms* and an epigram from John Dewey's *Art as Experience* ("The value of ideals lies in the experiences to which they lead") to open the Epilogue of this book. And I take part of this significance to be that, in Phillips's judgment, the sensibility or temperament of James and Dewey is akin to that of Darwin and Freud.

15. Phillips, *Darwin's Worms,* 133 (emphasis added).

16. William James, *A Pluralistic Universe* (Cambridge: Harvard University Press, 1977), 129.

17. Ibid., 116.

18. Experience is *incorporated* in our conscious memory and, to a *far* greater extent, in our largely unconscious habits. Hence, when I assert that our experience is a record of our loss, I mean this rather exactly: for these losses and our various habits and strategies of dealing with loss are inscribed, most of all, in the operative habits of what Dewey called the body-mind.

19. John Herman Randall, Jr., tends to give, in his interpretation of Dewey, too central a place to the classic tradition of Western philosophy. In a text upon which I will draw heavily, Randall suggests that: "'The classic tradition' [and this should be taken in Dewey's own sense: the cultural traditions of ancient Greece and medieval Europe] and 'present realities'—for Dewey both were essential, and each was to be used to illuminate and to criticize the other. This is the source of the power of Dewey's thought. He was neither the mere traditionalist . . . nor the mere contemporary experimentalist . . ." ("John Dewey, 1859–1952," in *Dewey and His Critics,* ed. Sidney Morgenbesser [New York: Journal of Philosophy Publications, 1977], 3–4). But, for Dewey present realities need to be interpreted and evaluated in reference to a wide range of cultural traditions, not simply or even primarily the classic tradition.

20. Dewey was, for the most part, writing for a Western audience confronted with the encompassing forces of modern culture (scientific, technological, economic, etc.). The scenes of *our* losses are those confronting historically and culturally situated actors, living at a specific time and place.

21. This is nowhere better expressed than in Dewey's autobiographical essay "From Absolutism to Experimentalism": "Nothing could be more helpful to present philosophizing than a 'Back to Plato' movement; but it would have to be back to the dramatic, restless, cooperatively inquiring Plato of the Dialogues, trying one mode of attack after another to see what it will yield; back to the Plato whose highest flight of metaphysics always terminated with a social and practical turn, and not to the artificial Plato constructed by unimaginative commentators who treat him as the original university professor" (LW 5:155).

22. Cf. Mary Douglas, *Natural Symbols: Explorations in Cosmology* (New York: Pantheon, 1982); also Catherine Bell, *Ritual: Perspectives and Dimensions* (New York: Oxford University Press, 1997).

23. Cf. William James, *The Principles of Psychology* (Cambridge: Harvard University Press, 1981), 1260; also his *Varieties of Religious Experience* (New York: Mentor Books, 1958), Lecture III ("The Reality of the Unseen") and Lecture XX ("Conclusions").

24. Phillips, *Darwin's Worms,* 134.

25. Ibid.

26. Dewey in *Human Nature and Conduct* exhibits an explicit awareness of these important features of human experience. See, e.g., (MW 14:71, 73).

27. See Louis Menand, *The Metaphysical Club: A Story of Ideas in America* (New York: Farrar, Straus & Giroux, 2001). Also see Philip P. Wiener, *Evolution and the Founders of Pragmatism* (New York: Harper Torchbooks, 1949). Dewey wrote a foreword to this work in which he stresses: "One realizes the ineptitude of the method of pigeonholing classification of philosophical writings when one compares it with the method of placing them in the setting of a new and vital movement in culture which extends far beyond the confines of technical philosophy" (xii). The goal of my essay is, in part, to read Dewey in light of a radical shift in Western consciousness, wherein an ontology of evolved and evolving forms replaces that of eternal and immutable species.

It is significant that in his recollection of Dewey at the time of his death, John Herman Randall, Jr., stressed: "Dewey's enduring contribution to philosophy is not to be found in those places where he exhibits himself primarily as the critic of a too narrow tradition. . . . But Dewey's enduring contribution is to be found where he extends and broadens the classic tradition by setting it in the context of the wider experience of modern knowledge" ("John Dewey, 1859–1952," 4).

28. But defenders of traditional religious orthodoxy who contest the heresy of Darwin have mounted, especially in recent years, a renewed campaign to discredit the Darwinian approach. For a survey and critique of

these defenders, see Frederick Crews, "Saving Us from Darwin" (Part I), *New York Review of Books* 48, no. 15 (October 4, 2001): 24–27; "Saving Us from Darwin" (Part II), 48, no. 16 (October 18, 2001): 51–55.

29. In "The Work of Mourning," Francine du Plessix Gray recalls that the original German title of Freud's "Mourning and Melancholia" was *Traüer Arbeit.* She stresses, moreover: "Mourning, Freud constantly reminds us, is hard, slow, patient work, a meticulous process that must be carried out 'bit by bit' (that phrase is repeated a half dozen times [in his classic essay]), over a far vaster amount of time than twentieth-century society has allotted to any ritual of grief" (*American Scholar* [summer 2000]: 8).

30. This is, of course, an echo of Ludwig Wittgenstein, who in his *Philosophical Investigations,* trans. G. E. M. Anscombe (New York: Macmillan, 1953), makes much of our ability to go on.

31. Cf. Friedrich Nietzsche, *The Gay Science,* trans. Walter Kaufmann (New York: Vintage Books, 1974), §295 ("Brief Habits"). Of course, also see John Dewey, *Human Nature and Conduct* (e.g., MW 14:49–53, 91). In *Darwin's Worms,* Phillips observes: "The habits that sustain us can be deadly; it is we, in Darwin's characteristically quiet irony, that are among the many other cases [of species that can lack the flexibility to adapt to changed circumstances]. If we, like other creatures can prefer our habits to our lives—if we love our routines more than our futures—then we are fatally addicted to the past. Sometimes old, habitual associations need to be turned into looser ends" (134).

32. For Dewey's recollection of James at the time of his time, see the two texts bearing the same title: simply "William James" (MW 6:91–97, 98–102). It is instructive to compare these tributes to James at the time of his death with two recollections of James in commemoration of the centennial of his birth. See "William James and the World Today" and "William James as Empiricist" (LW 15:3–8,9–17). For his eulogy at the memorial service of George Herbert Mead, see "George Herbert Mead as I Knew Him" (LW 6:22–28). Early in his eulogy Dewey asserted: "If I do not speak of the more intimate things [regarding Mead and his wife Helen] which throng in my memory, of their genius for friendship, of their unwearied and unremitting pouring forth of their generous natures, it is not because of coldness to these things but because I do not trust myself to speak of them" (LW 6:22; MW 6:98). For a brief account of Dewey's address at the memorial for Mead in Bond Chapel at the University of Chicago, see George Dykhuizen, *The Life and Mind of John Dewey* (Carbondale: Southern Illinois University Press, 1973), 270–71. See also Dewey's tributes to James Hayden Tufts, with whom he wrote *Ethics* (LW 15:321–23,324–25).

33. Hanna Segal, "The Achievement of Ambivalence," *Common Knowledge* 1 (1992): 12. It is important to stress that this is a matter of *experiencing* ambivalence, of living through it, not simply conceptualizing it.

34. Ibid., 10.

35. Ibid., 13.

36. Part of my preoccupation in this paper will be with prefixes (most notably, the English prefix *eu*-echoing the Greek one ευ- and the English prefix *re*-), part of it will be with a cluster of interrelated topics such as mourning, eulogy, elegy, etc. In the case of eulogy, these two preoccupations come together.

37. John Herman Randall, Jr., "John Dewey, 1859–1952" in *Dewey and His Critics,* ed. Sidney Morgenbesser (New York: Journal of Philosophy Publications, 1997), 4. Cf. my essay on "The Eclipse of Piety" in *Journal of Chinese Philosophy* 24 (1997): 466–77.

38. John Herman Randall, Jr., *Nature and Historical Experience: Essays in Naturalism and in the Theory of History* (New York: Columbia University Press, 1958), 2; emphasis added. Cf. John Herman Randall, Jr., *How Philosophy Uses Its Past* (New York: Columbia University Press, 1963), 47–64.

39. Randall, *Nature and Historical Experience,* 2.

40. Randall, "John Dewey, 1859–1952," 3.

41. In *Nature and Historical Experience,* Randall appropriates Ernst Cassirer's notion of *Aufgabe:* "Cassirer's *Aufgabe,* the 'task imposed,' is a rather better term than 'problems.' It means something imposed, that must be faced, *faciendum*. 'Problems' is too weak: it suggests that men 'thought them up,' and could escape them if they wanted to" (60). In one sense, this might be taken as an implicit criticism of one of Dewey's central notions—that of a problematic situation. But, in a deeper sense, this is better read as a suggestion for what is implied in Dewey's understanding of the problems of men and women in their actual historical circumstances. We do not make up these problems so much as they make us up: we *are* our conflicts. The apparently irenic character of Dewey's philosophical project is predicated on an abiding sensitivity to the agonistic dimension of human existence. Our conflicts are constitutive of who we are; our handling of these are further constitutive of who we are.

42. Cf. Richard Rorty, "On Ethnocentrism: A Reply to Clifford Geertz," in *Philosophical Papers,* vol. 1 (Cambridge: Cambridge University Press, 1991), 203–10.

43. See John Dewey, *A Common Faith* (LW 9:18, 56–58). Cf. George Santayana, *Reason in Religion,* vol. 3 of *The Life of Reason* (New York: Collier Books, 1962), chap. 10; also, Steven Smith, "Piety's Problems," in

Scottish Journal of Religious Studies 16 (spring 1995): 4–24; finally my "Eclipse of Piety," 457–82.

44. Erik H. Erikson, *Identity: Youth and Crisis* (New York: W. W. Norton, 1968), 138–39.

45. John Lachs, "Both Better Off and Better: Moral Progress amid Continuing Carnage," in *Journal of Speculative Philosophy* 15, no. 3 (2001): 173–83.

46. Randall, "John Dewey, 1859–1952," 3–4.

47. Ibid., 4.

48. Ibid.

49. Smith, *Experience and God,* 13.

50. See Sigmund Freud, "Mourning and Melancholia" in *The Freud Reader,* ed. Peter Gay (New York: W. W. Norton, 1989), 584–89; also Julia Kristeva, *Black Sun: Depression and Melancholia,* trans. Leon S. Roudiez (New York: Columbia University Press, 1989). In "What's the Use of Calling Emerson a Pragmatist?" in *The Revival of Pragmatism: New Essays on Social Thought, Law, and Culture,* ed. Morris Dickstein (Durham, N.C.: Duke University Press, 1998), Stanley Cavell argues that whatever the pragmatic conception of work might mean, it can *not* mean grief-work. The concluding pages of my essay address Cavell's conception of grieving as a process of working through loss, a work allegedly falling outside of the scope of pragmatism.

51. See Hanna Segal, "Achievement of Ambivalence," 9–15.

52. Smith, *Experience and God,* 57.

53. See Dewey, *Human Nature and Conduct* (MW 14: 227) and *A Common Faith* (LW 9:56–57).

54. In *The Philosophy of History* (New York: W. W. Norton, 1981), John William Miller approvingly recalls that: "In *The Ancient City,* Fustel de Coulanges centers the sense of personal identity, as it was felt by [ancient] Greeks and Romans, on ancestral piety. The dead still belonged to the family, and the family to them. They guarded the living members and received daily homage. Not to share in such a tradition was to be an outcast or a slave. These practices went beyond private sentiment. They had, indeed, nothing to do with the separated person but only with those whose individuality grew from, and depended on, a community stretching into the past. This membership was the locus of obligation" (110).

55. Jane Addams, *The Excellent Becomes Permanent* (New York: Macmillan, 1932), chap. 6 ("Gordon Dewey"). Gordon died in Ireland when he was eight years old, while he and his family were on an extended trip to Europe. Afterwards on this same trip, John and Alice Dewey adopted an Italian boy named Sabino, about the same age as their recently deceased child. In the introduction to *The Excellent Becomes the*

Permanent, Addams explained: "One memorial is for a child, Gordon Dewey, for whom a service was held in the Hull-House theatre while his parents were still abroad. The place was filled, not only with their friends but with his own as well. I recall my gratitude that afternoon to a member of the philosophy department of the University of Chicago who, although his words naturally centered upon the child of his colleague, interpreted for us the many promising children we had known at Hull-House whose brief lives had been prematurely extinguished" (11–12).

56. In contrast, see Dewey, *Experience and Nature* (LW 1:40–41).

57. When Paul McCartney learned of John Lennon's murder, he went into the studio to write music. Countless other examples of this response to death might be cited.

58. See, for example, Dewey, "Beliefs and Existences" (MW 3:94). See also *Human Nature and Conduct* (MW 14:226–27).

59. Friedrich Nietzsche, *Thus Spoke Zarathustra,* trans.Walter Kaufmann (Princeton: Princeton University Press, 1954), 72.

60. See George Dykhuizen, *Life and Mind of John Dewey,* 79, 115.

61. Ibid.

62. Cavell, "What's the Use of Calling Emerson a Pragmatist?" 73.

63. Ibid., 79.

64. Ibid., 73.

65. Ibid., 79; emphasis added.

66. In reference to gender and other specific aspects of human embodiment, Shannon W. Sullivan in *Living Across and Through Skins* (Bloomington: Indiana University Press, 2001) details how some important gaps in Dewey's transactional account of human experience can be filled in.

67. Bharati Mukherkee, *Jasmine* (New York: Fawcett, 1989), 29 (emphasis added).

68. See Dewey (MW 14:200) and James, *Varieties of Religious Experience,* Lectures VI and VII ("The Sick Soul"), 118ff.

69. In this discussion Dewey draws the distinction between the chair as something at which we gaze and something upon which we sit, granting primacy to the former. This distinction is akin to one drawn by Martin Heidegger, namely, the distinction between that which is ready-to-hand *(zuhanden)* and that which is present-to-hand *(vorhanden)*.

70. See John E. Smith, *Purpose and Thought: The Meaning of Pragmatism* (New Haven: Yale University Press, 1978), chap. 3 ("The New Conception of Experience"); also his *America's Philosophical Vision* (Chicago: University of Chicago Press, 1992), chap. 1 ("The Reconception of Experience in Peirce, James, and Dewey").

71. Cavell, "What's the Use in Calling Emerson a Pragmatist?" 79–80.

72. In "Body-Mind and Subconsciousness: Tragedy in Dewey's Life and Work," in *Philosophy and the Reconstruction of Culture: Pragmatic Essays After Dewey,* ed. John J. Stuhr (Albany: State University of New York Press, 1993), Bruce Wilshire offers a corrective to the facile characterization of John Dewey as a philosopher who lacked any sense of the tragic (257).

Contributors

Thomas M. Alexander is Professor of Philosophy at Southern Illinois University. He is the author of *John Dewey's Theory of Art, Experience and Nature: The Horizons of Feeling.*

Raymond D. Boisvert is Professor of Philosophy at Siena College. He is the author of *Dewey's Metaphysics* and *John Dewey: Rethinking Our Time.*

James Campbell is Professor of Philosophy at the University of Toledo. He is the author of *The Community Reconstructs: The Meaning of Pragmatic Social Thought* and *Understanding John Dewey.*

Vincent Colapietro is Professor of Philosophy at Pennsylvania State University. He is the author of *Peirce's Approach to the Self: A Semiotic Perspective on Human Subjectivity* and *A Glossary of Semiotics.* His latest book, entitled *Fateful Shapes of Human Freedom,* is being published by Vanderbilt University Press.

Michael Eldridge is the author of *Transforming Experience: John Dewey's Cultural Instrumentalism.* A former community organizer, he now teaches philosophy at the University of North Carolina at Charlotte.

William J. Gavin is Professor of Philosophy at the University of Southern Maine. He is the editor of *Context over Foundation: Dewey and Marx* and the author of *William James and the Reinstatement of the Vague* and *Cuttin' the Body Loose: Historical, Biological, and Personal Approaches to Death and Dying.*

John Lachs is Centennial Professor of Philosophy at Vanderbilt University. His books include *In Love with Life, Intermediate Man,* and *The Relevance of Philosophy to Life.* He is interested in the relations between ethics and human natures.

Joseph Margolis is Laura H. Carnell Professor of Philosophy at Temple University. He is the author of more than thirty books, including a four-volume series under the general title *The Persistence of Reality,* which includes: *Pragmatism Without Foundations, The Truth About Relativism, The Flux of History and the Flux of Science,* and *Interpretation Radical But Not Unruly.*

Gregory Pappas is Associate Professor of Philosophy at Texas A&M University. He is the author of "Dewey and Feminism: The Affective and Relationships in Dewey's Ethics," and "William James and the Logic of Faith."

Sandra Rosenthal is Provost Distinguished Professor of Philosophy at Loyola University, New Orleans. She has published eleven books and approximately 175 articles on pragmatism and its relation to various issues and movements, and has presented invited formal lectures on pragmatism in China, Poland, and Germany, among other places. She is on the editorial boards of several journals and books series, and has served as president of various professional organizations, including the Charles Peirce Society, the Society for the Advancement of American Philosophy, and the Metaphysical Society of America, and on the executive committee of the APA, Eastern Division.

Shannon Sullivan is Assistant Professor of Philosophy and Women's Studies at Pennsylvania State University. She teaches and researches in the areas of feminist theory, American pragmatism, critical race theory, and Continental philosophy. Her book, *Living Across and Through Skins: Transactional Bodies, Pragmatism, and Feminism,* was published in 2001 by Indiania University Press. Her next project, tentatively entitled *Race, Space, and Place: Pragmatist Reflections on Racial Experience,* explores how spaces and places become constituted by race, and how the category of race is composed in part by peoples' relationships to space and place.

Index